The 1500s

HEADLINES IN HISTORY

Books in the Headlines in History series:

The 1000s

The 1100s

The 1200s

The 1300s

The 1400s

The 1500s

The 1600s

The 1700s

The 1800s

The 1900s

The 1500s

HEADLINES IN HISTORY

Stephen Currie, *Book Editor*

Bonnie Szumski, *Editorial Director*
Scott Barbour, *Managing Editor*

Greenhaven Press, Inc., San Diego, California

Every effort has been made to trace the owners of copyrighted material. The articles in this volume may have been edited for content, length, and/or reading level. The titles have been changed to enhance the editorial purpose.

Library of Congress Cataloging-in-Publication Data

The 1500s / Stephen Currie, book editor.
    p. cm. — (Headlines in history)
  Includes bibliographical references and index.
  ISBN 0-7377-0538-8 (lib. bdg. : alk. paper)—
ISBN 0-7377-0537-X (pbk. : alk. paper)
    1. Civilization, Medieval. 2. Sixteenth century. 3. Europe—
Civilization—16th century. I. Currie, Stephen, 1960–
II. Headlines in history (San Diego, Calif.)

CB367 .A165 2001
940.1—dc21
                                                              2001017056

Copyright © 2001 by Greenhaven Press, Inc.
P.O. Box 289009, San Diego, CA 92198-9009

Printed in the USA

CONTENTS

demonstrated that the English could more than hold their own by using tactics and smaller, faster ships.

Chapter 3: Life and Culture in Sixteenth-Century Europe

enslavement of Africans and others by Europeans. The beginnings of the transatlantic slave trade more or less coincided with the start of the sixteenth century.

Brazil. The official chronicler of the voyage recorded his impressions of the journey, the land, and particularly the people.

3. The Fall of the Inca
The fate of the Inca of Peru was much the same as the fate of the Aztecs. Indeed, the tactics that Spanish leader Francisco Pizarro used to capture the Inca leader Atahuallpa were strikingly similar to the tactics Hernán Cortés had used to capture the Aztec ruler Montezuma. Once Atahuallpa had been captured, the Spanish found it relatively easy to destroy the rest of Inca power in South America.

FOREWORD

Chronological time lines of history are mysteriously fascinating. To learn that within a single century Christopher Columbus sailed to the New World, the Aztec, Maya, and Inca cultures were flourishing, Joan of Arc was burned to death, and the invention of the printing press was radically changing access to written materials allows a reader a different type of view of history: a bird's-eye view of the entire globe and its events. Such a global picture allows for cross-cultural comparisons as well as a valuable overview of chronological history that studying one particular area simply cannot provide.

Taking an expansive look at world history in each century, therefore, can be surprisingly informative. In Headlines in History, Greenhaven Press attempts to imitate this time-line approach using primary and secondary sources that span each century. Each volume gives readers the opportunity to view history as though they were reading the headlines of a global newspaper: Editors of each volume have attempted to glean and include the most important and influential events of the century, as well as quirky trends and cultural oddities. Headlines in History, then, attempts to give readers a glimpse of both the mundane and the earth-shattering. Articles on the French Revolution, for example, are juxtaposed with the then-current fashion concerns of the French nobility. This creates a higher interest level by allowing students a glimpse of people's everyday lives throughout history.

By using both primary and secondary sources, students also have the opportunity to view the historical events both as eyewitnesses have experienced them and as historians have interpreted them. Thus, students can place such historical events in a larger context as well as receive background information on important world events.

Headlines in History allows readers the unique opportunity to learn more about events that may only be mentioned in their history textbooks, or may be ignored entirely. The series presents students with a variety of interesting topics that span cultural, historical, and political arenas. Such a broad span of material will allow students to wander wherever their curiosity will take them.

From Medieval to Modern

The story of the sixteenth century is in many respects the story of the increasing dominance of western Europe in the world. In earlier centuries—the tenth, say, or the thirteenth—little distinguished the greatest European societies from the other empires of the world. Neither European learning, technology, nor government were stronger or more advanced than similar societies elsewhere. The Ming Chinese, the Maya of Central America, the Mongols of Genghis Khan's time, the kingdoms of western Africa, all routinely matched western Europe in art, science, and military strength.

During the sixteenth century, however, Europe began to dominate the world as it never had before. Certainly, some cultures beyond Europe continued to be strong and influential. A few even flourished. The Ottoman Empire in present-day Turkey expanded until quite late in the century; the power of India under the Mughal dynasty was just beginning during this period. But the story of many non-European cultures during the 1500s was far from happy. During this century western Europe began to flex its collective muscles at the expense of other cultures—those cultures it found smaller, weaker, or technologically less advanced than Europe itself. The power of the Aztec Empire of Mexico, for example, was destroyed forever early in the century. So was that of the Inca of Peru. The sixteenth century also marked the beginning of the importation of African slaves to the New World. These events were not isolated; they began a process of European colonialism and imperialism that persisted for many more hundreds of years.

To be sure, not all of Europe's rise came at the expense of other nations. Much of the increase in the continent's influence was a result of new conditions at home. The sixteenth century was a time of great innovation and curiosity, traits that revealed themselves in the science, learning, and art of the time. The century, too, was a period of fairly rapid social and political change. All at once, the rules were no longer the same as they had been before. Religion, social structure, painting, literature, government—all was new, different, and exciting. Part of Europe's domination of the era stemmed from this ferment of ideas and the resulting mix of experiences that the century offered Europeans.

A Century of Change

Indeed, more so than many historical periods, the sixteenth century stands out as a time of tremendous social, cultural, and political change. From Europe to South America and from East Asia to the Middle East, sixteenth-century life was marked by quick and sudden shifts. These shifts occurred in many different areas of life: in cultural styles and standards, in types and forms of government, in new knowledge of the world and its peoples. So great and far-reaching were the changes that typical Germans, Mexicans, or Japanese alive at the beginning of the century would scarcely recognize their world as the same if they could be suddenly transported to century's end.

The changes are not difficult to spot. Many of them dealt with politics, government, and military strength. England, for example, had been a relatively unimportant seafaring nation early in the century. Politically, geographically, and culturally, it stood off to the side of Europe. It was scarcely the equal of Portugal or the Netherlands, let alone France or Spain. Yet during the sixteenth century England rose from obscurity to the forefront of European influence and power.

The history of England's ascension includes a broad range of themes: the political and religious struggles between King Henry VIII and the Roman Catholic pope; the careful diplomacy of Queen Elizabeth I and the attempt of her cousin Mary, queen of Scots, to seize the crown; the cultural influence of Shakespeare; and the technological and military know-how that allowed the English to defeat the Spanish Armada in 1588. The combination of these factors helped make England among the most feared European powers by 1600, well on its way to establishing an empire that would encircle the globe.

In contrast, the mighty empires of the New World had flourished as the century opened—and lay in ruins by the midpoint of the period. China saw a much more gradual decline in its wealth and influence. So did Spain, loser of the attack on England. France was shaken by brutal civil and religious warfare. Even the powerful Ottoman Empire was on the defensive as the century wound down. The sixteenth century saw perhaps more than its share of conquerors and crushing defeats. With few exceptions, the list of great powers at the beginning of the century had little in common with the list of similar powers at century's end.

Cultural changes were significant, too. As the sixteenth century began, the Italian Renaissance was drawing to a close. Painters and sculptors of the fifteenth century had brought new techniques, subjects, and styles into vogue, and the artists of the sixteenth continued the trend toward novelty and experimentation. The so-called Mannerist school of painting of the late sixteenth century, for instance, veered toward exaggeration of line and form, unusual color schemes, and works with subject matter reminiscent of twentieth-century cubism and surrealism—a far cry from the works of Michelangelo, Leonardo da Vinci, and other masters of the early part of the 1500s.

Similar changes took place in music and literature. During the sixteenth century the madrigal, an unaccompanied melody sung in parts on a secular topic, and the advent of conservatories specifically intended for music education were developed. In drama, the last decades of the century marked the period of William Shakespeare's greatest output. Shakespeare's plays had roots in English culture, of course, and were foreshadowed by other plays and dramatic styles popular earlier in this period. However, Shakespeare's genius moved theater well beyond anything that had ever been seen before.

From Medieval to Modern

Many of the sixteenth century's most important changes signaled the coming of a new worldview. Very broadly, it is fair to say that the century—at least within Europe—represented the start of a shift away from a medieval society and a medieval way of thinking to a much more modern perspective on the world. This change did not come all at once, of course, but occurred gradually throughout the period. It took place more slowly in some regions of the world and more quickly in others. Likewise, it affected the upper classes and the educated of European society more than it did those at the bottom of the social structure. Still, the overall trend was clear.

Some of these changes are evident. By the sixteenth century the old feudal system prevalent during the Middle Ages was gone. Knights, lords, and manors had lost most of their importance. Still, they had yet to be replaced by participatory democracy; even the English Parliament was dominated by nobles and could not be counted on to stand up to despotic kings and queens. More peasants were independent farmers during the sixteenth century than had been true a few hundred years earlier, when most who worked the land were lowly serfs only a few steps removed from slavery. But although the peasants in most of Europe were moving toward a greater freedom, they had scarcely achieved it by twentieth-century standards. Fighting was the same. Swords, spears, and bows and arrows were beginning to fall from favor during the 1500s, but firearms had not yet come into widespread use.

There were more subtle signs of change, too. The medieval period, for example, had been marked by a deep reliance on superstition. Men and women searched for signs, portents, and omens. The birth of a two-headed calf, say, might signify an impending natural disaster. Other odd and unusual events might presage a good harvest, a propitious time for marriage, or a poor time to attack an enemy. The existence of witchcraft and sorcery was accepted by nearly all peoples. To people of medieval times, the answers lay in the stars. Determining cause and effect was only a matter of accurately reading the signs.

The world in medieval times, moreover, had often seemed to be a simple and straightforward place. Life may have been hard, but at least it appeared to be free of complexity. The countries of western Europe, and many of those in eastern Europe as well, were united under one religion—Roman Catholicism—with one clear path toward salvation. The roles of men and women were fixed; class divisions were sharp and difficult to erase. People lived their entire lives in the same village, and professions tended to be handed down, like land, from one generation to the next. Compared to modern life, or even to life in the seventeenth or eighteenth centuries, medieval Europe was a rather static and unchanging place.

During medieval times, too, the world outside Europe was little known and considered dangerous. Muslims and Jews, even the Orthodox Christians of eastern Europe, were viewed as infidels. In all likelihood, Europeans feared that East Asians and Africans were worse. Dragons and giants were rumored to roam distant lands, while hundred-foot-high whirlpools and boiling seas lurked in the oceans. Only a few ships ventured out past the sight of land, and only a few travelers braved trade routes that led toward other continents. To medieval Europeans, Europe was the center of the world; and since the world was the center of the universe, according to astronomical thought of the time, Europe was at the midpoint of everything. The rest of the world was valuable only in supplying spices, cloths, and a few other materials unavailable in Europe itself.

Reliance on superstition did not disappear during the sixteenth century, of course. On the contrary, superstitious belief was relatively common, especially in the early part of the 1500s. The great explorer Ferdinand Magellan, for example, scarcely dared to make a move without consulting his staff astrologer. Nor did people of the sixteenth century immediately discard the notion of the world as a simple place with clear and easy answers or stop mistrusting everything that lay outside the borders of Europe. Still, there is no doubt that many people during this time did adopt a more modern perspective—an attitude toward the world around them much more in tune with today's views. The late sixteenth century, along with the years immediately following its end, increasingly began to see the world as a more complicated place than the medieval population had wanted to admit.

Of all the events and ideas of the century, three themes in particular sparked and encouraged that shift in worldview. These themes may have dealt with specific areas of sixteenth-century life, but they had an impact that went far beyond the narrow confines of those categories. Individually and together, geographical discoveries, scientific progress, and new questions about religion all added shades of gray to a previously black-and-white world.

The Age of Exploration

Among the most important hallmarks of the sixteenth century was a dramatic increase in geographical knowledge caused by a surge in the number of journeys of discovery. To be sure, the people of the sixteenth century were hardly the first to investigate the world's oceans and landmasses. The ancient Greeks had been a seafaring people. So had the Vikings. So had the Polynesians, who may have had a greater knowledge of navigation and the Pacific Ocean than anyone until the 1500s or, perhaps, beyond.

Similarly, caravans and trade routes had sprung up through the occupied continents. The Romans built roads stretching from Spain to Arabia and from Ethiopia into Britain. The Inca of Peru knew the countryside around them for many miles. Thirteenth-century Italian Marco Polo and fourteenth-century Moroccan Ibn Battuta were both veteran travelers who had journeyed across much of the Old World—and written about their adventures.

The fifteenth century, too, had seen a significant increase in geographical knowledge. Portugal's Prince Henry the Navigator had sent ships down the coast of Africa and toward the East Indies. Christopher Columbus had sailed to America. Ships grew in size, and captains grew in confidence. During the medieval period, maps either included large empty spaces, showing lands no European had visited—or imaginative drawings of dragons, whirlpools, and other flights of fancy, showing precisely the same. During the 1400s the spaces on those maps began to be filled in, and the imaginative creatures began to disappear for good.

Still, the sixteenth century represented the major breakthrough. During this time Europeans sailed almost everywhere they could manage to sail. When sailing was impossible, they walked. Vasco Núñez de Balboa crossed the isthmus of Panama and became the first European to see the Pacific Ocean from that side. Ferdinand Magellan's crew sailed completely around the world. The English and the French sent ships to the northeastern parts of North America, beginning colonization attempts that would eventually give rise

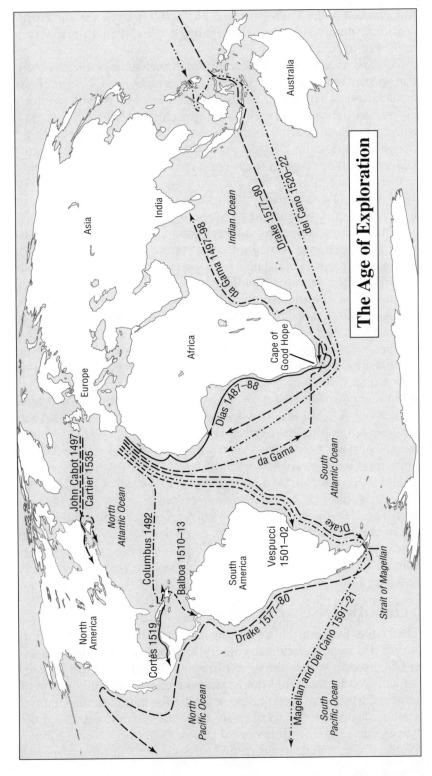

North America

John Cabot 1497
Cartier 1535

North
Atlantic Ocean

Columbus 1492

Balboa 1510–13

Cortés 1519

South
America

Vespucci
1501–02

Drake

Strait of Magellan

Drake 1577–80

Magellan and Del Cano 1591–21

South
Pacific Ocean

North
Pacific Ocean

Europe

Africa

Asia

India

Dias 1487–88

da Gama 1497–98

Indian Ocean

Cape of
Good Hope

da Gama

South
Atlantic Ocean

Drake 1577–80

del Cano 1520–22

Australia

The Age of Exploration

to Canada and the United States. The Spanish explored the North American plains and desert. The Portuguese and the Dutch sent ship after ship to Asia.

By the end of the 1500s geographical understanding had ballooned. Europeans knew about Brazil and Patagonia and Ceylon, about Canada and Zanzibar and Japan. Once Europe had considered itself essentially the center of the earth, surrounded only by oceans and a few African and Asian nations impossibly far off. New geographic knowledge made this a harder attitude to justify. Increasingly, Europeans looked outward, not inward: Out in the world they saw new markets, new sources of revenue, new possibilities for colonies. By 1600 the era of colonialism was in full swing—an era that would have been nearly unimaginable just a hundred years before.

But, of course, the effects of exploration were not felt only in Europe. European ships brought the rest of the world closer together, too, whether it wanted to be or not. Some cultures benefited from European trade. For other non-European peoples, however, the ships often spelled disaster. Sometimes the disaster was intentional, as when Hernán Cortés and the Spanish wrested political control of Mexico from the Aztec Empire, or when African slaves began to be shipped in great numbers across the Atlantic Ocean to Brazil and the Caribbean. Sometimes the disaster was an unforeseen by-product of contact, as when New World peoples caught European illnesses: Even relatively mild diseases, like chicken pox, mumps, or strains of the flu, could kill people who had never encountered them before. Of course, the problem of disease worked both ways. Once in the tropics of Africa or the Americas, many Europeans succumbed to unfamiliar diseases such as malaria.

For good or for ill, however, the increased contact between peoples across the world changed life irrevocably in the sixteenth century. The 1500s were a time when cultures came together and influenced one another as never before. From the cloth they wove to the spices they sought, from the foods they ate to the gods they worshiped, the effects of the age of exploration were widespread, quick, and long-lasting.

Scientific Discovery

The sixteenth century also saw the stirrings of a new scientific curiosity. Through the fifteenth century, Europeans had made little scientific progress since the days of ancient Greece and Rome. Biological and medical knowledge was sketchy at best; dissection of human corpses was frowned upon by the Roman Catholic Church, making it difficult for scholars to study the various systems of the body. Astronomers still accepted the ideas of the ancient scientist Ptolemy, who had determined that the sun—and all other stars and planets—revolved around the earth. And while the Muslim world was steadily moving toward better mathematical understanding, Christian Europe was not keeping pace.

All that began to change during the sixteenth century. The period was full of exciting new scientific discoveries. In 1528 the Swiss physician Paracelsus wrote Europe's first manual of surgery. Later in the century, when the ban on dissection was relaxed, other scientists explored the function and structure of the brain, the eyes, and other parts of the human body. A number of Italian mathematicians worked out solutions to cubic equations and other high-level math problems. The modern sciences of geology, mineralogy, and ballistics were developed during this period, and Galileo carried out many of his greatest experiments in physics and motion at the end of the century.

Perhaps the greatest change of all, however, was the work of Nicolas Copernicus, a Polish astronomer whose work demonstrated that Ptolemy was wrong. The sun, Copernicus proved, did not revolve around the earth: Rather, the earth revolved around the sun. Most other discoveries of the period had extended the limits of human knowledge or organized what people already knew into somewhat more formal categories or into slightly different groupings. Copernicus's discovery, however, was of another sort altogether. It contradicted what was known and what seemed obvious, even undeniable, to any observer. Perhaps more seriously, it removed the earth from its special position at the center of creation. An earth-centered universe implies a special role for humankind; a sun-centered universe, in contrast, may not. Copernican thinking reached far beyond science itself and into religion and culture as well. Though the full impact of Copernicus's work would not be felt until the seventeenth century, few scientific discoveries have had such an effect on thought and worldview as the realization that the earth travels around the sun.

There were several reasons for the sudden rise in scientific discovery. One was the sixteenth century's interest in exploration. Traveling to distant seas called for better maps, faster ships, and better systems of navigation, which in turn led to new work in the realms of mathematics and engineering. Europeans designed more capable astronomical instruments to make finding a ship's position easier, and they tackled the question of determining a ship's longitude—or distance east or west around the globe—by constructing more and more accurate clocks. Physicists investigated the properties of magnets and compasses. Many of the great mapmakers and geographers lived during the sixteenth century, among them Gerardus Mercator, whose method of depicting the earth on a flat sheet of paper is still used by many cartographers today.

Another reason for the rise in scientific discovery had to do with the artists of the time. As a general rule, Renaissance artists brought the outside world into their art much more than artists of the medieval period. Whereas earlier artists had been content to paint full-length portraits and sculpt statues, Renaissance artists wanted to understand how the bodies they painted and sculpted worked. Which muscles made certain poses possible? How did a tightly clenched fist affect the way a robe hung from a subject's upper arm? Which joints moved which ways, and why? Questions like these led artists such as Leonardo da Vinci to study anatomy. They wanted realism in their art, and science was necessary to fulfill that goal. Other artists studied mathematics, engineering, or other scientific disciplines for much the same reasons. Germany's Albrecht Dürer, for example, wrote a geometry textbook and sketched out plans for a wartime flying machine, which was never built.

Of course, change in the way people thought about science was not accomplished overnight, or even during the course of the century. For many years after the 1500s, subjects such as alchemy and astrology were still considered scientific disciplines. Nevertheless, a new scientific ethic was moving through Europe.

The Reformation

Besides exploration and science, the sixteenth century stands out in a third way, at least in Europe. This was perhaps the most prominent of all, and it involved religion. For centuries western Europe had one Christian church, the Roman Catholic Church. Catholic leaders had dealt swiftly, and usually harshly, with the few breakaway Christian sects that had formed over the previous few centuries. The pope was in charge of all matters ecclesiastical, along with many civil concerns as well. To be sure, not every king and prince paid close attention to papal pronouncements on governmental issues, but the problems there were political rather than religious. As the century opened, western Europe presented a united Catholic front to the world.

However, that unity was beginning to fracture. Shortly before the dawning of the sixteenth century, a number of Christian thinkers had begun to challenge the policies and teachings of the official church. Late fourteenth-century English scholar and theologian John Wycliffe, for example, had questioned the authority of priests and bishops. Wycliffe preached that the church belonged to the people. In his view, every person could come to salvation without the intervention of the church hierarchy. In his view, the church had become bureaucratic, arrogant, and so sure that it was right that it had grown distant from the people it was supposed to serve. Church services of the time were held exclusively in Latin, a tongue incomprehensible to the average northern European of the time; Wycliffe translated the Bible into English so it would be accessible to ordinary people, and he urged its use in services. The church responded to Wycliffe's ideas and writings by stripping him of his teaching post, but it did not address the underlying concerns Wycliffe raised.

Later reformers took up Wycliffe's cause. Fifteenth-century Czech thinker Jan Hus was warned to stop advocating for changes. When he refused, he was excommunicated; when that failed to silence him, he was burned at the stake. Throughout the 1400s, the church continued to stamp out disaffection wherever it appeared. The more officials refused to listen to complaints or consider reforms, the more people came to agree—or at least sympathize—with Hus and Wycliffe.

Finally, in the early part of the 1500s, the time was ripe for change. A young German monk named Martin Luther grew more rebellious about the policies of the church and the leadership's unwillingness to make even small changes. Luther's concerns were many, but the most burning involved the so-called sale of indulgences. An indulgence was a remission of sin; when the church sold indulgences, it was essentially pardoning people's sins for a fee.

Offering these indulgences was nothing new, but by Luther's time the practice was becoming more widespread; church officials no longer seemed even slightly embarrassed about it. Luther, on the other hand, was scandalized at the notion. He believed that only God could pardon sins, and he felt that the sale of indulgences was another example of the church putting itself as an institution ahead of the God it was supposed to serve. In 1517, angered and frustrated by the sale of indulgences and by the church's refusal to change, Luther decided he would make his dispute public. That October he posted a list of ninety-five complaints about the Roman Catholic Church on the door of the church in Wittenberg, Germany.

The reaction was quick. Luther was ordered to a church tribunal in Augsburg, Germany, where he was told to recant his complaints. He refused, citing conscience. Negotiations between Luther and the pope's officials continued for several years, but the end of the debate was already clear. In 1520 Pope Leo X excommunicated Luther. When Luther burned the document to show what he thought of it, he was imprisoned.

The story might have ended there, as had Wycliffe's and Hus's, but unlike those earlier reformers, Luther had allies. By this time, many others were as angry as Luther himself. Other formerly Catholic theologians took Luther's part or used his ideas as springboards for promulgating their own: Huldrych Zwingli in Switzerland, Thomas Münzer in Germany, and John Calvin in France. Much of northern Europe stood behind Luther, too, partly for theological reasons and partly because of politics: The civil authority of Catholicism had largely worked to the benefit of the Italians and the French, and those removed from those centers of influence were anxious for a change. Luther's fight quickly became larger than himself. Before long, he had sparked the Protestant Reformation—the founding of new forms of Christianity, born of protest and a desire to reform the Catholic Church.

The story was not yet done. The pope and his allies fought back. Church officials excommunicated priests sympathetic to Luther and tried to reclaim church property—buildings, artwork, and other valuables—in areas that were now solidly Lutheran. Religious wars broke out across western Europe. In 1555 the Peace of Augsburg brought an end to some of the violence in Germany. The treaty recognized Protestant principalities and put them more or less on equal footing with states in which the rulers still were Catholic. However, battles between Protestants and Catholics continued to rage across France, the Netherlands, and other countries.

The Reformation ranks as one of the most influential events in European history. The protest was at once theological and political, opportunistic and based on conscience. It led to a fracture in the standard way of thinking and to the establishment of something entirely new. The Reformation led to a diversity of thought in Europe. It provided options and alternatives; Western Christianity no longer spoke with one voice, no longer choked off all debate on religious matters. The two sides initially viewed one another with hostility—and in some places, such as Northern Ireland, still do today. In the long run, however, the Reformation helped strengthen Europe by establishing an atmosphere in which discussion could be fruitful and questioning orthodoxy was entirely appropriate.

The Beginning and the End

Together, these three themes—the rise of exploration, the emphasis on scientific learning, and the Reformation—set the tone for the century. Each theme had an immediate effect on the lives of the people who lived during the sixteenth century, but each theme influenced people's understanding of the world around them as well. Exploration was not simply about maps and ships, for example. Exploration also sparked study in technology and mathematics, established connections between different and often hostile cultures, and helped begin the modern idea of interdependence between societies. Likewise, the Reformation was more than a revolution in religious thought; it was just as much about the relationship between politics and religion, and it tore down traditional ideas about the role of religion in society.

The three major themes, too, highlight the sixteenth century as a time of flux and a period of great change. Not quite medieval but not yet modern, the 1500s represented a bend in the river, a connection between two vastly different eras. The sixteenth century was at once the beginning of one period and the end of another.

Politics and Government in Europe

L ike most other centuries before and since, the sixteenth century in Europe was a time of intrigue, war, and shifting alliances. Civil wars rocked Germany, France, and other areas. It also saw any number of battles and outright wars, both small and large. The Danes fought the Swedes, and the Spanish sacked the Low Countries. The fringes of Europe were affected as well: The Turks conquered Hungary, and the Russians used military strength to dominate much of eastern Europe. As an indication of the complexity of political issues during the time, at various points throughout the century Spain waged war against both England and France—though England and France were scarcely allies and considered themselves more enemies than friends.

Indeed, military might and the struggle for power in many ways dictated the course of the sixteenth century within Europe. Part of the reason involved the voyages of discovery that helped define the period. With exploration increasing and population booming, the stakes were high. The nations that controlled the oceans could control trade, choose the best sites for overseas colonies, and win the inside track on gold, spices, and other valuable materials only available outside the borders of Europe. In earlier, more static centuries, wars and political alliances had been mainly about one country trying to take control of resources owned by another—resources, though, that already existed. That sort of conflict still took place in the sixteenth century, but now a new layer had been added. The pool of land, minerals, and raw materials had suddenly grown much larger, and the wars between powerful nations were increasingly more about access to these apparently limitless resources than about taking what another country had amassed.

Religious conflict spilled over into the political and governmental realm as well. The Reformation established a new axis of division. Once European conflicts had been mainly the result of troubles between ethnic groups and personalities who sought power; now, religious identity had been added to the list as Protestants and Catholics turned on one another. Religious differences joined with more traditional political concerns, too. The long-running feud between Elizabeth of England and Mary, queen of Scots, for example, was at once a struggle for governmental power and a more theoretical fight for religious supremacy.

Where government was concerned, the sixteenth century was far from modern. To be sure, a few nations held parliamentary sessions and allowed some people to vote. Still, the primary rulers were hereditary monarchs, kings and queens who could do more or less as they chose. Individual citizens had few rights, and even members of the nobility thought twice about incurring the ire of their leaders. No nation escaped the basic pattern: not the Netherlands, more tolerant of diversity and dissension than most, nor England, with one of the continent's strongest traditions of public involvement in government. Unresponsive governments sometimes led to civil wars and revolutions, although usually any change in leadership simply replaced one tyrant with another. More often, though, rebels were brutally suppressed. Any move toward greater democracy across Europe would have to wait for a future century.

Elizabeth I and Mary, Queen of Scots

Alison Plowden

Certainly among the most compelling story lines of the sixteenth century was the intrigue between two British queens. Elizabeth I was queen of England. Her first cousin once removed Mary Stuart, or Stewart, was queen of Scotland. Elizabeth was a Protestant, Mary a Catholic. Elizabeth never married and had no children to take the throne after her death; Mary, twice married, produced a son, James. Both women claimed the throne of England by right, but Elizabeth had more power on her side and so ruled as queen.

Mary was a threat to Elizabeth, however. Her very existence served as a reminder that many Catholics challenged Elizabeth's right to the crown. Mary's ties with other Catholic nations such as France and Spain also concerned Elizabeth, who could easily envision their rulers declaring war on her to support Mary's claims to England. In 1568, after many years in which Mary frequently demanded her rights, Elizabeth decided to put her cousin under what amounted to house arrest. That did not silence Mary, however, leading some of Elizabeth's advisers to call for her execution.

Finally, in 1586, Mary was implicated in the so-called Babington Plot, a conspiracy led by a disaffected English Catholic anxious to help Mary take the throne away from Elizabeth. Messages were passed to and from Mary by means of a secret code. The plot involved Elizabeth's assassination. This excerpt, drawn from *Elizabeth Tudor and Mary Stewart* by Elizabethan specialist Alison Plowden, describes the events of Mary's subsequent trial.

Excerpted from *Elizabeth Tudor and Mary Stewart* (Totowa, NJ: Barnes & Noble Books, 1984) by Alison Plowden. Copyright © 1984 by Alison Plowden. Reprinted with permission from Sutton Publishing.

M ary began expectably by refusing to recognize the jurisdiction
of the court. She was a sovereign princess. She was not the
Queen of England's subject and therefore not bound by English law.
It was a nice legal point, but the time for nice legal points had passed.
All the same, the commissioners spent the best part of two days pa-
tiently trying to induce the Queen of Scots to appear before them, until at last Lord Burghley [Elizabeth's Secretary of State, William Ce-
cil] told her bluntly that if she persisted in her refusal they both could
and would proceed without her. . . . In the end, it seems to have been
[Elizabeth's friend and adviser Sir] Christopher Hatton who persuaded
her to lay aside the privilege of royal dignity, appear in judgement and
show her innocency, lest by avoiding a trial she should draw suspicion
upon herself and lay an eternal blot upon her reputation.

The actual trial occupied another two days and was neither more
nor less inequitable than any other 16th century treason trial. All the
evidence—the letters, the confessions and the sworn statements—
were painstakingly rehearsed and Mary defended herself with elo-
quent dignity, answering 'with a stout courage, "That she knew not
[conspirator Anthony] Babington; that she never received any letters
from him, nor wrote any to him: that she never plotted the destruction
of the Queen; and that to prove any such thing, her subscription under her own hand was to be produced."' It would, after all, she pointed
out, have been only too easy for someone to have counterfeited her
ciphers.

It was perfectly true that, to [investigator Francis] Walsingham's
disappointment, the Queen of Scots' original draft of the letter to
Babington had not been found among her papers at Chartley; nor had
the original letter itself, forwarded by Phelippes, ever been recovered—the Casket Letters [an attempt to implicate Mary in which her
enemies forged private letters] all over again. This time, though, the
circumstantial evidence was overwhelming and Mary's cry that she
would never 'make shipwreck' of her soul by conspiring the hurt of
her dearest sister rang hollow in the ears of the commissioners.

The issue was not in doubt—or was it? Certainly the court would
have proceeded to judgement without further ado had its members not
been suddenly called back to London by royal command. Francis
Walsingham feared the worst, 'I see this wicked creature ordained of
God to punish us for our sins and unthankfulness' he lamented in a
letter to the Earl of Leicester.

On 25 October the commissioners re-assembled in the Star Chamber to hear the evidence once more passed solemnly in review, while
[Elizabeth's secretaries Claude] Nau and [Gilbert] Curle were produced to repeat in person the statements previously made in writing.

The panel then unanimously pronounced its verdict, finding the Queen of Scotland 'not only accessory and privy to the conspiracy but also an imaginer and compasser of her Majesty's destruction.'

Four days later Parliament met at Westminster. It was an extraordinary session. All normal business went by the board as the Lords and Commons, united as seldom before or since, concentrated their energies on what had become the issue uppermost in everyone's mind—ensuring that the Scottish Queen should 'suffer the due execution of justice, according to her deserts.' Elizabeth had won some notable battles of will with Parliament in the past and could no doubt have won again—when she had made up her mind on a matter of principle she was immovable—but on this occasion her battle was with herself, and that her indecision and distress were both genuine and agonising there can be no question,

She felt no personal malice against Mary, she told a deputation of twenty peers and forty MPs [members of Parliament] on 12 November. Although her life had been 'full dangerously sought', her strongest feeling was grief that another woman, another Queen and her near kin should have fallen into so great a crime. Even now, if 'we were but two milkmaids with pails upon our arms', with no more depending on the matter but her own life and not the safety and welfare of the nation, she would 'most willingly pardon and remit this offence.'

Two days later she sent a message to the Commons asking if they could suggest any alternative to execution. Again the question was debated and again the decision was unanimous—Mary must die. Still Elizabeth hesitated. What would the world say 'when it shall be spread abroad that for the safety of her life a maiden queen could be content to spill the blood even of her own kinswoman?' And yet, as she told another deputation which had made the journey to Richmond, where she had withdrawn in a deliberate gesture of dissociation from the proceedings at Westminster, and yet—'I am not so void of judgement as not to see mine own peril, nor yet so ignorant as not to know it were in nature a foolish course to cherish a sword to cut mine own throat.'

Foreign Reaction and Doubt

It was an awesome, unprecedented dilemma, but even now, at this eleventh hour, if Elizabeth could have found a way of keeping Mary alive, she would undoubtedly have done so. For one thing, although the Scottish Queen had come to represent such an intolerable threat to internal security, she also, paradoxically enough, remained England's best protection against attack from abroad. While she lived, Philip of Spain was likely to go on hesitating about launching the much discussed Holy Enterprise [that is, a religious war] against the Protestant island and its anathematized [religiously banned] Queen. The success of such an endeavour might well store up treasure in heaven for the

Most Catholic King, but he would still be lavishing earthly treasure (always in painfully short supply) on elevating the half-French, half-Guise [a French territory] Mary to the English throne. Once that had been achieved, it was not to be supposed that either she or the Duke of Guise would remain so devoted to Spanish interests and the end result would be the close Anglo-French alliance which the Hapsburg family had laboured for generations to prevent. Once Mary was dead, the situation would look quite different to a King who could, after all, trace his own remote descent from [14th century English ruler] John of Gaunt.

There was French reaction to be considered, too, and, nearer home and more crucial, Scottish reaction. James [Mary's son, King of Scotland] was making, at least in public, what appeared to be a genuine effort to save his mother's life. In private, though, it was pretty plain that anxiety lest her execution should in any way affect his own title to the succession far outweighed considerations of filial piety, and [16th century historian] William Camden records that his special envoy, the Master of Gray, 'many times buzzed into the Queen's ear that saying *Mortua non mordet . . .* a dead Woman biteth not.' But James was still only twenty years old and under considerable pressure from a chauvinistic nobility and people who, although they had once only with difficulty been restrained from executing Mary themselves, were now showing every sign of outrage that the English should presume to usurp their privilege.

Meanwhile time was running out. It was more than a month since sentence had been passed on Mary and still it had not even been published, . . . looked very much as if she [Elizabeth] meant to do nothing after all—to try and defuse the situation by a series of endless delays and postponements. Then, in a sudden flurry of behind-the-scenes activity during the last week of November, the Queen changed her mind again. She agreed to shorten the recess to mid-February and on 4 December, two days after Parliament had risen, finally authorised a proclamation of the sentence under the Great Seal—possibly as a result of persuasion by the Earl of Leicester, who had just returned briefly from the Low Countries,

The news was taken to Fotheringay, and on 19 December Mary sat down to write her last letter to Elizabeth. After affirming her 'constant resolution to suffer death for the maintenance of the Apostolic Roman Catholic Church', she asked to be buried in holy ground in France, near 'the late Queen my mother', begging that her cousin would permit 'free sepulture [burial] to this body when the soul is separated, which when united could never obtain liberty to live in peace.' And, she went on, 'because I fear the secret tyranny of those into whose power you have abandoned me, I beg you not to allow me to be executed without your knowledge—not from fear of pain, which I am ready to suffer, but on account of the rumours which would be spread concerning my death if it were not seen by reliable witnesses. It is for this reason that I require that my attendants remain to be spectators of my end in the faith of my Saviour and in the obedience of His Church. . . . In conclusion, I pray the God of Mercy that He will deign to enlighten you by His Holy Spirit and that He will give me grace to die in perfect charity. . . . Do not accuse me of presumption if, on the eve of leaving this world, I remind you that one day you will have to answer for your charge as well as those who are sent before. Your sister and cousin wrongfully imprisoned, Marie, Queen.'

Queen Elizabeth

Mary, naturally enough, was now in daily expectation of her death, but Christmas came and went, the New Year came in, the days began to lengthen and still there was no word from London. Towards the end of January a sudden spate of rumours that the Scottish Queen had escaped began to sweep the country, together with other frightening stories that a Spanish fleet had been seen off Milford Haven; that the Scots were over the Border and the northern parts up in rebellion; that the Duke of Guise had landed in Sussex with a strong army; that there was a new conspiracy on foot to kill the Queen and set London on fire—even that the Queen was dead. On 3 February, the Mayor of Exeter, much perplexed by an outbreak of panic in his area, applied to Lord Burghley for guidance, but by this time Elizabeth had at long last signed Mary's death warrant.

Walsingham was ill again and William Davison, the second Secretary, in attendance. As he was about to leave her presence, with the precious document in his hands, the Queen 'fell into some complaint of Sir Amyas Paulet [Mary's jailer] and others that might have eased her of this burden' and gave orders that Walsingham and Davison should write 'to sound his disposition in that behalf.' Her meaning was plain enough. There were other ways for a Queen to die than at the hands of the public executioner.

Meanwhile, Elizabeth's councillors were taking no chances. The warrent had passed the Great Seal with scarcely an hour's delay and two days later was despatched to Fotheringay by the hand of Robert Beale [Walsingham's brother-in-law] without further reference to her Majesty who, it was agreed, had now done 'as much as in law or reason' could be expected of her.

On 4 February, the Queen called William Davison to her again and told him, smiling, how she had been troubled in the night by a dream that the Scottish Queen was executed, which had put her in such a passion against him that she could have done she knew not what. Davison, uneasily conscious of Mr Beale already on the road, asked her what she meant, and whether 'she had not a resolute meaning to go through with the said execution according to her warrant.' Her reply, as he later recalled it, was yes, confirmed with a vehement oath, but she wanted to know if there had been any word from Paulet.

His letter arrived that night. He would do anything for the Queen, he would die for her any time she liked to say the word, but he would not shed blood without law or warrant. This episode has scandalised many latter day historians, but at the time Elizabeth had good reasons for wanting, if at all possible, to avoid scandalising her fellow monarchs, to whom the idea that one of God's anointed should suffer judicial execution was not only sacrilegious—it set a grimly dangerous precedent. Unfortunately, though, Paulet was a practical man of the world, who knew the rules of this particular game quite as well as did his sovereign lady. Morally, no doubt, he was in the right, but he had signed the Bond of Association [an oath to kill Mary should there be violence against Elizabeth] as readily as anyone and the Queen had a good deal of justification for her complaints about the 'daintiness' and, as she called it, perjury of all those devoted subjects who, contrary to their Oath of Association, persisted in casting the burden upon herself. Precise fellows, she grumbled, who in words would do great things for her surety, but in deed perform nothing. Probably, though, she had never expected anything else. Like Amyas Paulet, she knew the ways of the world too well.

Execution

So, on the morning of Wednesday, 8 February 1587, Mary Stewart went to keep the appointment which had been waiting for her ever since she had sailed from Calais just over a quarter of a century before. She was forty-four now and the glowing, graceful beauty of the young Queen of Scotland had long since vanished. She had put on weight, become round-shouldered, double-chinned and 'lame of her limbs', but that scarcely mattered. All the evidence indicates that the officials in charge at Fotheringay that day were in a state of acute nervous tension, while Mary's serene self-command was total. As Mr Beale, in his capacity of Clerk to the Privy Council, read out Queen Elizabeth's warrant, she seemed calm, even cheerful, and, says one

eye-witness, 'listened with so careless a regard as if it had not concerned her at all.' She was ready to play her last scene, secure in the
knowledge that every eye in the crowded Great Hall was fixed upon
her, aware that to many in the carefully selected audience of some two
hundred knights and gentlemen she represented a figure of romance,
almost of legend, the Princess in Dolorous Guard for whose sake so
many men had died, that some at least of those present in their secret
hearts thought of her as rightful Queen of England.

Throughout her life Mary had failed and failed again, but she
might yet triumph over the last enemy—by martyrdom she might
yet be revenged on the woman who had won every round of their
long struggle—her death might rally Catholic Christendom to bring
about the destruction of Elizabeth Tudor. If she played her last scene
well, then the enigmatic motto she had used in her captivity ['In my
end is my beginning'] might yet prove a true prophecy—in her end
there might indeed be a beginning. She had been denied the comfort
of her own chaplain and scornfully refused the Protestant ministra-
tions of the Dean of Peterborough—the days when she had been prepared to flirt with Anglicanism were long past. 'Trouble not yourself,
Mr Dean nor me', she told him, 'for know that I am settled in the ancient Catholic and Roman religion and in defence thereof, by God's
grace, I mean to spend my blood.' Her faith had become a weapon
now, as, crucifix held high, Mary flung the Latin prayers—familiar
from childhood to everyone in her audience over the age of forty—in
a kind of defiance at the world which, though it had rejected and imprisoned her and was about to kill her body, had never been able to
defeat her restless, indomitable spirit. But her last public prayers were
in English, for the peace and unity of Christendom, for the conversion
of England, for her son, for the soul of her cousin Elizabeth.

It took two strokes of the axe to kill her, and there was one further
ceremony to be performed. But when the executioner stooped for the
head to display it to the company, an elaborate auburn wig came away
in his hands, and the head itself appeared 'as grey as if she had been
three-score and ten years old', the hair cropped close to the skull, the
face so altered that none could recognise it.

When the news that the Queen of Scots was dead at last reached London, the citizens rejoiced and gave heart-felt thanks for the lifting of
what had grown into an intolerable burden of dread. To them it seemed
'as if a new era had begun in which all men would live in peace.'

Their Queen was less optimistic. At Greenwich the court was
plunged into mourning, and it was more than anyone's place was
worth to have been seen to rejoice. Despite the pleadings of his col-
leagues, the unlucky William Davison was committed to the Tower [of
London prison] for the crime of having allowed Mary's death warrant
to leave his possession and, to the alarm of her friends, Elizabeth was

even threatening to hang him out of hand. To King James she wrote: 'I would you knew, though not felt, the extreme dolour which over-whelmeth my mind for that miserable accident which far contrary to my meaning hath befallen.'

Although James's most honest emotion was undoubtedly relief, it is embarrassing for any reigning monarch to see his mother beheaded in a neighbouring realm, and the King of Scots was going to need all the help his good sister and cousin could give him if he was to avoid the unwelcome obligations of family honour. She certainly did her best, and detailed descriptions of her confusion, her rage and her sorrow were hastily circulated to the courts of Europe.

Elizabeth had always been a consummate actress—'a princess who can play any part she pleases'—and there may well have been an element of playacting in the performance which was currently dazzling the public. But it went deeper than that, for it is clear that in the weeks which followed Mary's execution the Queen of England came close to a complete nervous breakdown. Her violent reaction cannot be explained by political considerations alone, any more than it can by personal regrets for the Queen of Scots—theirs had been a duel to the death and both had known it. But while Elizabeth Tudor had no cause to mourn the passing of that daughter of debate who had sown discord in her realm for the past eighteen years and been a nuisance and source of anxiety for longer than that, to one of her background and training there was something inherently atrocious in the very idea of subjecting an anointed queen to the process of earthly trial, and Elizabeth was suffering now in part from the superstitious revulsion of one who had violated a sacred tabu.

And there was something else. Ever since the day when she had first come to her throne to try the unprecedented experiment of a single woman ruling a notoriously turbulent and intransigent nation, all her energies, all the resources of her formidable intellect and subtle, analytical mind had been necessarily devoted to one end—to staying on top in a world dominated by the ambitious, thrustful, impatient male, to preserving her independent judgement and freedom of action, to never allowing herself to be manoeuvred into a position where any man or group of men would be able to say to her 'you must.' So far always she had succeeded by using her own special brand of magic—that artful mixture of authoritarianism, 'I will have here but one mistress and no master', and feminine blandishment, fishing for men's souls with so sweet a bait that no poor fool could escape her network.

But in the matter of the Queen of Scots the magic had not worked. Step by inexorable step Elizabeth had been driven back to the point from which there was no retreat. The trial of the Babington conspirators had made Mary's trial inevitable, and once Mary had been tried and convicted there was no way by which the men who formed the inner circle of power could have let her live. Always in the past this inner circle—Burghley, Leicester, Hatton, even the dour Francis Walsingham—had contrived to keep a toehold in Mary's camp, to find ways of assuring her privately of the reversion of their loyalty were she to succeed Elizabeth in the course of nature. But once they had sat in judgement on her at Fotheringay that road was closed. The Queen of Scots had to die.

The End of the Episode

Elizabeth knew this. . . . She also knew that once the warrant had been signed there would be no question that it would at once be executed. But she still realised she had been trapped and seems to have been overcome by an irrational, near hysterical panic—the worst of her wrath being reserved, as is so often the way, for her best friend, good, faithful old Burghley, who remained in black disgrace for several months. Walsingham, too, though he had been fortunate enough—or wise enough—to be off sick during the most critical period, felt the icy wind of royal displeasure. 'If her Majesty could be otherwise served, I know I should not be used' he wrote to Leicester in March.

It was not a comfortable time to be at court—'I think your lordship happy to be absent from these broils', remarked another of Leicester's correspondents. But, as it became apparent that there would be no thunderbolts from Scotland or France, that the skies were not about to fall, that the Queen's authority had not really been impaired, the storm began slowly to abate. William Davison, the official, necessary scapegoat, remained in the Tower until other events had diverted attention from him and was then quietly released. By June, Elizabeth had recovered from her devastating emotional *crise* and made it up with Lord Burghley and at the end of July the coffin containing the mortal remains of the Queen of Scots was at last taken from Fotheringay to be given Christian (Protestant) burial in Peterborough Cathedral near the tomb of Catherine of Aragon [Henry VIII's first wife], that other tragic queen who, had she been able to bear a living son, might have saved Mary from her deadly inheritance.

The rights and wrongs of the case of the Queen of Scotland have been exhaustively rehearsed over the centuries. But, in truth, Elizabeth Tudor and Mary Stewart were trapped by history in a life and death struggle over which they had very little control—cousins foredoomed to enmity by their blood and birth. The image of Mary as a helpless, hapless victim persistently and wickedly traduced, which she herself promoted enthusiastically during the years of her captivity, dies very hard, but it surely does her less than justice. The Queen of Scots was a 'bonnie fechter' [fighter] and a lioness of the royal breed. Unhappily, though, her grasp of reality was often as tenuous as that of so many of her partisans, and she was handicapped by a fatal lack of judgement which led her so often to fight the wrong enemies with the wrong weapons at the wrong time. 'The circumstances of her suffering 'tis not my business to relate', observed a 17th century Master of Balliol [college], 'but the event gives way to this note upon it, viz: How dangerous a thing it is, first to lay claim to a crown and afterwards to fly for succour to the head that wears it.'

That Mary had coveted Elizabeth's crown ever since the days when, as Queen of France, she had quartered the English royal arms on her shield, is not really in question. Just how deeply she was involved in the plots to seize that crown by violence will probably always remain a matter of debate. But by 1587 her 'guilt' or 'innocence' had long ceased to have any relevance. The mere fact of her existence had become insupportable and England, feeling itself threatened by aggression from without and subversion from within, quite simply could no longer contain the rival queen.

After her death the fear of the enemy within the gates began to lose its urgency, for, while the English Catholics could have welcomed the peaceful succession of Mary Stewart with clear consciences, only the lunatic fringe would ever have accepted Philip of Spain as their king, and when the dreaded Armada actually appeared in the English Channel the nation, Catholic and Protestant alike, could unite against a common enemy.

The problem of the succession, too, which had dominated the English political scene for a generation, now at least ceased to be an issue. Although James, like his mother before him, nagged for recognition and like her failed to get it, his claims [to the English throne] were never seriously challenged—especially after he married a Protestant princess and began to raise a family. The brutal truth is that the Queen of Scots had served her historical purpose on the June day in 1566 when she gave birth to her son at Edinburgh Castle, and from then on that brilliant, fascinating, dangerous woman was destined to become a mere supernumerary to be discarded or used as it suited the purposes of others. That, perhaps, was the real tragedy of Mary Stewart.

The Battle of Lepanto: The Last Crusade

Robert F. Marx

For several centuries, Christian and Muslim forces had battled frequently for both political and religious superiority. The Crusades of the Middle Ages were an attempt by Christian Europeans to win the Middle East from the native Muslims. Later in the medieval period, the Muslim Ottoman Empire, with Turkey as its home base, spread into southeastern Europe. During most of the fourteenth century, all of the fifteenth, and much of the sixteenth, the Turks were the dominant power in the eastern Mediterranean, a seemingly invincible foe to expanding western European nations.

That situation might have continued for many more decades, but in the latter half of the sixteenth century Christian Europe decided to band together against the Ottoman menace. Combining fleets from Austria, Spain, and various Italian city-states, the Christians met the Ottomans and their Muslim allies in the 1571 Battle of Lepanto. Fought off the coast of Greece, the naval battle ended in a decisive victory for the Christians. The power of the Turks was broken. Though they were never completely driven out of Europe, the Ottomans attempted no new attacks to the west and soon signed a peace treaty with Spain.

As Robert F. Marx explains, the religious element in this fight was never far from the warriors' minds. Both sides were well aware that this was a struggle between Christian and Muslim as much as between nations. Because of the religious zeal with which the Christians, in particular, approached the fighting, the battle of Lepanto has often been called

Excerpted from *The Battle of Lepanto, 1571* (Cleveland: World Publishing, 1966) by Robert F. Marx. Copyright © 1966 by Robert F. Marx. Reprinted with permission from the author.

the last of the Crusades. From a western European perspective, it was also perhaps the most successful.

Editor's Note: The story begins here on the day of the battle, with the two forces facing each other. Don Juan of Austria was the Christian commander, Ali Pasha the Ottoman leader. The Turks had slightly more ships than the Christians, but the Christians were better poised to take advantage of the wind. The ships used in the fighting were primarily galleys and galleasses, large ships that could be sailed or rowed and which were loaded with cannon and other weaponry.

Now the fleets were only two miles apart. The westerly breeze died out completely, leaving the Gulf of Lepanto flattened in an eerie, glasslike calm that continued for the rest of the day. The smooth waters mirrored an awesome sight: over six hundred ships stretched across the whole width of the gulf, covering an area of many square miles. On the vessels of both fleets more than one hundred thousand men waited tensely for the impending clash. The warlike spirit on both sides was heightened by religious fervor, for since childhood both Moslems and Christians had been taught that the others were sacrilegious monsters, and that to strike a blow against them was the duty of every devout believer.

Suddenly a shattering din arose from the Turkish fleet. Soldiers and sailors bellowed war cries, fired muskets and other weapons, blew horns, and clashed cymbals to express their excitement and to unnerve the enemy. The contrast was impressive. Complete silence was maintained throughout the Christian fleet except for the creak of the rigging and the steady swish of the great sweeps as they plunged in and out of the water. Then at a solitary trumpet blast from [Christian commander] Don Juan's [of Austria] flagship, every man in the entire fleet from the commander on down knelt on the decks in prayer. A crucifix was raised aloft on each vessel, while a long-robed friar sprinkled holy water over the bowed heads and pronounced a general absolution of the warriors' past sins. When the Christians ended their devotions and stood to their guns or in orderly ranks, each galley in the long battle line, with the noonday sun blazing on the armor and polished weapons, seemed to be on fire. The Turkish vessels were an equally splendid sight, with the brilliant uniforms of the Janissaries [Ottoman warriors] topped by fanciful crests and plumes, the many pennants flying from every point, and the variegated colors of the painted woodwork.

The Turks seemed the more eager for action, opening up with a very noisy but ineffective round of artillery fire long before the enemy fleet was within range. Only one of the shots touched a Christ-ian vessel—Juan de Cardona's galley, which was carrying orders from Don Juan to the advanced galleasses [large ships that could be rowed or sailed]—and the shot only broke off the mast point. The Christians were relying on their galleass squadron to lead off, and minutes after noon a flash was seen from one of the center galleasses. This single shot, aimed at the Turkish flagship, passed through its rigging and then carried away the three large lanterns on the galley's stern near which [Muslim commander] Ali Pasha had been standing and giving orders only seconds before.

The Battle Begins

This first shot was a signal from the commander of the galleasses, and four of these immediately began pouring a murderous fire into the Turkish center and right wing. The other two were rendered totally useless, however, because Aluch Ali, the commander of the Turkish left wing, had realized at first sight the danger of these floating fortresses and had wisely kept his squadron beyond range of their fire. As each cannon ball struck the other two Turkish sections, great splin-ters of wood and men's bodies were seen flying through the air. With the very first barrage two Turkish galleys were sunk and over a score badly damaged. The galleasses were able to fire many more rounds before the Turks recovered from the shock produced by the sight of such amazing devastation. Some of Ali Pasha's ships actually made a suicidal rush for the galleasses with the intention of overpowering them by a joint attack, but their commander recalled them from this futile attempt and ordered all his forces to close in on the main Chris-tian fleet, leaving the deadly galleasses behind.

The Turkish right wing, led by Mohammed Sirocco, attempted not only to get safely beyond the galleasses, but also to circumvent the an-tagonists on the Christian left. [Christian commander Agostino] Bar-barigo was quick to observe this maneuver and ordered his captains to close off the gap between the tip of the Christian line and the northern shore of the gulf. But being less familiar with those waters than the ad-versary and fearing that they might run aground, the captains failed to seal the opening completely. About twelve of the Turkish galleys were able to slip past and attack from the rear, trapping Barbarigo's squadron in a dangerous cross fire. His galley held the end position, having ventured closest to shore. Suddenly Barbarigo found himself alone, surrounded by thirteen enemy ships led by Mohammed Sirocco himself, while the rest of the Turkish galleys fought to keep aid from reaching the solitary Christian vessel. As Barbarigo stood openly on his quarter-deck shouting orders and encouragement to his outnum-bered men, he became a conspicuous mark. All of the ten officers who were at his side the moment the attack began were killed within minutes, but Barbarigo seemed to be immune to the arrows that fell so thickly about him. Finally one of these pierced through his left eye and the mortally wounded leader was rushed below to the surgeons.

By this time many of the Turkish Janissaries had slain over half of the defenders with their shower of musket balls and poison-tipped arrows and were gaining a foothold on the decks of the galley. Then another Christian galley, captained by Barbarigo's own nephew, managed to break through the Turkish blockade. He too was killed moments after leading his own men to repel the boarders, but his lieutenant assumed command immediately and, rallying the men from both galleys, was able to drive the Turks back to their own ships. Moreover, he sent the surrounding vessels to flight by having his men set the Turks' own arrows on fire and shoot them back. One of the vessels fleeing these fire arrows lost its rudder in a collision with another Turkish galley and, temporarily disabled, was grappled by the two Christian galleys, one on each side. After an hour of heavy fighting it was captured, the first Christian prize of the battle.

The Battle Heats Up

All during this time the rest of Sirocco's and Barbarigo's squadrons were engaged in fierce struggles, usually one galley pitted against another, and the Christians were suffering the worst of it. At first the Turks did not try to board. They could cause more damage with their showers of deadly arrows than could the Christians with their more modern harquebuses [musket-type guns] and muskets, since the archers could let loose one arrow after another without pausing, but the firearms had to be cleaned and reloaded after each shot. As soon as they began to run out of arrows, the Turks decided to grapple and board the enemy galleys, and here, in hand-to-hand combat the Christians were more than a match for them. In fact, they fought with such incredible ferocity that the battle soon became a slaughter. Sirocco's flagship was jointly attacked by two Venetian galleys and soon captured, and Sirocco himself, later found floating on a piece of wreckage, mortally wounded, was mercifully beheaded, his suffering thus ended quickly. The defeat of the Turks' right wing was complete. Not one galley escaped. Those that were not sunk, burned, or grounded ashore were captured by their Christian opponents.

The fiercest action of the day was that fought in the center, focused on the fleets' two flagships. As the gap between the two main squadrons closed, Don Juan and Ali Pasha each directed his helmsman to steer for the galley of the enemy admiral, both easily recognized by their massive size and ornate decorations. The wisdom of Don Juan's decision to cut away each galley's ramming prow [the piece of the ship that juts out at the front; Don Juan had ordered this to be done before the battle] soon became apparent; for the Turks had to open artillery fire while still a fair distance away, but the Christians were able to train their guns at a downward angle, unobstructed by any prow, and wait until the last minute to fire into the enemy ships with deadly effect. Then the Turkish commander tried to ram Don Juan's galley amidships but, in swinging away to avoid this, Don Juan crashed into the adversary's bow with tremendous force. Locked together in this way, the two flagships become one bloody battlefield on which the elite of the Sultan's Janissaries were pitted against the flower of Spain's infantry.

At the moment of impact, both flagships had about the same number of soldiers aboard them; four hundred harquebusiers on Don Juan's galley and three hundred of the same, plus one hundred archers, on Ali Pasha's. The Turkish commander was so determined to capture the rival flagship that he had ten galleys and two galliots [small coasting ships] filled with troops positioned close to his stern, connected by ladders, so that he could be supplied with replacements, and after the battle began he also ordered the galley of [Turkish captain] Pertev Pasha to come alongside to aid him. On the other side, Don Juan's lieutenant, [Luis de] Requesens, was close by the Christian flagship with two galleys, from which he sent a steady stream of reinforcements, but [Christian captains Sebastian] Veniero and [Marc Antonio] Colonna were too hotly engaged by other Turkish galleys to lend their leader any assistance according to the original battle plans.

The contest between the rival flagships was fought with great skill and bravery on both sides. During the first ten minutes that passed after the galleys locked together, over seventy-five of the one hundred troops in the bow of the Christian flagship were killed or seriously wounded, and only the timely aid from Requesens' galley prevented this sector from being overwhelmed. Ali Pasha himself was seen firing arrows against the Christians, and he probably holds the distinction of being the last naval leader who ever drew a bowstring, for by that time the bow and arrow were becoming obsolete as weapons of war.

The Christians Gain the Advantage

Although both sides were equally matched in numbers and in bravery, it became apparent after the first furious hour of battle that the Christian firepower was more effective than that of the Turks. Twice the main deck of Ali Pasha's galley was swept clear of defenders and twice the Spaniards rushed aboard and nearly captured the vessel, but each time hundreds of Janissaries from the nearby Turkish galleys swarmed aboard to save their flagship. Every time this occurred the Turks counterattacked and tried to overwhelm the forces on Don Juan's ship, but they were unable to gain a real foothold. The third Christian attack was led personally by Don Juan, who carried a huge broadsword in one hand

and an ax in the other. Advancing slowly from the bow, every inch gained only at the price of many dead and wounded, the attackers slipped repeatedly on the blood covering the decks and the oil deliberately spread by the retreating Turks. Ali Pasha rushed forward from the stern hoping to meet Don Juan in personal combat. Stopped by a harquebus shot in the head, he tumbled onto the rowing benches, where a Christian galley slave, grabbing a nearby scimitar, severed the brave admiral's head, which was then raised high on a Spanish soldier's pike. After two hours the battle was over. Seeing their leader's head, the remaining Janissaries lost heart and jumped overboard to swim to the other Turkish galleys. Don Juan ordered the standard of Islam cut down from the mainmast and a large Holy League banner [symbolizing the alliance of Christian nations] raised in its place for Turks and Christians alike to see. The slaughter in the struggle had been immense: over three thousand Turks and one thousand Christians had lost their lives on board both vessels, and many more were wounded.

During the struggle between the two flagships, most of the other Christian vessels in the main squadron had been locked in heated combat. Colonna, Veniero, and Cardona all distinguished themselves, setting examples for their men by their deeds of personal valor and directing the fighting with such skill that several galleys were captured or sunk by each of their ships. One of the Papal galleys had the good fortune to capture the Turkish paymaster's ship, which not only carried a great treasure in coin aboard, but also turned out to be one of the Papal galleys captured by the Turks in the battle of Djerba [in the Mediterranean Sea] ten years before.

The battle seemed all but ended, but when Don Juan climbed to the lofty sterncastle of the captured enemy flagship he was dismayed by what he saw. The Turkish left wing under Aluch Ali was rapidly bearing down on the exposed flank of the main squadron, while the Christian right wing led by [Gian Andrea] Doria was moving away to the south in the opposite direction. It looked as if the Genoese admiral [that is, Doria], who had been accused of treachery in the past and who had opposed the plan of seeking out the enemy during this campaign, was now trying to run away. But whatever may have been the motives for his past actions (and excessive caution could be one explanation), in this case he had simply been outmaneuvered by his opponent. Aluch Ali and Doria, both experienced veterans, had been trying to outbluff each other, and the crafty Algerian had won. Aluch Ali had attempted first to get past Doria and attack him from the rear, as Sirocco had done to Barbarigo, and had failed. But while foiling this tactic, Doria's squadron was drawn steadily southward, away from the battle line. Seeing the ever-widening gap, Aluch All had ordered a rapid change of direction and sped toward the unprotected right flank of Don Juan's center squadron, a maneuver that Doria had somehow failed to foresee.

Nearest to the advancing Moslem wing was a Maltese galley under the command of an Italian Knight of Malta named Giustiniani, an old foe of the Algerian corsairs who had twice wounded Aluch Ali in personal combat. When Aluch Ali recognized this ship, which was towing four captured Turkish galleys from its stern, he bore down rapidly and rammed it with such tremendous force that it almost capsized. His troops quickly boarded, joined by soldiers from six other Algerian galleys nearby. The struggle that followed was one of the most savage and intense of the entire battle, second only to the one fought on the rival flagships in the number of casualties. Aluch Ali's troops were still fresh, this being their first action of the day, whereas the Christian soldiers under Giustiniani and those from the two other galleys of the Knights of Malta that rushed to the aid of their leader had been fighting for hours, and soon every one of them had fallen before the Turkish onslaught. Giustiniani himself was thought to be dead also, lying on the deck with five arrows in him and many slash wounds from the curved Turkish scimitars.

Aluch Ali was very pleased with himself. Not only had he rescued the four Turkish galleys that had been under tow and captured all three ships belonging to the Knights of Malta, but also he had rid himself of his lifelong enemy, Giustiniani. A sudden puff of wind cleared the smoke from an area to the north, and he sighted the Christian reserve squadron under Alvaro de Bazán bearing down on him at full speed. Cutting adrift the captured Maltese galley, which slowed him down, he escaped quickly to rejoin the main body of his squadron to the south. One of Bazán's vessels was detached to recover the Maltese galley and, stepping aboard, its officers were met with the grisly sight of almost five hundred Christian and Moslem corpses strewn all over the deck. But Giustiniani was found still breathing and, after several months of hospital care in Rome, he lived to sally out on many other forays against the Moslems, especially the Algerian pirates.

A Moslem Victory?

In the meantime the rest of Aluch Ali's ships, after sweeping past Doria's squadron, had wheeled around again and attacked it from the rear, sending the Christian ships into great confusion. It looked as if the Moslems would gain a total victory in this sector, and even when Bazán's reserve force appeared the issue was still in doubt. But Don Juan, seeing that his own squadron was doing a thorough job of finishing off the few remaining enemy ships in the center area, rushed south to Doria's aid, and as more and more galleys were able to follow his lead, the Algerians' victory turned into a thorough disaster. As soon as he recovered from his astonishment at being outmaneuvered so deftly, Doria more than compensated for his tactical error by excelling all the other Christian captains in skill and bravery during the combat. Aluch Ali, realizing that the main battle had already been lost and seeing his own ships captured one after another, decided to save what he could and fled with sixteen galleys, in hopes of reaching a safe haven in the port of Lepanto. Juan de Cardona's eight galleys were the only obstacle to his flight and, even though they gallantly strung themselves in a line to cut off his escape route, the desperate Algerians charged them in such a ferocious attack that they were able to break through, leaving behind eight crippled ghost ships with barely fifty survivors among them.

The whole battle was over by four o'clock that afternoon, even though many of the Christian galleys were still giving chase to Aluch Ali's ships and other solitary escaping Turkish vessels. Wreckage from the many vessels destroyed was everywhere in sight. The waters of the gulf for miles around were stained red from the great amount of blood shed that day and the sea was strewn with the bodies of both victors and vanquished. Small boats moved among the floating debris to salvage anything of value and to search for wounded survivors, but any unfortunate Moslem found clinging to a piece of wreckage was quickly put to the sword. Some of the captured enemy ships were so damaged that they had to be burned, along with a Papal galley that was almost on the point of sinking unaided. On board the vessels of the Christian fleet there was much to be done: surgeons were especially busy trying to save the lives of the many thousands who had been wounded in the battle; the able-bodied seamen and soldiers were all employed in making necessary repairs to the hulls and rigging.

At sunset there were signs of approaching bad weather, so that Don Juan ordered the fleet to regroup quickly and head for a sheltered bay near the northwestern limits of the gulf, proceeding under sail because the rowers were completely exhausted from the day's furious rowing. Around midnight they anchored in the bay and immediately all the fleet's leaders, with the exception of those badly wounded, came on board Don Juan's galley to congratulate him and celebrate the victory. Extra rations of victuals and wine were issued to all the men in the fleet and most of the night was passed in great merriment, the elated spirits undampened by either fatigue or the thunder and rain squalls that soon arrived.

The Huguenots and Catholics in France

Richard S. Dunn

The late sixteenth century witnessed several religious-based wars between Protestants and Catholics. Feelings ran high in many parts of Europe—in Germany, where many people followed Martin Luther and others stayed loyal to the Catholic Church; in the Netherlands, where the Protestant population rebelled against Spanish Catholic rule; and in England, where Henry VIII set up a Protestant Anglican Church in direct opposition to the authority of the pope.

Perhaps the greatest troubles, however, were in France. Although French Protestants, known as Huguenots, represented only about one-fifteenth of the population, warfare raged over several decades between the Huguenots and the Catholics. Religion and religious doctrine was one issue. Perhaps as important, however, was the question of political power. Catholicism was the official state religion of France. The French monarchs were Catholics; so were most of the nobles who strongly supported the royal family. In contrast, those nobles who became Protestant tended to be political opponents of the monarchy. Their interest in Protestantism was partly a matter of religious dogma and partly a matter of political power; they wanted to decentralize authority, embarrass the monarchy, and set up rules for their own feudal holdings, and Protestantism seemed to offer them that opportunity.

The quarrel began as a war of words but soon developed into something more significant. Several attempts to broker a compromise between the two factions failed. Catholics would not consider giving up any religious and civil authority, and Huguenots insisted on gaining at least some political and religious control. Over time, positions on both sides hardened, and the war of words became a war of weapons. Together, the political and religious concerns led to a war that lasted nearly forty years and attracted the attention of several nearby nations, including England and especially Spain. This excerpt, from Richard S. Dunn's *The Age of Religious Wars*, details the course of the conflict over time.

Editor's Note: The excerpt opens with a massacre that began the French religious wars. Henry, duke of Guise, was a leading Catholic of the time; it was his intemperate outburst described by Dunn that helped start the war. The duke was by no means the only Catholic leader to take part in the war. Charles IX, king of France at the time, was a Catholic. So was Charles's mother, the queen regent, Catherine de Medici. Some of the leading nobles on the Protestant side were the prince of Conde, Admiral Gaspard de Coligny, and Prince Henry of Navarre.

In 1562 the duke of Guise, passing the little town of Vassy with his troopers, was infuriated to see a congregation of Huguenots worshiping in a barn, and ordered his men to kill them. This incident triggered the French religious wars. Once started, the fighting was almost impossible to stop. The Huguenots formed far too small a minority to conquer France, but their armies became so expert at defensive campaigns that they could not be disbanded. Noncombatants suffered more than the soldiers: for every pitched battle there were numerous forays, sieges, lootings, and massacres. Peace treaties were repeatedly arranged only to be quickly broken. The original commanders on both sides were soon killed, not in battle but by assassins—the duke of Guise in 1563 and the Bourbon prince of Condé in 1569. These murders launched a blood feud in which the Catholic and Huguenot zealots strove for retaliation by ambushing and slaughtering the remaining leaders. Both sides were able to keep troops in the field for years at a time, their operations financed largely by tax money diverted from the royal treasury, and led by vagabond aristocrats who loved fighting and freebooting.

After ten years of inconclusive combat, the Huguenots seemed to be gaining the upper hand. In August, 1572, during an interval of peace, the cream of the Huguenot nobility gathered in Paris to celebrate the marriage of their chief, the young Bourbon prince Henry of Navarre (1553–1610), to the sister of King Charles IX. Not everyone joined in the rejoicing; to young Henry, duke of Guise (1550–1588), and to the queen mother, this wedding was bitter evidence that the Huguenots were capturing the king and the country. Admiral Coligny was now Charles IX's chief adviser and had just about persuaded the pliable king to reverse French foreign policy, declare war against Spain, and assist the Dutch Calvinist [Protestant] rebels. This was too much for Catherine de Medici. Insanely jealous of Coligny's influence over her son, she hired an assassin to murder the Admiral. On August 21, three days after the wedding, the assassin shot Coligny but merely wounded him. Now Catherine threw caution to the winds and hastily joined the Guise faction in a scheme to wipe out the entire Huguenot leadership. She insisted to Charles IX that the Huguenots, headed by Coligny, were plotting to kill him and seize power; playing upon the wretched king's jagged nerves as a musician bows his violin, she got Charles to agree to ambush *all* the traitorous Huguenot leaders.

Shortly after midnight on August 24, St. Bartholomew's Day, armed squads broke into the houses where the Huguenots lodged. The duke of Guise personally killed Coligny, in revenge for the murder of his father. Prince Henry of Navarre managed to save his life by promising to turn Catholic. By dawn the whole hysterical city was taking up the bestial cry, "Kill! Kill!" Women and children were senselessly hacked to death and dumped into the Seine. The great scholar Petrus Ramus was cut down while he knelt at prayer, and his pupils dragged his body through the streets. Debtors murdered their creditors. Looting continued for days. Such was the St. Bartholomew massacre, in which at least three thousand Huguenots were killed in Paris. As word spread throughout the country, thousands more were killed in the provincial towns. When the news reached the pope, he was so delighted that he gave a hundred crowns to the messenger. Catherine de Medici laughed exultantly when she saw Henry of Navarre attending his first Mass. Charles IX, on the other hand, sickened with guilt at having abused his royal responsibilities. Charles was wiser than his mother, for the massacre discredited the Valois monarchy without breaking the Huguenots or ending the conflict.

When Charles died in 1574, he was succeeded by his even more neurotic brother, Henry III. The new king was quickly hated for the money and affection he lavished on his *mignons*, effeminate court dandies, to say nothing of the degenerate royal ballets and masquerades, where (according to a scandalized Paris lawyer) the king "was usually dressed as a woman, with a low-cut collar which showed his throat, hung with pearls." Henry's feckless extravagance was inherited from his mother, but not his sudden spasms of religiosity, during which he took up the hermit's life or walked barefoot on penitential pilgrimages. Under this last Valois king, the Catholic-Huguenot conflict reached its climax. Ultra-Catholics and Huguenots alike saw Henry as a dissembling hypocrite. They repudiated his efforts at peacemaking, and did their utmost to dismantle the French state. The Huguenots, despite their loss of many aristocratic leaders in the St.

Bartholomew massacre, still held important western towns, such as La Rochelle. They were strongest in the south, and Languedoc became virtually independent. The ultra-Catholics formed a Holy League in 1576 and vowed to exterminate heresy and to seat a Catholic champion, such as Henry, duke of Guise, on the French throne. Leaders of both religions preached rebellion. In the most famous Huguenot tract, the *Vindiciae contra tyrannos* (1578), Calvin's political theory was rewritten to show that a tyrannical king has violated his contract with the people and should be overthrown. Jesuit writers argued the League position that a king who betrays the Church must be overthrown. Both sides had strong commanders. For the League, Henry of Guise was a perfect bandit captain, brave, dashing, and arrogant, with a saber scar etched across his cheek. But the Huguenots could boast the heir apparent to the throne, Prince Henry of Navarre, who quickly renounced his forced St. Bartholomew conversion. Henry of Navarre was an easygoing extrovert with one priceless virtue: he was the only late sixteenth-century French political leader who honestly tried to serve his country as well as himself.

The War of the Three Henries

The turning point in the French crisis came in 1588–1589, with the War of the Three Henries: Guise versus Valois versus Navarre. The conflict began when the duke of Guise made his supreme bid to capture the monarchy. He had to move carefully, for he was in the pay of Philip II, who had his own claim to the French throne! (Philip's third wife had been a Valois princess.) In 1588 the Spanish king directed Guise to stage a revolt in Paris in order to prevent Henry III from interfering with the Spanish Armada when it attacked England. Accordingly, Guise entered Paris against Henry III's express orders. He incited the city mob to disarm the king's guards and besieged him inside the Louvre palace. Before Guise could summon the nerve to assault the Louvre and kill the king, his intended victim fled the city. Nevertheless, Guise now had virtual control. He forced Henry III to make him chief minister, he dictated policy, and he managed the Estates-General which convened at Blois in 1588. The only trouble was that by this time Guise's patron, Philip II, had been badly beaten by the English and was unable to protect his French agent.

The royal château at Blois was Henry III's last retreat. This rambling palace, with its famous open staircase, myriad paneled rooms, and secret passageways, lies in the heart of the Loire Valley. Nearby are Amboise, where Henry's brother escaped conspiracy, and Chenonceaux, where his mother squandered a fortune on new construction. Catherine de Medici could no longer intervene, for she lay mortally ill. Imitating Catherine's role in the St. Bartholomew massacre, Henry III plotted to murder Guise. "He does not dare," said the duke contemptuously, but for once he underestimated the Valois. On December 23, 1588, the king's bodyguard closed in on Guise and cut him down. The old queen mother could hear the uproar as the dying duke dragged his assassins through the royal chambers above her sickbed.

Henry III now joined the Huguenots in an all-out effort to crush the Catholic League. He threw himself into an alliance with Henry of Navarre, whom he recognized as his heir, and the two men marched together against Catholic Paris. But retribution for Guise's murder came fast: in July, 1589, Henry III was himself assassinated, by a fanatical monk who had secreted a dagger in the sleeve of his habit. Only one of the three Henries was left. Could the French Catholics be induced to accept this heretical prince as King Henry IV?

The Politiques

The new king's strongest asset was the mounting popular revulsion against anarchy. Many Frenchmen, derisively called *politiques* because they preferred merely political goals to spiritual ones, had long craved for peace and stability. The skeptical essayist Michel de Montaigne (1533–1592) was a *politique*, disgusted with cannibalism in the name of divinity. So was the profound political theorist Jean Bodin (1530–1596), whose *Six Books of the Republic* (1576) pleaded for the establishment of centralized sovereign authority in the hands of a purposeful prince. In Henry IV, the *politiques* saw at last a French prince who could be trusted with sovereign authority, who was a statesman of humanity and honesty (unlike Catherine de Medici), with a suitably jocose, pragmatic temper. Yet it took Henry IV a full decade to end the war. With Guise dead, the Catholic champion became Philip II, who intended once he had conquered Henry IV to put a Spanish infanta on the throne. In the early 1590's, Spanish troops repeatedly swept down from Flanders and blocked Henry IV's efforts to occupy his capital city. The Parisians continued to believe their League priests, who taught that a good Catholic would eat his own children rather than submit to a heretic. In 1593, Henry concluded that he must undergo the humiliation of abjuring Protestantism. "Today I talk to the Bishops," he told his mistress. "Sunday I take the perilous leap" (that is, attend Mass). Henry's politically motivated conversion scandalized the ultra-Catholics even more than the Huguenots, but the pope felt compelled to grant him absolution. Paris opened its gates to the king who, hat in hand, saluted all the pretty ladies in the windows as he entered the city.

In 1598, Henry IV and Philip II finally made peace, restoring the terms of 1559. Spain had gained nothing. In this same year, Henry bought off the last of the Catholic League nobility with grants of money and titles and conciliated the Huguenots with the Edict of Nantes. With this edict, Henry established a lasting religious truce. He declared Catholicism the official French religion and prohibited the reformed worship within five leagues of Paris. Yet any nobleman who chose to do so could practice the reformed religion in his own household, and bourgeois and lower-class Huguenots could also worship in certain specified places. The Huguenot residents of some two hundred towns, mostly in the south and along the Bay of Biscay, were granted full religious freedom, including the right to set up schools and printing presses. About half of these towns were fortified and garrisoned by the Huguenots at royal expense. In addition, Huguenots throughout the country were promised "perpetual and irrevocable" liberty of conscience, full civil rights, and eligibility for public office. The king appointed special courts (half Catholic, half Huguenot) to adjudicate breaches of his edict.

The close of the French religious wars, with the Edict of Nantes, was to some extent a Catholic victory. France was hence forth a Catholic country with a Catholic king. Yet Henry IV temporarily expelled the Jesuits and repudiated the fanaticism of the ultra-Catholic League. At the same time, his edict was to some extent a Protestant victory, since it granted the Huguenots an entrenched position within the country. Yet the Huguenots had lost their leader; toleration was a gift of the king. In most ways, the compromise of 1598 signalized the triumph of political expediency over religion. The chief lesson of the French religious wars was a political one, that strongly centralized government was the only possible alternative to rebellion and social chaos. Upon this foundation would be built the magnificent seventeenth-century absolute monarchy of Louis XIV.

Russia and Ivan the Terrible

Ian Grey

Ivan IV of Russia was a brutal ruler and a brutal man, an emperor known as "the Terrible" in the sense of "terrifying." It was a nickname richly deserved, though Ivan was capable of acts of kindness. Ivan's significance in world history, however, goes beyond his cruelty. Russia in the early sixteenth century was a relative backwater, an insignificant country surrounded by hostile powers. During Ivan's reign, Russia consolidated its gains, established a good-sized army, and began to move toward being a world power.

This excerpt, from Ian Grey's book *Ivan the Terrible,* discusses the year 1547, in which Ivan was crowned czar, married his queen, Anastasia, and faced down civil rebellion pitting aristocrats known as boyars against Ivan's relatives, the Glinsky family of princes. The passage sheds light on Ivan's cruelty, but also provides a good picture of Russia as it was at the beginning of Ivan's reign. Ian Grey, Australian by birth, spent many years in Russia and has written biographies of several other leading Russian rulers.

A nastasia herself possessed all the womanly virtues, prized among Orthodox Russians, of humility, charity, and devoutness, which made her a gentle and obedient companion. Women in Muscovy were completely subservient to their men, and their lives were hard and often miserable. [Russian ambassador Sigismund von] Herberstein noted that the Muscovites "consider no woman virtuous unless she live shut up at home and be so closely guarded that she go out nowhere". They were not even free to go to church on public occasions. Relegated to the *terem*, their special apartments, the women of noble families led a life of idleness in which the monotony was relieved by spinning and needlework. Their sole function was to bear children, for servants carried out all domestic duties. Among the poorer people the women were not shut away, but they worked so hard that they were no more than beasts of burden. A woman of character might exercise a strong influence within her family, but this was exceptional. The wife of the autocrat was, of course, required to lead an exemplary life.

On 13 February the Metropolitan [a religious leader] performed the marriage ceremony in the Uspensky Cathedral. The couple then showed themselves to the people who called out their blessings. Muscovites gave themselves up to celebrations, lasting several days. But Ivan and Anastasia devoutly withdrew and, although the countryside was in the freezing grip of winter, they walked together in stages the forty miles to the Troitsa monastery, where they spent the first week of Lent, praying daily at the tomb of Saint Sergius.

Such piety, deeply felt and sincere, was part of the daily life of all Muscovites, and it was expected of the autocrat. But in this harsh age, not only in Muscovy but throughout Europe, Christian devotion went hand in hand with cruelty and inhumanity. In Ivan this capacity for devoutness, even tenderness, and savagery were combined to an extraordinary degree. He was capable of affection; in fact, the few who managed to set aside his morbid suspicions and to win his trust found a gentle spirit, longing to love and be loved. Anastasia awakened such feelings in him and he was always to treat her with gentle affection and respect. In time she was to bring a calming influence to bear on him. But she could not at once assuage his hatreds or exorcize his mistrust of others. Confronted by hostility or even simple opposition, he at once felt himself to be surrounded by enemies and his fury was unleashed.

At this time, despite the Christian vows enjoined on him as Tsar at his coronation, and the example of Christian piety displayed by his Tsaritsa, Ivan was intoxicated by his new-found power. He was autocrat; nothing could be denied him; no one could gainsay him. He indulged his coarsest tastes for entertainers, drinking bouts, and cruel sports, and he played with power, raising up and striking down whomsoever he wished. The government of the country remained in the hands of the Glinsky who, apart from meeting the least whims of the Tsar, were free to pursue their own interests, preying on boyars and people alike. The *nastavniki* or governors, whom they appointed, ruled corruptly and those who suffered had no redress.

The people of Pskov . . . had a tradition of freedom and independence, and were more ready than the people of central Russia to voice their complaints and to demand justice. Boldly they decided to petition the Tsar about the malpractices of their *nastavnik*, Prince Turuntai-Pronsky.

The seventy citizens of Pskov, chosen to present the petition with accusations and proofs against him, made the journey to Moscow and confronted Ivan in the village of Ostrovka. He refused to hear them. Their presence alone was to him a form of sedition. In a rage he shouted, abused, and condemned them. He had hot wine poured over their heads and some had their hair and their beards singed by fire. He ordered them to strip and to lie naked in the snow. Bewildered and re-signed, they obeyed, expecting now to be summarily executed, and this was almost certainly the fate awaiting them. But at this moment messengers galloped into the village with news of a terrible fire in Moscow. Ivan at once mounted his horse and rode away with his suite to the city. The petitioners of Pskov were forgotten and to this they owed their lives.

Fire!

Fires were frequent in Moscow. The houses, built of logs, were heated in winter by crude stoves and dried out until they were like tinder in the short hot summers. The yards surrounding most houses often helped prevent fires from spreading, but it needed only a wind to carry the sparks and then whole districts were aflame. The city had suffered many major fires, but none within recent years.

Moscow was, however, now growing rapidly. Established as the seat of the Tsar and the principal city of Muscovy, it attracted people from all over the country. Houses sprang up wherever there was space. Richard Chancellor, the English sea captain, considered Moscow "greater than London . . . but it is rude and standeth without all order". Herberstein wrote that the great number of houses, said to exceed 41,500, was "scarcely credible", while the Kremlin was so large that it not only contained "the very extensive and magnificently built stone palace of the prince", but also spacious timbered houses of the Met-ropolitan, the leading boyars, and many churches. Within and with-out the Kremlin and even in the newer suburbs the new huddled with the old dilapidated houses, and the congestion, caused by the rapid growth of the city, made the spreading of fires a far greater hazard.

On 12 April 1547 a serious fire broke out in Kitai Gorod, the middle town and merchant quarter. All the stalls and warehouses of the mer-chants and traders perished. A tower, used to store gunpowder, exploded, blowing parts of the city wall into the Moskva river. This fire then died down, but no doubt smouldered and a few days later new fires destroyed the district beyond the Yauza river, where the smithies and tanneries were concentrated. Again the fires died down or were dormant with only minor outbreaks, but then after several weeks came the great confla-gration, the most devastating fire that Moscow had yet experienced.

A high wind was blowing when on 21 June fire first broke out in the Arbat, a suburb to the west of the Kremlin. The church of Vozdvizhenskoe quickly burnt to the ground. The fire spread rapidly, reducing to ashes the whole of the western part of the city up to the banks of the Moskva river. At this stage the wind changed direction, carrying the fire on to the Kremlin which was soon ablaze. The palace, the treasury, armouries, all the state offices, private houses, the Metropolitan's palace, the cathedrals and churches, all were destroyed. The books and manuscripts, the treasures of the Kremlin, the holy ikons with few exceptions, but including the miracle-working ikon of the virgin of Vladimir, perished. The Uspensky Cathedral with its renowned ikonostasis and gold vessels was partly spared, but the structure of the cathedral was seriously damaged. The great bell of Moscow fell from its burning belfry to fracture on the ground below. Adding to the horror of the people in the smoking inferno, which the whole city had become, were the explosions of gunpowder in the state arsenal.

At the first outbreak of fire Metropolitan Makary had gone to the Uspensky Cathedral to pray for the deliverance of the city. The smoke almost suffocated him, but he managed to escape carrying with him the holy ikon of the Mother of God, painted by the Metropolitan Peter. He was followed by several priests and an archpriest, bearing the ancient church statutes, which had been brought originally from Constantinople. He made his way along the city wall by means of a secret passage, but once again the smoke overwhelmed him. The priests, accompanying him, then lowered him from the Kremlin wall by means of a wooden platform. The rope broke and the Metropolitan fell heavily to the ground. He was almost unconscious as he was carried off to the Novospassky monastery.

Reaction Against Ivan

Driven by the high wind, the fire had swept across the city. Few buildings had escaped damage and most districts had been reduced to smouldering ruins. At least 1,700 people, not including many children, had lost their lives. For days heavy clouds of smoke hung over the city. The survivors, with singed hair and blackened faces, searched hopelessly among the charred ruins for missing members of their families and traces of their property. Everyone had suffered some loss and, bowed down by personal tragedy, sought consolation that was not to be found. The bewildered sorrowful mood of the people began to turn to resentment, especially towards their autocrat who had completely failed to succour or to consider them in this time of need.

At the outset of the disaster Ivan with his wife, brother, and boyars had ridden away to safety in the village of Vorobiovo, not far from the city. There, watching the pall of smoke rising from Moscow, he remained while fire raged. Apparently he had no thoughts for his people for their sufferings, but he and several boyars gave prompt instructions for the rebuilding of their palaces in the Kremlin.

On the day following the fire, Ivan rode with his suite to the Novospassky monastery to pay his respects to the Metropolitan, who was recovering from exhaustion and the shock of his accident. There Ivan's chaplain, Archpriest Feodor Barmin, Boyar Prince Feodor Skopin-Shuisky, Ivan Chelyadin, and others, known to be hostile to the Glinsky, told him that black magic was responsible for the fires and the burning of Moscow. Sorcerers had torn out the hearts from human corpses, soaked them in water, and then had sprinkled this water on the streets of Moscow; this had caused the fire.

Ivan was astonished, but ready to accept this explanation. Witchcraft, a stubborn and powerful relic of pagan religions, was widely practised in Muscovy and Western Europe in the 16th century, as the innumerable trials and the general persecution of witches bore witness. Fervently believing in the devil, people had no difficulty in accepting the existence of witches as his agents. To a young man of Ivan's temperament, witchcraft was a very real force, a manifestation of the devil's evil influence, to be guarded against by prayer. He at once ordered his boyars to conduct an investigation and the method they adopted in carrying out this investigation suggested that either the charge of witchcraft was invented as part of a careful plan to overthrow the Glinsky or that the boyars seized on a popular rumour to achieve this purpose.

Blame

On the fifth day after the fire, without the usual interrogations or assembling of evidence, the boyars called the homeless and desperate people of Moscow to the square in front of the Uspensky Cathedral. There they put to the crowd the question, "Who set fire to Moscow?" Spontaneously they shouted in reply, "Princess Anna Glinskaya with her children made the magic. . ." and they recited the details concerning the use of human hearts. Whether because this explanation was the popular belief or because it had been well planted among them beforehand, the crowd needed no prompting. Moreover, they spoke from a burning hatred of the Glinsky and at the same time, since the Glinsky were of his family and his current favourites, they were censuring their young Tsar, who had thought only of his personal safety.

Prince Yuri Glinsky, Ivan's uncle, was with the boyars on the Kremlin Square and heard the crowd condemn him and his family. He quietly slipped away to seek sanctuary in the Uspensky Cathedral. The boyars, themselves opposed to the Glinsky as much as the people, then sent the angry mob in pursuit of him. They swept into the cathedral and, ignoring the fact that they were on consecrated ground and in a place of special sanctity, they killed him near the altar. They then dragged his corpse from the Kremlin to the place of execution on the Red Square, where they exposed it for all to see.

Their fury unabated, the mob stormed through the city in pursuit of the supporters and attendants of the Glinsky and they killed all whom they found. Three days later, still thirsting for blood, the mob made its way to Vorobiovo. They took up a stand before the Tsar's residence, shouting demands that his grandmother, Princess Anna, and his uncle, Prince Mikhail Glinsky, whom they believed to be hidden there by the Tsar, should be handed over to them.

To Ivan this was treasonable conduct and an affront to him personally, such as he could never tolerate from his own subjects. He showed no fear of the mob and not only refused their demands, but had many of the rioters seized and summarily executed. The rest of the mob, not having expected that their young Tsar would act so severely, took fright and made their escape back to the city. The riot and the talk of black magic had come to an end. . . .

The riots had made a deep impression on [Ivan], not only because of the strength of the popular antagonism towards the Glinsky, but because it was also directed at him. Popular discontent had been stirring throughout his reign, but it had always been concentrated against the boyars who were equally his enemies. It came as a shock to him to find himself coupled with a hated faction in the popular mind, and the shock was salutary.

Freebooters and Sea Dogs: Pirates of the Spanish Main

Hamilton Cochran

Although seagoing vessels of almost every era have had to deal with the possibility of pirates, the threat was never greater than in the period beginning with the sixteenth century. Indeed, this time has been called the "golden age of piracy." Some pirates, known as privateers or corsairs, worked more or less directly for governments; British and French ships patrolled the Caribbean and the Atlantic in search of Spanish galleons, large slow ships loaded with gold and other riches from North America. Other pirates were independent of any government; they preyed on whomever they wished. All pirates used small, quick ships and the element of surprise to overcome their enemies.

This excerpt, from Hamilton Cochran's *Pirates of the Spanish Main*, discusses the English sea robbers who made life miserable—and dangerous—for the Spanish galleon captains. To the English, men like Sir Francis Drake were heroes, patriotic Englishmen doing their best to enrich England at the expense of its Spanish enemy. To the Spanish, of course, Drake and others of his kind were criminals. As attacks against Spanish vessels increased throughout the century, the tensions between the two nations increased as well. These tensions culminated in outright war in 1588, a war unexpectedly won by the English. Indeed, partly due to the efforts of the English pirates, the balance of power between England and Spain shifted significantly during the sixteenth century. When the century began, England was weak and Spain powerful; matters were very different when the century ended.

Excerpted from *Pirates of the Spanish Main,* by Hamilton Cochran. Copyright © 1961 by Forbes, Inc. Reprinted with permission from American Heritage, a division of Forbes, Inc.

To the lordly Spaniards of the early sixteenth century, England was an insignificant island that could not compare in natural wealth to Spain's newly settled isle of Española (Hispaniola) in the West Indies. English shipping was also of little account, consisting mostly of fishing smacks. Henry VII, the first Tudor king, encouraged an English merchant marine. But he had been too busy with problems at home to give explorer Columbus the financial backing requested of the English in 1489.

Soon after Columbus' discovery of the New World for Spain, Ferdinand and Isabella, fearful that England might seize unsettled parts of the Spanish Main [that is the Spanish New World claims], took possession of the Isthmus of Darien (Panama). Such an idea had never entered Henry's mind. Yet many of his seagoing subjects were looking westward. In the dockside taverns of English ports seamen who had sailed the Caribbean told of great riches to be plundered from the Spaniards; of slaves and parrots and silver ingots and lovely Indian girls—all there waiting to be taken by Englishmen with keen blades and a touch of daring. So it happened that English freebooters (in the succeeding reign of England's new king, Henry VIII) began entering the forbidden waters of the New World to vie with French corsairs for their share of Spain's newfound wealth.

The French corsairs (privateers working for Francis I of France, the great rival of the new ruler of Spain, Emperor Charles V) were the first seamen to prey on the Spanish treasure galleons. The Spanish considered corsairs such as Juan Florin, Juan Terrier, and Jean d'Ango—who sailed from the ports of Dieppe, Brest, and Bordeaux—a great menace to the prosperity of Spain's valuable trade with her New World colonies. Florin is said to have captured two of the galleons Cortés sent back to Spain loaded with gold from the conquest of Mexico. An official chronicler of the reign of Charles V tells how Florin was later captured by the Spanish navy and beheaded—by personal order of the Emperor. The chronicler reports that Florin confessed that he had "robbed and sunk 150 ships and galleys and galleons."

Henry VIII of England built a navy bristling with cannon, for he shrewdly realized that England's destiny lay at sea. With staunch vessels to carry them, his English sea dogs would prove that they were able navigators, persistent merchants, and stubborn fighters against the Spaniards.

The Hawkins Family

It was William Hawkins, a mariner of Plymouth, who was one of the first Englishmen to exploit the trade in "black ivory," as Negro slaves were sometimes known. Hawkins captured Negroes on the west coast of Africa and smuggled them into the Spanish colonies. The chief wealth of the Spanish in the West Indies was coming to be based on the working of great plantations for raising sugar and other crops. Therefore, the Spanish had to have great numbers of slaves to perform the necessary labor. Slave running in those days was considered a respectable business from the English standpoint, for William Hawkins in later life was twice elected mayor of Plymouth, became a member of Parliament, and died a wealthy man in 1553.

Five years later, Queen Elizabeth, a Protestant, ascended the throne. She feared Spain, not only because it was Catholic, but because the Spaniards were growing rich and powerful from their enormous overseas possessions. So it was quite logical that she would take an interest in the privateering voyages and adventures of another Hawkins, named John, son of old William. The Queen gave him financial backing, as did a number of nobles and the lord mayor of London.

The Spaniards called John Hawkins a pirate, but he was actually a privateer and smuggler of slaves. Like his father, he robbed the Portuguese of their Negroes on the Guinea coast of Africa and sold them to the Spaniards in the West Indies.

On his second voyage, in 1564, he was refused permission to sell his Negroes. Infuriated, Hawkins landed a hundred armed men, marched to the town of Barbarotta (near present-day Puerto Cabello, Venezuela), and forced the Spanish governor to grant him a license unless he wanted to fight. By means of threats and persuasion, Hawkins sold all his Negroes and returned to England a hero. He was knighted by the Queen.

Bluff and Strategies

Hawkins' third privateering venture, in 1567, turned out quite differently. By now the king of Spain threatened the most severe punishments to any of his subjects who bought slaves from those Protestant English dogs. Spanish America, he declared, was his private preserve; none but licensed Spaniards could trade there.

Among the fleet of six vessels commanded by Hawkins were two that belonged to Queen Elizabeth, the *Jesus of Lübeck* and the *Minion*. Another little vessel, the *Judith*, was captained by a twenty-two-year-old Devon mariner named Francis Drake. After again robbing the Portuguese of their slaves, Hawkins arrived off the Spanish Main. "We skirted the coast from one settlement to another," he wrote, doing "good business" smuggling Negroes to the Spaniards.

Then, loaded with pearls, gold, and silver, Hawkins started home by way of the Yucatán Channel. All went well until a frightful storm harried the fleet and forced Hawkins to put in to Veracruz for repairs.

The citizens were expecting the king of Spain's fleet at any moment, and Hawkins knew that if he sailed into the harbor under his own flag, he would be saluted with shots from the fort. So he hoisted Spanish colors. When the eager Spaniards came aboard and saw the hated English, they were thunderstruck. Merchant Hawkins got right down to business. He trained his guns on the town, sold the last few of his slaves, and repaired his ships.

When the Spanish fleet appeared, Hawkins bluffed the new viceroy into coming to terms to avoid a fight. But the wily viceroy, breaking his word of honor, staged a surprise attack and caught Hawkins off guard. Trapped in the narrow bay near San Juan de Ulúa, the little English fleet tried desperately to escape. Drake got out first, but the *Jesus of Lübeck* and hundreds of men were lost or taken prisoner. Hawkins returned to England, minus four ships and all his treasure.

Francis Drake had also arrived home with nothing to show for his adventure except a leaky ship and a handful of survivors. But he had learned that a fortune could be his for the taking in Spanish America.

Francis Drake

So began the spectacular career of Francis Drake and his one-man war against Spain. Few characters in history have matched his adventurous life. His fellow countrymen respectfully called him Admiral and the Prince of Privateers. Spaniards prayed Heaven to punish that "Francisco Draque," whom they sometimes called The Dragon, and other names even less flattering.

Drake's next voyage to the Main after the disastrous experience with Hawkins was mainly to spy out the coast. Then, in 1572, he set sail from Plymouth with two privateers, the *Pasha* and the *Swan*, manned by seventy-three men and boys. His first objective was the town of Nombre de Dios, then only a small pest-ridden place on the Isthmus of Panama. It was the terminus of the trail that led across the jungle on the Isthmus. Over the trail came mule trains, their bells gaily jingling, loaded with silver from the rich mines of Potosi. For months Drake lay in wait, knowing that the arrival of the treasure train at Nombre de Dios was timed to coincide with the appearance of the Spanish fleet sent to fetch it home. Drake's patience paid handsome dividends. The treasure arrived on schedule. With the aid of friendly maroons (Negroes, escaped from slavery and often living with the Indians; their name is a shortening of the Spanish word *cimarrón,* which means "wild," "untamed," "free"), Drake surprised and attacked the heavily laden string of two hundred mules. The booty that Drake captured in this 1572 attack included thirty tons of heavy silver ingots. When Drake arrived home in Plymouth, the town and, in fact, all of England went mad with joy.

Using part of the loot to finance a new expedition and again with the backing of the Queen, Drake once more set out across the Atlantic in the *Golden Hind* with four other small privateers. It was December 13, 1577. Only he knew their destination: he was sailing for the Pacific. He had viewed that ocean from a "goodly and great high tree" the same year he captured the treasure at Nombre de Dios. Reverently he "besought Almighty God of his goodness to give him life and leave to sail an English ship on that sea."

To South America

Now, pointing into the sunset once more, Francis Drake would be the first Englishman to round Cape Horn and to raid the weakly defended coastal towns of Chile, Peru, and Mexico.

As he was prowling off the coast of Ecuador, Drake captured the great plate ship *Nuestra Señora de la Concepción*. Then sailing north to California, at Drake's Bay, just north of San Francisco, he put in to careen [turn the ship on its side], scrape, and repair the hull of the *Golden Hind*. He left a bronze tablet on a post there, which claimed "New Albion" for England.

With his treasure safely under hatches, Drake then sailed eastward across the Pacific, touched at the Moluccas and Java in the East Indies, rounded Africa's Cape of Good Hope, and dropped anchor in Plymouth in 1580 after an absence of two years and ten months—the second man [after Ferdinand Magellan] ever to sail around the world.

After some hesitation, Queen Elizabeth ignored the fury of King Philip II of Spain and knighted Drake in honor of his world-girdling exploit. A fair share of the immense booty he brought back to England "passed quietly into the royal hands."

Another Voyage

In 1585, as the inevitable war with Spain was approaching, Drake set out again with the greatest and most heavily gunned English fleet yet to cross the Atlantic. His object was highly practical: to weaken Spain by seizing her important Caribbean ports and to shut off her golden flow of wealth. Santo Domingo, on Hispaniola (in the present-day Dominican Republic), the "ancientest and chiefly inhabited place" in all the West Indies, paid a disappointing ransom of 25,000 ducats as well as guns, ships, and provisions. Next came Cartagena, where Drake's armored English pikemen breached the walls and drove the defenders back into the city and forced them to surrender.

Casualties and fever forced Drake to abandon his plan for making Cartagena his main base for attacks on other Spanish towns. He contented himself with exacting a heavy ransom just as he had in Santo Domingo—burning the city block by block until the ransom was paid; he then sailed to Florida by way of Cuba. He captured St. Augustine but did not linger. By July, 1586, he was in home waters once more. . . .

There were Englishmen other than Sir Francis Drake who tried to seize the wealth and break the power of Spain. In 1591 Sir Richard Grenville was killed in an attempt to seize a fleet of Spanish treasure ships in the Azores. The famous courtier Sir Walter Raleigh also tried to claim some of the gold of South America for England. His expedition up the Orinoco River in 1595 in search of El Dorado yielded only some gold ore samples. His second expedition, in 1617, brought him no gold at all, and his capture of a Spanish town in Venezuela brought a demand from Spain that he be executed in England. He went to the block in 1618.

Sir Richard Hawkins, son of the famous Elizabethan privateer Sir John Hawkins, and grandson of the equally adventuresome slave runner William Hawkins, followed his family's tradition and became a rover. He served under Drake in the Caribbean in 1585, commanded a ship for England in the fight against the Spanish Armada in 1588, and in 1593 set out as a privateer aboard his own ship, the *Dainty*. After sailing down the Brazilian coast, he sailed into the Pacific through the Strait of Magellan and plundered the town of Valparaiso, Chile. He was captured by the Spanish after his successful attack and imprisoned first in Lima, Peru, and then in Spain until 1602. On his release he returned to England, became a famous admiral, and often served to defend the English coast against pirate attack.

A distinguished nobleman financed and led the last of Queen Elizabeth's great privateering expeditions against Spain, in 1598. Lord George Clifford, Earl of Cumberland, started financing and sometimes leading privateering expeditions in 1586 in order to build up his sadly reduced family fortune. In 1598 he sailed from England with twenty ships for the Spanish stronghold of San Juan, Puerto Rico. He wanted to sack the town and also take it over as an English base. On June 6, Clifford's ships arrived at San Juan and laid siege to the city. The city surrendered and was occupied by Clifford and his men. Soon after, however, Clifford's troops became ill of a tropical fever and had to abandon San Juan.

The Spanish Response

The Spanish were determined to rid themselves of the English sea dogs and to preserve the Caribbean as a private Spanish sea. In Drake's time and later, all foreign ships found in the Caribbean—whether merchantmen, privateers, or pirate craft—could be seized by the Spanish and confiscated. Their crews were often tortured to death or imprisoned. For two reasons the English were more harshly treated by the Spanish than were members of any other nation. First of all, England was the leader of Europe's Protestants. The Spanish Inquisition—the much dreaded attempt by Spain to purify the Catholic Church itself from heresy from within and also to curb the spread of both Protestantism and Islam in the world—was active in Europe and in the New World. Its sentences were cruel, but in the sixteenth and seventeenth centuries the English courts and the disciplines of the English navy could be equally cruel. The Inquisition first set up its religious courts and police system in Cuba in 1516. In 1571 Mexico received its own courts of the Inquisition; in 1581 the Inquisition came to Peru. Between 1581 and 1776 fifty-nine heretics were burned at the stake in Lima. Englishmen who were caught in Spanish waters ran the danger of being turned over to its courts. Prisoners from John Hawkins' expedition of 1567 fell into the hands of the Inquisition in Mexico City. Two were sentenced to death. A few were set free. Others were imprisoned, flogged, or sent to the galleys.

Secondly, English smugglers were trying to break Spain's trade monopoly over her colonial empire in the New World. And even though Spain could supply her colonies with only a small fraction of their needs, smugglers might be killed if captured. So the Englishmen who sailed into the Caribbean were risking much for gold.

And of all those brave rivals, Sir Francis Drake was the luckiest, the most gallant, and by far the most successful of the sea dogs who fought for Queen Elizabeth.

Henry VIII and Thomas More: Conscience Versus Politics

Peter Ackroyd

One of the great dramas of the sixteenth century involved Henry VIII of England and his lord chancellor Thomas More. Henry wished to divorce his wife, Catherine of Aragon, and marry Anne Boleyn. When the Roman Catholic pope refused to grant Henry a divorce, Henry took matters into his own hands: He divorced Catherine, cut England's ties to Catholicism, and began his own national church.

Henry received opposition, though, from More, a lawyer and a staunch Catholic. Henry tried to cajole and coax More into agreeing with his decision. When those attempts failed, Henry resorted to threats. He insisted that More accept both the divorce, and the supremacy of the English sovereign over the Catholic Church. As British writer Peter Ackroyd explains in this excerpt from *The Life of Thomas More,* More could not conscientiously do so and refused—with disastrous consequences. The story of More and Henry has inspired artists, writers, dramatists, and others who have taken stands based on conscience.

Editors Note: In the winter of 1534, the English Parliament passed the so-called Act of Succession at Henry's behest. This act announced that

Excerpted from *The Life of Thomas More*, by Peter Ackroyd. Copyright © 1998 by Peter Ackroyd. Reprinted with permission from Doubleday, a division of Random House, Inc.

the marriage between Catherine and Henry was null and void. It also held that no earthly power could sanction the marriage, a statement that directly defied the authority of the pope. Furthermore, the act obligated all the subjects of the king to swear an oath, the Oath of Succession, which announced their willingness to abide by the act.

To this point, More had been loud in his criticism of the king's actions, but had suffered little for his beliefs. That was about to change. As one government official after another took the oath, More realized that he could not conscientiously do the same. He had hoped that somehow he would escape being forced to sign it, but that was not to be. In April 1534 More was summoned to Lambeth Palace in England. He was brought before some of the most powerful political and religious leaders of the time and specifically asked to swear his allegiance to the king by accepting the Act of Succession. More knew that his position was a difficult one. It was clear that the government was going to make an example of him and insist that he sign the oath—or accept the consequences. Neither was a pleasant prospect. One, he knew, might mean a death sentence, but the other would mean a loss of self-respect and a violation of his conscience. For More, the choice was not in doubt. Refusing to sign the oath, he was beheaded in 1535, and canonized in 1935.

[M]ore] was led before [the Earl of Essex Thomas] Cromwell, [archbishop of Canterbury Thomas] Cranmer, [Lord Chancellor Thomas] Audley and William Benson, the Abbot of Westminster. They asked him if he was now ready to swear the oath and he expressed a wish to see it; a small slip of parchment, beneath the impress of the Great Seal, was handed to him and he read it carefully. Then he requested a copy of the Act of Succession itself, which was given to him in the form of a 'printed roll'. He read this, too, and in his precise way he compared the oath to the Act. The commissioners were waiting impatiently for his answer and, finally, after detailed consideration of both documents, he spoke out. 'My purpose is not to put any fault either in the Act or any man that made it, or in the oath or any man that swears it, nor to condemn the conscience of any other man. But as for myself in good faith my conscience so moves me in the matter, that though I will not deny to swear to the succession, yet unto the oath that here is offered to me I cannot swear, without the jeopardizing of my soul to perpetual damnation.' It may be supposed that this statement, constructed in the manner of a lawyer to avoid prejudice, had been rehearsed during More's sleepless nights. All along he had known the opinion of his family. His wife had told him that 'God regardeth' the heart rather than the tongue and that the meaning of the oath thereby 'goeth upon that they thinke, and not upon that they say'. But More was not capable of such dissimulation. Instead he made a careful point to the commissioners. 'If you doubt whether I do refuse the oath only for the grudge of my conscience, or any other fantasy, I am ready here to satisfy you by my oath. Which, if you do not trust it, why should you be the better to give me any oath? And if you trust that I will herein swear true, then I trust of your goodness you will not move me to swear the oath you had offered me, perceiving that for to swear it is against my conscience.' So he was invoking the dictates of his conscience for his refusal, but at no stage did he explain what they were.

Lord Chancellor Audley then replied to him. 'We all are sorry to hear you say thus, and see you refuse the oath. On our faith you are the first that has ever refused it, and it will cause the King's highness to conceive great suspicion of you and great indignation toward you.' He then showed More a printed roll, with the signatures of the Lords and Commons [members of Parliament] inscribed upon it [that is, those who had signed the oath], but More simply reiterated his first statement. 'I myself cannot swear, but I do not blame any other man that has sworn.' He was then silent, and was asked to walk down into the garden for further reflection or meditation. But it was a hot day and he decided to rest in 'the olde burned chamber' on the first floor, which overlooked the garden and the river; this was a 'waiting' room, next to the guards' chamber, that had suffered a fire in the time of Archbishop Warham. As he lingered there he saw [religious reformer] Hugh Latimer walking with some of the Lambeth clergy; Latimer was laughing and joking with the chaplains, putting his arm around the shoulders of one or two of them 'that if they had been women, I wolde haue went he had been waxen wanton'. Latimer was of strongly Lutheran tendencies, and had been continually under threat of imprisonment because of his beliefs; but he was laughing now, in the knowledge that half of his cause was won. More looked on and perhaps raised his eyes to the ever-flowing river.

A fateful spectacle was then played out before him. Dr Nicholas Wilson, a scholar and divine, was escorted from the interview chamber; he was 'brought by me', according to More, 'and gentilmanly sent straight into the Towre'[the Tower of London prison]. He, too, had refused to swear the oath; he had been 'brought by' More as living proof of what would happen to all recusants. There was, for them, only one ultimate destination. More later learned that [the Bishop of Rochester] John Fisher had also been taken before the commissioners and dispatched to the Tower for the same reason. The anxiety and threat were too great for some to endure and the vicar of Croydon, Rowland Phillips, well known for his orthodox opinions and his devotion to the old faith, swore to the oath and signed his name. More heard that he had then gone down to the 'buttry barre' and ordered drink 'either for gladnes or for drines [dryness], or else that it might be sene'. He might also have called for drink, of course, as a way of slaking his conscience as well as his thirst. In a description of the scene to his daughter More used a phrase from the gospel of St John, with the clear implication that he himself was in the position of St Peter just before he denied Christ. Yet there would be no denial from him. More called all these events a 'pageant', and indeed it might have been devised as a theatrical scenario for the state of the realm—a reformer rejoicing, an orthodox cleric bowing to the king's will and a defiant scholar sent to the Tower.

Another Attempt

It was at this point that he was once again led before the commissioners. They revealed to him the number of the London clergy who had sworn the oath that day, even as he had waited in the burned chamber, but he still would not be drawn. He simply repeated his position that he could not join them in their assent. They asked what particular aspect of the oath disturbed him. More replied that he had offended the king already, but 'if I should open and disclose the causes why, I shall therewith but further exasperate his Highnes, which I will in no wise do, but rather will I abide all the danger and harm that might come toward me than give his Highnes any occasion of further displeasure." His was a subtle strategy of silence and non-compliance, but it had its dangers. The commissioners immediately accused him of stubbornness and obstinacy, but More knew the law better than any of them. 'But yet it thinketh me,' he told them, 'that if I may not declare the causes without perill, than to leave them unde-

Henry VIII

clared is no obstinacy.' No man is obliged to condemn himself. [Archbishop Thomas] Cranmer then intervened. More had agreed that the swearing of the oath was 'uncertain and doubtfull', precisely because his own conscience did not match that of others; but since it was his certain duty to obey his prince, why not take the less doubtful course and swear? More saw the force of the argument and could reply only that 'in my conscience the trouth seems on the tother side'. The Abbot of Westminster then asked him to estimate the weight of his conscience, when opposed by so many of the clergy and the parliament, but More answered that he could claim in his support 'the generall counsail of Christendome'. This was his central argument; the derivation of 'conscience' suggests knowledge-with-others, which for More included the communion of the dead as well as the living. It was this understanding which afforded him the strength and confidence to continue what seemed, to almost everyone, a foolish and futile struggle.

Thomas Cromwell, recognising More's position to be unalterable, swore 'a gret oth' that he would rather have seen his own son beheaded than be a witness to More's refusal. The mention of a beheading here was surely significant. Cromwell went on to suggest that the king would now 'conceiue a great suspicion' against More. . . . Their conference ended soon after, with More apparently conceding that he might swear to the succession if the oath was differently framed. He did not elaborate upon the necessary alterations, but once more invoked the principle of human conscience and finally declared that 'me thinketh in good faith, that so were it good reason that euery man should leaue me to myne'.

A Prisoner

He was now, effectively, a prisoner. He had rejected the oath and was therefore to be charged with 'misprision of treason'. But he had refused to give his reasons for his fatal decision and, at this moment, he entered silence. Or, rather, silence entered him. In a sense it was no longer his own choice; he ceased to be aware of himself, and at this level of conscience or knowledge he became part of the larger world of faith and spirit. He had always followed the imperatives of duty and service, but now that duty had turned irrevocably from his society to his God. If the will of heaven is vouchsafed to a human being in a wholly private way, demanding an act of faith as it had once been demanded of Abraham, then he cannot speak to the world. The world will not understand.

But if he did not explain the specific legal reasons for refusing the oath of succession, it is perhaps possible to reconstruct them. He told his daughter later that he had refused the oath because it was 'not agreeable with the statute'; by which he meant that, in his careful consideration and rereading of the two documents, he had realised that the oath itself went far beyond the matter of the royal succession. It required obeisance not only to the Act of Succession itself, in other words, but also to 'all other Acts and Statutes made since the beginning of the present Parliament'. This included all the antipapal legislation within the Acts of Annates, of Appeals, of Dispensations, and of Peter's Pence. If More had sworn the oath, as presented to him with this wording, he would have concurred in the forcible removal of the

Pope's jurisdiction and the effective schism of the Church in England. This he could not do, even at the cost of his life. He might have been willing to swear to a differently phrased oath, as he had suggested, as long as it did not include any other matters.

After the formal interrogation was over More was delivered into the custody of the Abbot of Westminster, under whose supervision he remained for the next four days. The truth was that no one knew precisely what to do with him. . . . Cranmer wrote to Cromwell suggesting that More . . . should be asked to swear only to the Act of Succession itself, thereby avoiding all the problems of acceding to the other Acts; he also suggested that [More's] compliance, if it came, 'should be suppressed' or concealed until the right moment for its publication. [More's] oath of loyalty to the new royal family would be advertised, in other words, for the maximum possible effect upon the king's opponents. The importance being attached to More . . . was clear. But when Cromwell put Cranmer's arguments to the king, Henry refused to countenance any such compromise; he argued, with some justification, that it might act as a precedent. What if any others refused to swear to the entire oath?

Consequences

So More's last hope of freedom was gone. On 17 April he was sent by river from Westminster to the Tower of London. He was wearing his gold chain of livery, as a solemn token of his service to the king, and he was advised to deliver it into the safekeeping of his family; but he refused, with a characteristic piece of irony: 'For if I were taken in the field by my enemies, I would they should somewhat fare the better by me.' The boat steered its course towards Traitor's Gate, where a great oaken wicket was opened to receive the prisoner. The wooden gate may be taken as an image for a subsequent conversation.

More: Well met, my lord, I hope we shall soon meet in heaven.

Fisher: This should be the way, Sir Thomas, for it is a very strait gate we are in.

At the landing stage beneath St Thomas's Tower More was met by the lieutenant of the Tower, Sir Edmund Walsingham, and by the porter of the wicket. It was an old custom for the porter to request the 'upper garment' of any new prisoner. More proffered him his hat and explained that 'I am very sorry it is no better for you'.

'No, sir,' came the reply, 'I must have your gown.'

More would have known perfectly well the tradition of handing the man his gown, and his offering of the hat may be construed as an example of that humour which always emerged in the most grave situations. Sir Edmund Walsingham led him up the narrow spiral stairway, with its thick stone and worn steps, the darkness punctuated briefly by slits carved in the massive outer wall. It was fortunate, perhaps, that Walsingham was a 'good friend and old acquaintaince' of More's; he took him to his cell, or chamber, and 'desired him that he would accept in such cheare as he was able to make hym'. His famous prisoner replied that 'if any here like it not, turne hym out of dores for a churle'. If I complain, in other words, then eject me from the Tower. It is not at all certain in which part of the building More was imprisoned, but it seems most likely to have been within the Bell Tower or the Beauchamp Tower. It is reasonable to suppose, however, that he was moved during the period of his imprisonment.

He was taken to one of those apartments which were reserved for the more influential or privileged 'guests' of the lieutenant. His was a pentagonal stone chamber, with a vaulted ceiling; it was some nineteen feet in height, with a floor space of approximately eighteen feet by twenty feet. The walls themselves were between nine and thirteen feet thick, the floor flagged with rough and uneven stone, the windows merely arrowslits or 'loops'. More's furnishings were of the simplest; they included a table and chair as well as a 'pallet' bed. There was a small brick stove, to heat this cold room, and More arranged for mats of straw to be placed upon the floor and against the walls. He described it as 'metely feyre' and 'at the lest wise it was strong ynough'; indeed he would not have necessarily been uncomfortable. His old servant, John Wood, was allowed to attend him; board and lodging, for both of them, amounted to fifteen shillings a week, which was more than adequate for food and clothing.

Conscience

Wood remained his faithful servant through the entire period of More's imprisonment and might himself, if anything else were known of him, provide an interesting study in loyalty and affection. But he is only ever mentioned as a silent attendant upon his unfortunate master. When Wood and More were first shown the prison chamber by Walsingham, for example, More insisted that his servant swear an oath to the effect that if he, More, ever said anything to the king's detriment then Wood must report his comments to the lieutenant of the Tower. His master was not held with any strict discipline, however; it was appropriate for a prisoner of his rank to be given permission to walk within the 'liberties' of the Tower and to stroll in its gardens. More's fascination for animals was such that he perhaps visited the royal menagerie, where he might refresh his memory of the lions which 'in the night walken'. Much more importantly, however, he was allowed to attend Mass each day to pray for his own salvation and for the spiritual comfort of those close to him.

He wrote to his daughter, Margaret, soon after his arrival in order to calm her fears. 'I am in good health of body, and in good quiet of minde,' he told her, and beseeched their creator to 'make you all mery

in the hope of heauen'. This letter was written 'with a cole', or piece
of charcoal, because More then had no other pen. He wished to console them because he knew in what desperate need of comfort they
stood; the [family] house in Chelsea was searched on more than one
occasion, and in a dialogue he composed in his cell a young man described how 'our pore famely be fallen into suche dumpes, that scantly
can any such comfort as my pore wyt can give them, any thyng ass-
wage [soothe] their sorow'. They spoke of More constantly, as Margaret told her father later, and repeated to each other the proverbs and
dicta by which he had tried to fortify them.

Yet he also was obliged to console himself. It has been recorded
that a new prisoner is so overwhelmed with feelings, on his first ad-
mittance to his cell, that he does not notice the hardness of his bed until the second night. We cannot hope to follow More's unwritten med-
itations, but on several occasions he accused himself of being 'faint-
hearted' and prey to many fears. There were the natural concerns for
his family, who might now be reduced to penury; there was his constant anxiety for the safety and future of his Church. But he also suffered from the stronger and more deadly fear that he would not be
courageous enough to sustain his lonely course and that he would, in
the end, surrender. His great fear was of torture, of 'duresse and harde
handelinge' and 'violente forceble waies'. He confessed that he considered 'the very worst and the vttermost that can by possibilite fall',
and that he found 'my fleshe much more shrinkinge from payne and
from death, than me thought it the part of a faithfull Christen man';
indeed he seems to have had some compulsion to dwell upon all the
vagaries of anticipated torment.

The Rise of England as a World Power

PREFACE

The sixteenth century had its share of political success stories, but none stand out more than England's. The English had had their share of success stories in earlier centuries—as one example, they had defeated the French at Agincourt in 1415, thus ending the Hundred Years' War—but the sixteenth century found them in political disarray. The Wars of the Roses in the fifteenth century, a massive civil conflict, had sharply weakened England's military forces and had been enormously costly. The early sixteenth-century king Henry VIII, though an effective leader in many ways, had gotten involved in a personal quarrel with the pope; in the process, Henry had managed to cut ties with some former allies and bring the wrath of several other powerful nations down upon England.

To make matters worse, Henry's death had resulted in a succession struggle that would last through the rest of the century. And his daughter Elizabeth, who eventually claimed the throne, was an unmarried woman who seemed to have little chance of preserving England's independence. If she did not succumb to the one-sided marriage proposals offered by the kings of Spain and France, then she would certainly fall before the military threats they presented. Most observers of the time believed that England was in serious trouble.

But, in fact, it was England and Elizabeth who carried the day. A skilled politician, Elizabeth was wise enough to surround herself with intelligent and thoughtful advisers. Though she may have been an anomaly, an unmarried queen in an era dominated by men, she did not let others make decisions for her; she listened to her counselors but acted on their advice only when it made sense to her. The image of weakness turned out not to apply. Instead, popular with her people and feared by those whom she disliked, Elizabeth began to project an image of strength and tenacity—an image that was quite accurate, and one that helped enormously in winning respect from outside the country.

Elizabeth had another advantage. The age of exploration was virtually made to order for the English, a small island nation with a proud seagoing tradition. English ships sailed all over the map but particularly to North America. There, they gradually began to lay claim to much of that continent—an opportunity unavailable to landlocked nations.

The queen also built up her naval forces and hired the very best captains, shipbuilders, and navigators she could find. She decided to reject all marriage proposals, even knowing that such rejection might lead Spain to a declaration of war. If war was inevitable, Elizabeth reasoned, then England would be ready. She sent out pirates in fast ships to attack and harass Spanish vessels carrying treasure and other goods, and eventually she even sent a captain into Spanish waters to damage the Spanish fleet. When direct battle began, the smaller English ships proved more maneuverable than the ponderous Spanish fleet; the result was a crushing defeat for the mighty Spanish Armada and a glorious victory for the English. England had arrived as a dominant power within Europe—and by extension, in the world itself.

The Lost Colony: Roanoke

William S. Powell

The first permanent English settlement in what is now the United States was established at Jamestown, Virginia, in 1607. Jamestown was not England's first attempt at colonization, however. This excerpt, from William S. Powell's *North Carolina: A Bicentennial History*, describes the efforts of Elizabethan explorers and rulers to found a colony and lay claim to the New World. The best-remembered attempt was the so-called Lost Colony, established on Roanoke Island, North Carolina, in the 1580s. The fate of the men, women, and children of the colony is a matter of much historical debate even today.

E ngland's interest in the New World was demonstrated in 1497–1498 when John Cabot, sailing under a charter from Henry VII, discovered North America. Although he probably did not sail south of New England and quite likely not even south of Nova Scotia and Labrador, it was this voyage which gave England the claim to North America that she perfected.

The first step toward implementing England's claim was taken in 1578, when Queen Elizabeth granted a charter to Sir Humphrey Gilbert to discover and settle lands "not actually possessed of any Christian prince or people." His efforts were centered in Newfoundland, and it was there that he attempted to plant a colony in 1583, After about a month he gave up hope of establishing a lasting settlement and the colony returned home. On the way Gilbert was drowned when a severe storm struck his fleet.

Excerpted from *North Carolina: A Bicentennial History,* by William S. Powell. Copyright © 1977 by the American Association for State and Local History. Reprinted with permission from W.W. Norton & Co., Inc.

Queen Elizabeth renewed Gilbert's charter in the name of his half-brother, Walter Raleigh, on New Year's Day, 1584, which was March 25 under the now outdated Julian calendar that England retained until 1752. Raleigh's charter, like Gilbert's, provided that any traveler to or settler in the colony "shall and may have and enjoy all the privileges of free denizens [inhabitants] and persons native of England and within our allegiance, in such like ample manner and form as if they were born and personally resident within our said Realm of England, any law, custom, or usage to the contrary notwithstanding.". . . .

Raleigh set about in a most logical way to colonize his grant. He reasoned that financial support would be offered and that potential colonists would come forth when more was known of the prospects for a settlement. Just one month and two days after receiving his charter, Raleigh dispatched a reconnaissance expedition to America under Captains Philip Amadas and Arthur Barlowe, whom he employed at his own expense. A naturalized English subject, Portuguese-born Simon Fernandez, was engaged as pilot of the small fleet. Fernandez quite likely was with the de Coronas colony [a Portuguese attempt to settle in North America] in 1566 and he knew a desirable place near the Currituck [North Carolina] landing to begin the exploration. Sailing southwest through the West Indies, the ships encountered the Gulf Stream and soon were sailing up the Atlantic. They entered the sound through Ocracoke Inlet on July 4, 1584, landed on Roanoke Island, and quickly began exploring and collecting plants, rocks, soil samples, and other material to be examined and tested in England. When they weighed anchor in mid-September, they took back with them two willing and intelligent young Indian men, Manteo and Wanchese. This was an especially fortunate move as the Indians attracted a great deal of attention wherever they appeared in England and proved to be a valuable means of publicizing Raleigh's new plans for a colony. The reports made by Amadas and Barlowe were so full of promise for this "goodliest soile under the cope of heaven," as the region was soon being described, that Queen Elizabeth knighted Raleigh and named the new land Virginia in honor of herself, the Virgin Queen. From these reports Englishmen began to understand and to appreciate many qualities of the New World.

Financial support came rather quickly. A share in such an expedition as Raleigh proposed appeared to be a good investment. The queen furnished a ship and so did the secretary of state. Many individuals subscribed money, and by April 1585 a colony of 108 men sailed from Plymouth, Devonshire, for Roanoke Island. Queen Elizabeth recalled her servant Lieutenant Ralph Lane from Ireland and put him under Raleigh's command although she continued his pay herself. John White, a gifted artist, and Thomas Harriot, a professor at Oxford who was a noted mathematician and scientist and one of the most versatile men of the age, also sailed. Harriot had already learned some of the natives' language from Manteo and Wanchese, and undoubtedly they had also learned some English.

Settlement

By the middle of August this colony, England's first mainland American colony, arrived at Roanoke Island and began the construction of Fort Raleigh. The men were organized along military lines under Lane's command. Cottages were constructed nearby and a suitable base created for a variety of expeditions that set out in different directions. Some went north to the Chesapeake Bay and others into the backcountry a hundred miles or more. People in England were as anxious to know everything about the New World as we have been in recent times to know about the moon, Mars, and Venus. The written reports, the watercolor drawings of John White, and the collected specimens in some cases satisfied their curiosity, but many people wanted to know more. Indians proved to be good sources of information for the colonists, as many of the Englishmen were good students of Indian culture. From the natives Lane's men learned to make dugout canoes. They also learned to plant crops in rows and hills, as well as to keep weeds out of their gardens. This was a particularly important lesson for them. In England, where land had been tilled for generations, a field would be plowed and the seed broadcast over it. In America, however, the warm climate and the presence of weed seed would not permit this. Such a field would quickly be covered with vigorous weeds of many kinds. They also adopted the Indians' name for unfamiliar things, hence *moccasin, canoe, hickory, persimmon, opossum, raccoon, tomahawk, hurricane, hominy*, and a host of other Indian words began to enter the English language.

Supplies anticipated by Ralph Lane's colony were late in coming, and on June 1, 1586, when Sir Francis Drake visited Roanoke Island on the way back to England after an expedition against the Spanish in the West Indies, Lane decided to return home. To make room for the colonists Drake put ashore and apparently abandoned some black slaves who had been captured from the Spanish. A severe storm arose, and Drake felt obliged to leave quickly. Some of the collected specimens and perhaps even some of White's paintings were thrown overboard to lighten the boats as they passed from shore to ship. Lane also abandoned three of his men who had not returned from an expedition. Apparently it was only a few days after Lane and Drake left when Sir Richard Grenville arrived with the long-expected supplies. If Lane had remained but this brief time longer, his colony might well have been England's first permanent American colony.

Grenville, when he departed soon afterwards, left fifteen men with enough supplies for two years. He could easily have spared additional men thereby more certainly ensuring the permanence of the beach-head. Why he did not is merely one of many puzzles associated with these earliest English ventures in America.

A Second Attempt

Raleigh's personal fortune was dwindling, and if he expected to plant an English colony in America, he had to act quickly. By the spring of 1587 he had succeeded in enlisting the aid of nineteen merchants and thirteen gentlemen of London. He abandoned the idea of a military organization and instead created a civil government for his new colony, with a governor and a dozen assistants. He gave these men a charter and incorporated them as the "Governor and Assistants of the Citie of Raleigh in Virginia." The new colony consisted of one hundred twenty people, including seventeen women and nine children. John White was named governor, and he and the other leaders were instructed to sail by way of the West Indies to get some plants that might grow in Virginia and to round up some livestock abandoned there by the Spanish. The colony was then to stop at Roanoke Island for the men left by Lane and Grenville, to drop off Manteo, who had gone to England with Lane, and then to go to the Chesapeake Bay to settle at a place recommended by Ralph Lane. A colony at that location would have the advantage of a deep-water port that could be used by English ships as a base for attacking Spanish settlements in the New World as well as Spanish ships in the Atlantic.

The colony reached Cape Hatteras on the Outer Banks on July 22, and an advance party went ahead to Fort Raleigh, which was found to be damaged. The houses were deserted and covered with vines. The men left by Grenville had disappeared, but some human bones suggested that they had been killed. Pilot Fernandez refused to take the colony any farther, and White was unable to prevail over him. Fernandez seemed anxious to put to sea, perhaps to try to capture Spanish treasure ships for himself. The colony had no other choice than to disembark at Roanoke Island. Men began cleaning up the old houses and building new ones. They had brought over some brick and two thousand roofing tiles, perhaps intended for their most important buildings—a chapel and a house for the governor, which would also serve as a capitol for the colony. As soon as the people were moderately comfortable, the friendly Manteo was baptized and created Lord of Roanoke as Raleigh had directed. This was the first Protestant baptismal service in the New World and the first time an American was elevated to the peerage. Through these ceremonies Raleigh recognized Manteo as leader of the Indians of Virginia, and it was to him that the colonists were expected to turn for guidance in their relations with the natives.

On August 18 Eleanor Dare, daughter of Governor White, gave birth to a daughter, who was christened Virginia on August 24 because she was the first child of English parents to be born in Virginia. Her father was Ananias Dare, one of the assistants in the government. A few days later a child was also born to Dyonis and Margery Harvie, but Governor White recorded nothing further in his journal about this child.

One colonist who strayed too far away from the fort while searching for crabs along the shore was attacked by Indians who broke his skull with a wooden sword. Beyond that there was no suggestion of trouble with the natives. Indeed, the attacking Indian was from the mainland, not a local Indian. Still, all was not well with the colony. It arrived too late to plant crops, and the previous season had been such a poor one that the Indians had no food they could share. Officials of the colony persuaded a reluctant Governor White to return with the fleet to hasten the shipment of supplies. They agreed to care for his personal possessions; and if they carried out their intention of moving to a more suitable place, the name would be carved on a tree near the fort. A cross above the name would let him know when he returned that they had left in distress.

Croatoan

After a very rough voyage White arrived home late in 1587 to find all of England busily preparing to defend the country against the powerful Spanish Armada that was set for an invasion. The queen commanded that no ship could sail if it might be of any possible use in defending England. Nevertheless, by April 1588 White managed to find two small ships that could be spared. Loaded with supplies and with some additional colonists, the ships sailed for Roanoke. The captains, however, were less concerned about the welfare of England's pioneer American colony than with their own profits. Once in the Atlantic, the English crews turned to piracy, but instead of capturing treasure ships themselves, they were boarded by French pirates who took all the supplies intended to relieve Roanoke. There was nothing to do but return to port. It was not until 1590 that White was again able to sail. When he arrived at Fort Raleigh a few days before his granddaughter's third birthday, he found the place overgrown with melon vines and the houses abandoned. Nearly everything that could be moved was gone, but he found a half-buried chest of his own containing rusted armor and ruined pictures and maps. The word CROATOAN without the feared cross above it was carved on a tree. Before he could go out to Croatoan, now called Hatteras, on the Outer Banks where Manteo lived, a violent storm came up, and he was forced to leave in haste. Because of the damage to his ships he could not continue the search, and his colony became the "Lost Colony" of Roanoke. No trace of the colonists was ever found although Chief Powhatan later told Virginia colonists that most of the people from

Roanoke had been slaughtered as they made their way toward Chesapeake Bay. They were caught quite by chance, Powhatan explained to Captain John Smith at Jamestown, between two warring bands of Indians—one from the southwest that was invading the region and the other composed of local Indians trying to defend themselves. This seems to have occurred just a short while before the English colony arrived at Jamestown. As evidence of his account, Powhatan showed Smith some copper pots that he picked up after the battle ended.

Raleigh had invested a fortune in his efforts to plant an English colony in America, and many other people had also contributed generously to the scheme. Many lives had been lost, but all of this was a part of the price that England had to pay for America. Gerald Johnson called these first colonists "the expendables," yet their contributions were significant. They enabled England to try several forms of colonial government and to develop and test theories of colonization.

Singeing the King's Beard: The Exploits of Francis Drake

Richard Hakluyt

Richard Hakluyt was one of the great seafarers and writers of the late six-teenth century. In this excerpt, he gives a first-person account of the ex-ploits of Sir Francis Drake. Drake, a sea captain, was instructed by Queen Elizabeth I to attempt to undermine the more-powerful Spanish navy. Though England was at the time a minor sea power, Drake did exactly as he was told. He ended up destroying many Spanish ships as they lay in or near Spanish waters, an act celebrated in legend as "singeing the King of Spain's beard."

Hakluyt mentions various kinds of Spanish ships in the text, notably galleons, galleys, galleasses, caravels, and carracks. The differences have to do with the size and purpose of each ship; Drake's fleet had nothing resembling the largest Spanish ships in size. As Hakluyt points out, the success of the smaller ships against the large ships of Spain gave England hope for success in a sea battle.

A brief relation of the notable service performed by Sir Francis Drake upon the Spanish fleet prepared in the road of Cadiz: and of his destroying of a hundred sail of barks; passing from thence all along the coasts to Cape Sacre, where also he took certain forts: and so to the south of the river of Lisbon, and thence crossing over to the Isle of St. Michael, surprised a mighty carrack called the *St. Philip* coming out of the East Indies, which was the first of that kind that ever was seen in England: performed in the year 1587.

Her Majesty, being informed of a mighty preparation by sea begun in Spain for the invasion of England, by good advice of her grave and prudent council, thought it expedient to prevent the same. Whereupon she caused a fleet of some thirty sails to be rigged and furnished with all things necessary. Over that fleet she appointed General Sir Francis Drake (of whose manifold former good services she had sufficient proof), to whom she caused four ships of her navy royal to be delivered; to wit, the *Bonaventure*, wherein himself [that is, Hakluyt] went as general; the *Lion*, under the conduct of Master William Borough, Controller of the Navy; the *Dreadnought*, under the command of Master Thomas Venner; and the *Rainbow*, captain whereof was Master Henry Bellingham: unto which four ships two of her pinnaces [ships used for support purposes] were appointed as handmaids. There were also added unto this fleet certain tall ships of the city of London, of whose especial good service the general made particular mention in his private letters directed to Her Majesty. This fleet set sail from the Sound of Plymouth in the month of April, towards the coast of Spain.

The sixteenth of the said month we met in the latitude of forty degrees with two ships of Middleborough which came from [Spanish] Cadiz; from which we understood that there was great store of warlike provision at Cadiz and thereabout, ready to come for Lisbon. Upon this information our general, with all speed possible, bending himself thither to cut off their forces and provisions, upon the nineteenth of April entered with his fleet into the harbour of Cadiz; where at our first entering we were assailed over against the town by fire galleys, which notwithstanding in short time retired under their fortress.

There were in the road sixty ships and divers[e] other small vessels under the fortress. There fled about twenty French ships to Porto Reale, and some small Spanish vessels that might pass the shoals. At our first coming in, we sunk with our shot a ship of Raguza of a thousand tons, furnished with forty pieces of brass and very richly laden. There came two galleys more from St. Maryport, and two from Porto Reale, which shot freely at us, but altogether in vain, for they went away with the blows well beaten for their pains.

Booty

Before night we had taken thirty of the said ships, and became masters of the road in spite of the galleys, which were glad to retire under the fort. In the number of these ships there was one new ship of an extraordinary hugeness, in burden about twelve hundred tons, belonging to the Marquis of Santa Cruz, who was at that instant High Admiral of Spain. Five of them were great ships of Biscay, whereof we fired four as they were taking in the king's provision of victuals for the furnishing of his fleet at Lisbon; the fifth, being a ship of about a thousand tons in burden, laden with iron spikes, nails, iron hoops, horseshoes, and other like necessaries, bound for the West Indies, we fired in like manner. Also we took a ship of two hundred and fifty tons, laden with wines for the king's provision, which we carried out to sea with us, and there discharged the wines for our own store, and afterward set her on fire.

Moreover we took three flyboats of three hundred tons apiece, laden with biscuit, whereof one was half unladen by us in the harbour and there fired, and the other two we took in our company to the sea. Likewise there were fired by us ten other ships which were laden with wine, raisins, figs, oils, wheat, and such like. To conclude, the whole number of ships and barks, as we suppose, then burnt, sunk, and brought away with us, amounted to thirty at the least. There were in sight of us at Porto Reale about forty ships, beside those that fled from Cadiz.

We found little ease during our abode there, by reason of their continual shooting from the galleys, the fortresses, and the shore, where continually at places convenient they planted new ordnance [weapons] to offend us with: besides the inconvenience which we suffered from their ships, which, when they could defend no longer, they set on fire to come among us. Whereupon when the flood came, we were not a little troubled to defend ourselves from their terrible fire, which nevertheless was a pleasant sight for us to behold, because we were thereby eased of a great labour which lay upon us day and night in discharging the victuals and other provisions of the enemy. Thus by the assistance of the Almighty, and the invincible courage and industry of our general, this strange and happy enterprise was achieved in one day and two nights, to the great astonishment of the King of Spain. And this exploit so affected the Marquis of Santa Cruz, High Admiral of Spain, that he never enjoyed good days after, but within a few months died of extreme grief and sorrow.

Victory

Thus having performed this notable service, we came out of the road of Cadiz on the Friday morning, the twenty-first of the said month of April, with very small loss not worth the mentioning. After our departure ten of the galleys that were in the road came out, as it were in disdain of us, to make some pastime with their ordnance, at which time the wind scanted upon us [failed us], whereupon we cast about again, and stood in with the shore, and came to an anchor within a league of the town; where the galleys, for all their former bragging, at length suffered us to ride quietly.

We now have had experience of galley-fight: wherein I can assure that only these four of Her Majesty's ships will make no account of twenty galleys if they be alone, and not busied to guard others. There were never galleys that had better place and fitter opportunity for their advantage to fight with ships: but still they were forced to retire, we riding in a narrow gut, and driven to maintain the same until we had discharged and fired the ships, which could not conveniently be done except upon the flood, at which time they might drive clear of us. Thus being victualled with bread and wine, at the enemy's cost, for divers months (besides the provisions that we brought from home), our general dispatched Captain Cross into England with his letters, giving him further in charge to declare unto Her Majesty all the particulars of this our first enterprise.

After whose departure we shaped our course toward Cape Sacre, and in the way thither, we took at several times of ships, barks, and caravels well near a hundred, laden with hoops, galley oars, pipe-staves, and other provisions of the King of Spain for the furnishing of his forces intended against England; all which we burned, having dealt favourably with the men and sent them on shore. We also spoiled and consumed all the fisherboats and nets thereabouts, to their great hindrance; and (as we suppose) to the utter overthrow of the rich fishing of tunnies for the same year. At length we came to Cape Sacre, where we went on land; and the better to enjoy the benefit of the place, and to ride in harbour at our pleasure, we assailed the castle and three other strongholds, which we took, some by force, and some by surrender.

Thence we came before the haven of Lisbon, anchoring near where the Marquis of Santa Cruz was with his galleys. He, seeing us chase his ships ashore, and take and carry away his barks and caravels, was content to suffer us there quietly to tarry, and likewise to depart, and never charged us with one cannon shot. And when our general sent him word that he was there ready to exchange bullets with him, the Marquis refused his challenge, sending him word that he was not then ready for him, nor had any such commission from his king.

One Last Prize

Our general being thus refused by the Marquis, and seeing no more good to be done in this place, thought it convenient to spend no longer time upon this coast. Therefore with consent of the chief of his company he shaped his course toward the Isles of the Azores, and passing towards the Isle of St. Michael, within twenty or thirty leagues thereof, it was his good fortune to meet with a Portugal carrack called *St. Philip,* being the same ship which in the voyage outward had carried into the Indies the three princes of Japan that were in Europe. This carrack without any great resistance he took, bestowing the people thereof in certain vessels well furnished with victuals, and sending them courteously home into their country. This was the first carrack that ever was taken coming forth of the East Indies; which the Portugals took for an evil sign, because the ship bare the king's own name.

The riches of this prize seemed so great unto the whole company (as in truth it was) that they assured themselves every man to have a sufficient reward for his travail. Thereupon they all resolved to return home for England: which they happily did, and arrived in Plymouth the same summer with their whole fleet and this rich booty, to their own profit and due commendation, and to the great admiration of the whole kingdom.

And here by the way it is to be noted, that the taking of this carrack wrought two extraordinary effects in England. First, it taught others that carracks were not such bugbears but that they might be taken, and secondly, in acquainting the English nation more generally with the exceeding riches and wealth of the East Indies: whereby themselves and their neighbours of Holland have been encouraged—being men as skilful in navigation, and of no less courage than the Portugals—to share with them in the East Indies, where their strength is nothing so great as heretofore hath been supposed.

The Spanish Armada: Less than Invincible

Garrett Mattingly

The single event that did the most to propel England into the category of a world power was its defeat of the Spanish Armada in 1588. Spain was among the preeminent naval powers of the time, and its large ships dominated many of the world's seas. England, by contrast, was a much less important seafaring nation. Its ships were smaller, its overseas possessions fewer, its weaponry less powerful.

Earlier in the century relations between Spain and England had been friendly enough for King Philip of Spain to propose marriage to Queen Elizabeth of England. Over a period of thirty years or so, however, the friendship had begun to sour. Spain allied itself with Elizabeth's cousin and enemy Mary, Queen of Scots, and began pushing for England to officially become a Roman Catholic country. Little by little, the countries moved toward war. In 1588, Philip sent an armada, or naval fleet, to England to destroy his enemy. The English were given little chance of destroying the Spanish fleet, but in a series of battles during that summer the English did exactly that.

This excerpt, drawn from historian Garrett Mattingly's *The Armada*, describes the opening engagement between the two fleets. Fought near the western end of the English Channel, a few miles from England's coastline, the battle's result was a grave concern to the Spanish captains. While the English had not scored a dramatic and decisive victory, they had definitely carried the day, and the supposed Spanish advantages in firepower, ships, positioning, and strategy had been of no avail.

Excerpted from *The Armada,* by Garrett Mattingly. Copyright © 1959 by Garrett Mattingly, renewed 1987 by Leonard H. Mattingly. Reprinted with permission from Houghton Mifflin Co. All rights reserved.

Several more battles would be fought before the Spanish fleet, damaged almost beyond repair, gave in and crept home via Ireland, but this first battle set the tone.The Spanish, both sides realized, were not invincible.

Editor's Note: The battle described in this selection took place on July 31, 1588–July 21 according to the Julian calendar then in use in England. Fighting raged along England's southwestern coast between two landmarks: the Eddystone and Start Point. The Spanish were under the authority of Alonso Perez de Guzman el Bueno, the duke of Medina Sidonia; the English were commanded by Lord Admiral Charles Howard. Each ship, of course, had its own individual captain.

The Spanish fleet had well over a hundred ships in all, the English somewhat fewer. The ships on both sides went by many names— galleys and galleons, galleasses and pinnaces, carracks, galiots, and many more. The galleys and the galleons were the largest and most important; they were relatively slow and sluggish, but big. They cruised under sail and used oars when involved in battle. The Spanish had more of both these large ships than did the English.

Strategy played a large role in this and other battles throughout the summer. When it was clear that battle was about to begin, the Spanish placed their ships in a crescent formation. This formation was hard to achieve when all ships were either rowed or propelled by wind power, but it was worth the effort: it was considered extremely difficult to break through the formation. The Spanish, however, were also at a tactical disadvantage as the battle began. Because of some careful work by the English commanders, the English ships had sailed off to one side of the Armada and the wind was now against the Spanish; as Mattingly puts it, they had lost the weather gauge. Finally, each side's strengths suggested a particular plan of action. For the English, the goal was to fight from a distance, putting an emphasis on speed and tactics. The Spanish, on the other hand, hoped to create a melee, a large group of ships fighting one another from close quarters, which would put a premium on strength and brute force.

Appropriately enough, the first modern naval battle in history began with gestures out of the middle ages, out of romances of chivalry. The [Spanish] Captain General of the Ocean Sea [Alonso Perez de Guzman el Bueno, Duke of Medina Sidonia] hoisted to his maintop his sacred banner as a signal to engage, as Castilian commanders at sea had always done since first they sighted the Moorish galleys. And the Lord Admiral of England [Charles Howard] sent his personal pinnace [small ship], the *Disdain*, to bear his challenge to the Spanish admiral. . . . Then, his defiance delivered, at about nine in the morning, Howard led the English fleet in line ahead, *en ala* the Spanish called it, single file, one ship behind another, against the northern, shoreward tip of the Spanish crescent.

The wing attacked was [Spanish Commander Don Alonso] de Leiva's, mainly the Levant squadron [made up mainly of Italian ships], which had been the vanguard as long as the Armada had been reaching north towards the shore in an effort to cut off the leeward detachment of English ships. In most accounts of the battle de Leiva's squadron is still called "the vanguard," although in taking its new formation the Armada had changed front to flank, each ship turning east ninety degrees or more, so that de Leiva was on the left wing, and his Levanters formed the horn of the crescent projecting towards the rear on that side.

The rearmost ship, in the post of honor and of danger, was de Leiva's own *Rata Coronada*, and as Howard's *Ark Royal* began to cross his stern Don Alonso put down his helm, meeting the English flagship broadside to broadside and steering a course parallel with it across the chord of the arc formed by the Spanish crescent as he tried to edge to windward to close the range. Behind him swung into action [Spanish Commander Martin de] Bertendona's great carrack, *Regazona*, the biggest ship in the Armada, almost as big as the queen's *Triumph*, and following Bertendona, the rest of the Levant squadron. Howard, under the impression that the *Rata* was "the admiral," that is, the flagship of the Spaniards, "wherein the duke was supposed to be," exchanged broadsides with her for some time, "until she was rescued by divers[e] ships of the Spanish army." Or that is how Howard tells it. In fact, the Levanters, not the most weatherly ships in the Armada, were quite unable to close the range, and Howard had no intention of doing so, so the two lines kept well asunder. As far as we know, nobody got hurt in that part of the action, or was in the least in need of rescue.

Meanwhile, a group of English ships, led by [Sir Francis] Drake in the *Revenge*, and including [John] Hawkins in the *Victory* and [Martin] Frobisher in the *Triumph*, assailed the other wing of the Armada, the "rear guard," commanded by the vice-admiral, Juan Martínez de Recalde. They met a rather different reception. Recalde in the *San Juan de Portugal*, the largest of the galleons and a powerful ship, swung round to meet the attack, but the rest of the galleons sailed on. Later, when he discovered what was happening, Medina Sidonia seems to have been under the impression that Recalde either got separated from the rest of his squadron by accident or was deliberately deserted by them. His report to the king leaves both alternatives open. Neither

After the English defeated the Spanish Armada in 1588, Spain's naval supremacy declined rapidly.

seems at all probable. The galleons of Portugal were manned and commanded by veterans who would scarcely have panicked at the mere noise of a cannonade. Throughout all the rest of the fighting no squadron in either fleet behaved with greater gallantry. Nor can one easily imagine Recalde's own Biscayans [northern Spaniards] deserting him. On the other hand, of all the squadron commanders Recalde was the least likely to get into trouble by accident. He was famous for the way he handled his ships and almost equally famous for the way he handled his men. If he left the duke with a choice between two improbabilities, it must have been because he did not want to confirm the only likely conjecture, that he had disobeyed orders, parted from his squadron, ordering them not to follow him, and deliberately thrust himself into the midst of the enemy.

Recalde knew better than anyone that, now the fleet had lost the weather gauge [a positional advantage], its only chance of victory was to precipitate a general melee. He had seen enough of the action already to be sure that he had read the English admiral's intentions correctly, and that Howard meant to stand aloof and knock the Spanish ships to pieces with his culverins [long cannons] at a range at which his ships could not get hurt. But it was unheard of in the previous annals of war at sea for a single ship surrounded by enemies not to be boarded. Boarding was the only way a superior force could make sure of taking a valuable prize intact, and among the group bearing down on him Recalde saw one ship, surely larger than his, and with bow and stern castles at least as high. It would be strange if her captain could not be tempted to close. Recalde knew that if he could once get his grappling irons on one English galleon or, better still, on two, he could hold on until help came. Then, if the English in their turn should attempt a rescue, perhaps the general melee, on which everything depended, could begin. Even if he could lure the English close enough for him to use with full effect his big short-range ship-smashers, cannon and demi-cannon and perriers, he might accomplish something. It was worth risking a single ship for, even worth disobeying a formal order.

The Rest of the Battle

Drake must have read Recalde's mind as clearly as Recalde had read Howard's. *Revenge, Victory, Triumph* and their companions closed the range, but only to a cautious three hundred yards or so, and proceeded to pound Recalde with the long guns which were their principal armament. He could not get at them and they would not come to him, though Martin Frobisher in the *Triumph* must have been, as Recalde hoped, sorely tempted. So, for over an hour the *San Juan* alone withstood the battering of the English squadron, until the great [Spanish ship] *Grangrin* came up, followed by the rest of the Biscayans, drove the English away, and guarded *San Juan* back into the midst of the fleet where she could patch her wounds.

The rescue of Recalde's ship seems to have been begun by the movement of the *San Martin* which also led to the breaking off of the action. Recalde may have been willing to be bait in the trap a little longer, but whatever he had told his captains, he could, of course, have told the Captain General nothing. As soon as Medina Sidonia saw his vice-admiral in danger, he spilled the wind from his sails and put his helm hard over. Immediately all the fighting ships in the main body, the Andalusians, the Guipúzcoans [both from regions of southern Spain], and the rest of the galleons, imitated his action, waiting, with their sails flapping, until the slow drift of the rearguard fighting should come abreast of them or, if the English were completely preoccupied, perhaps even pass them, giving them the advantage of the weather gauge. Instead, at the critical moment, the English sheered off, out of range. That was the end of the first day's fight.

When the English broke off the action, about one in the afternoon, Medina Sidonia immediately went over to the offensive, and tried to get to windward of them. Since the crescent was strictly a defensive formation which could only be maintained with a following wind, the duke formed his fighting ships for attack in squadron columns, each squadron in line ahead, leaving the sluggish hulks to pursue their course to leeward. No doubt the galleons made a pretty sight, heeling over, close-hauled in the fresh breeze, but the English easily kept whatever distance they pleased, now and then tossing in a derisive salvo of round shot, and the abrupt rushes of the Spanish fleet, first to port and then to starboard, had less chance than the brave, blind rushes of the bull against his agile persecutors. For three hours the duke kept up his futile attempts; then he put up his helm and turned away, back towards the laboring hulks. "The enemy having opened the range," reads the official log, "the duke collected the fleet, but found he could do nothing more, for they still kept the weather gauge, and their ships are so fast and so nimble they can do anything they like with them."

For both sides the first day's fighting had been a somewhat frustrating experience. The Spanish were exasperated rather than hurt. No ship in the fleet had taken as much mauling as Recalde's, and its injuries amounted to no more than two cannon balls in its foremast, some stays and rigging shot away, and a handful of killed and wounded. But if the English long-range bombardment had inflicted, so far, only annoying jabs, they were jabs that had to be suffered, apparently, whenever the English chose, and with little prospect of effective retaliation.

As for the English, if they were not hurt, they were beginning to be alarmed. This was a bigger, tougher enemy than they had bargained for. Spanish seamanship and discipline all day had been impeccable, and the Spaniards had been as full of fight at the end as at the beginning. The Armada was more heavily gunned than they had looked for, with enough long guns to return their fire and, on its best ships, more short-range ship-smashers, cannon and perriers than the queen's galleons. If they could close the range sufficiently, the Spaniards could do serious damage, even without boarding. And if the Spanish guns had done no damage that day, why neither, so far as anyone could see, had the English. The Armada looked even more formidable at a nearer view than it had at a distance. At the end, as it stood away into the darkening afternoon, it was more than ever like an impregnable wooden wall, like a grim fortress bristling with towers.

The English were not proud of their performance. They had hunted the Spanish past Plymouth, and if the Armada had had any intention of looking in there (it had shown none), that, at least, was foiled. But now the Armada was proceeding with majestic deliberation, in unbroken order, up the Channel, towards its rendezvous with [the Duke of] Parma [Spanish captain and nobleman]. If that rendezvous were to be prevented, they would have to do better. Howard, who had been willing to encounter the whole Spanish fleet with some sixty-five sail, now hesitated to join battle again until the rest of the ships in Plymouth had come up, and was writing everywhere for reinforcements, men and ships. His council of war concurred. To [Secretary of State Francis] Walsingham he wrote, "We gave them fight from nine o'clock until one and made some of them to bear room to stop their leaks [this was rather what he hoped than what he knew]; notwithstanding we durst not adventure to put in among them, their fleet being so strong." Drake, warning [English captain Lord Henry] Seymour of the approach of the enemy, was even more laconic. "The 21st we had them in chase, and so, coming up to them, there hath passed some cannon shot between some of our fleet and some of them, and as far as we perceive, they are determined to sell their lives with blows."

Spanish Disaster

The first serious Spanish losses came after the battle, two accidents, unrelated to enemy action, but destined to cost the Armada two capital ships. The first seemed minor. Some time after four in the afternoon as the Spanish were re-forming their defensive crescent and the Andalusian squadron was closing up on the duke's right, its *capitana* [flagship], Pedro de Valdés's flagship, *Nuestra Señora del Rosario*, collided with another Andalusian and lost its bowsprit. Then, only a few minutes later, on the duke's left, there was a tremendous explosion. [Commander Miguel de] Oquendo's *almiranta*, the *San Salvador*, was seen to be ablaze; her poop and two decks of her stern castle had disappeared. Obviously, the gunpowder stored astern had blown up.

The farther we get from this event, the more detailed and dramatic does its story become. In the diary or smooth log of his voyage sent to Philip on August 21st, Medina Sidonia says simply that aboard the *San Salvador* some barrels of gunpowder blew up. Presumably the duke had made some sort of inquiry, and he had some of the survivors from the *San Salvador* aboard the *San Martín*, but if he found out no more than he reported, it would scarcely be surprising. Everyone anywhere in the vicinity of the explosion seems to have been killed. Naturally, various conjectures were soon bruited in the fleet. Fray Bernardo de Gongora, who ended his voyage aboard the *San Martín*, heard that the explosion was due to some gunner's carelessness, a plausible guess. On another ship it was said that a gunner had set fire to a powder barrel, nobody knew why. Probably he was an Englishman. Some deserters, not from the *San Salvador*, picked up after Gravelines [a later battle], had a much more definite tale. A Dutch master gunner, rebuked for carelessness, laid a train to the magazine, lit it and jumped overboard; his subsequent whereabouts not stated. In Amsterdam an enterprising newsmonger had a better idea. The master gunner (a Hollander, of course, and pressed for the service), reproved by Oquendo for smoking on the quarter-deck, calmly knocked out the dottle of his pipe into a powder barrel and so blew up the ship. . . . In Hamburg, some weeks later, the master gunner was a German whom a Spanish officer struck with a stick.

By the time [Italian journalist and chronicler] Petruccio Ubaldini took hold of it, the story was ready for the full treatment. The master gunner, a Fleming this time, was injured not only in his professional but his personal honor, the Spanish officer who reprimanded him had already cuckolded him, and was now threatening the happiness and safety of his daughter, both wife and daughter being, by some poetic

license, aboard the *San Salvador*. The Fleming fired a powder train
and sprang into the sea, destroying them all, and Ubaldini has a moving peroration on the folly of arousing in the human breast the savage
passion of revenge. The baroque luxuriance of Ubaldini's version
should have swept all before it, but it already had too many competitors, and northerners may have found it, as they found some Italian
baroque churches, a trifle too exuberant. In one form or another, however, the story of the liberty-loving, or patriotic, or revengeful, Dutch-
man, or German, or Englishman, or Fleming has become . . . firmly
imbedded in the Armada legend. . . .

The catastrophe it was invented to explain was real enough. Medina Sidonia acted promptly, fired a gun to call the attention of the fleet,
and steered back towards the *San Salvador*, meanwhile sending off
pinnaces and ship's boats with messages. Small craft converged on
the burning ship to tow her stern around away from the wind so that
the fire would not blow forward, to reinforce the depleted crew now
desperately fighting the fire amidships (there was another great store
of powder under the forecastle), to take off the maimed and burned
and transfer them to one of the two hospital ships among the hulks.
The *San Martín* stood by with the duke on the poop deck, within easy
hail, supervising and encouraging the operation, until two galleasses
appeared to tow the *San Salvador*, her fires now under control, in
among the hulks.

By this time it began to look like a squally evening, the sky lower-
ing, the wind blowing in unpredictable gusts, and a heavy, choppy sea
making up. Just as the ranks of the fleet opened to admit the two gall-
casses and their helpless charge, Pedro de Valdés's ship [that is, Nuestra Señora del Rosario], which was steering badly without the balance
of her head sails, was taken aback, and lost her foremast, weakened,
perhaps, by the collision and the breaking of the bowsprit. Again the
duke acted promptly. Again he fired a gun to stop the fleet, and stood
across to the *Rosario* where she wallowed in the rear. This time the
San Martin was first at hand. There were few better seamen in the Armada than the flagship's sailing master, Captain Marolín de Juan, and
rough as the sea now was, and wildly as the *Rosario* was behaving,
Captain Marolín succeeded in passing her a cable. The *San Martin*
herself would take the crippled *Rosario* in tow. Scarcely had the cable been secured, however, when *Rosario* bucked like a bronco, and
it parted. The wind was increasing, the sea was getting rough, and it
proved unexpectedly difficult to pass another line. The duke, on the
poop deck, stood watching the work with painful attention.

It had begun to grow dark, and a couple of pinnaces were standing
by, when Diego Flores de Valdés came charging up to the poop deck
to protest. An experienced officer, commander of the galleons of
Castile, he was serving on the flagship at the king's suggestion, as the

Captain General's chief-of-staff and principal adviser on naval and military matters. The duke, he declared, absolutely must resume his station, and the fleet must resume its course eastward. Standing by like this in this increasing sea, the ships might do each other mischief, and would certainly scatter so during the night that by morning the duke would not see half of them. It was impossible to continue this disorder in the face of the enemy, and to go on imperiling the success and safety of the whole fleet for the sake of a single ship.

There seems to have been a bitter, excited argument. Diego Flores was, apparently, supported by another officer, perhaps Bobadilla, *maestre de campo general*. Finally the duke gave way, though he insisted on standing by until he saw [Captain Augustin de] Ojeda, in the small galleon that was the flagship of the screen, coming up with four pinnaces to take over, and received word that his orders to one of the galleasses and to the *almiranta* of the Andalusians to assist in the rescue had been received. Then, at last, he turned away, took up his station in the main body, and the fleet, in close formation, resumed its march. It was disturbing to hear, some time later, out of the darkness astern where the *Rosario* was drifting, the thud of heavy guns.

The duke had been on deck all day and had eaten nothing since breakfast. He did not go below now. He had a boy bring him a crust and some cheese to the poop deck, and stood a long time, leaning on the taffrail, watching the wake and the blackness beyond. Abandoning the *Rosario* was his first real failure, and he knew that whoever advised it and however wise had been the advice, his would be the blame. Perhaps it was only then he remembered that Diego Flores de Valdés and Pedro de Valdés were not only cousins, but inveterate and implacable enemies.

Life and Culture in Sixteenth- Century Europe

PREFACE

The sixteenth century was a time of particular cultural and social upheaval in Europe. Old ways and ideas began to seem less compelling, and new ideas and systems of organization competed for the attention of Europeans. A century of scientific advance, the period was also one of great progress in artistic matters—and an era that marked the beginning of a shift from one worldview to another.

That shift, of course, did not happen all at once. While Nicolas Copernicus was developing his bold new idea that the sun was at the center of the solar system, peasants all over Europe continued to believe that mysterious forces caused events to occur. Their own actions, from whistling at the wrong time to impure thoughts, could cause a whole range of seemingly unrelated consequences, and there was no telling in what way God might decide to meddle randomly in the affairs of the world. Nevertheless, life in the sixteenth century did move gradually from a somewhat simplistic understanding of cause and effect and humanity's central place in the universe to a more subtle and nuanced way of looking at things.

The sixteenth century was a time of artistic and cultural achievement. The ideas and styles of the early Italian Renaissance set the tone for artistic works across the continent and throughout the rest of the century. These pieces of art were by no means all alike in style, form, and execution. The sixteenth century began with the production of such works as Michelangelo's painting of the ceiling of the Sistine Chapel and closed with the beginnings of the Dutch Old Master style that would be made famous by painters such as Rembrandt van Rijn in the century to come. In between, the century saw a whirlwind of changing fashions, ideas, and tastes—a mix that helped distinguish the art of one decade, or even of one small geographical area, from its neighbors in time and space.

Currents in the visual arts were matched in other areas as well. The sixteenth century was a time of swift change in fashions, music, and literature. By increasing travel and connections between nations, new systems of communication and transportation helped spread these new standards. No longer did it take decades for a new clothing style, say, to move from Italy to England. Trade routes, faster ships, and a greater awareness of other cultures made it possible for northern Europeans to emulate their southern counterparts much more quickly, if they wished to do so. Similarly, the plays of William Shakespeare, the music of the Italian composer Giovanni Palestrina, and the poetry of German author Hans Sachs—just to name a few—moved much more quickly throughout Europe, influencing and inspiring developments in literature and music far beyond the places where they originated. Culturally speaking, the European world was becoming a smaller and more tightly connected place.

Developments in science and learning were another way in which the sixteenth century distinguished itself. From the practical, such as the invention of the Gregorian calendar, to the more theoretical, such as the question of whether the sun revolves around the earth, a quest for understanding drove the scientists of the sixteenth century. No longer were they as content to carry out experiments that would prove what they already believed to be true. Instead, a new curiosity drove research during this period. Besides reforming the way scientists thought and carried out their work, that quest for scientific discovery impacted the cultural landscape of sixteenth-century Europe. Socially and culturally, in science, in art, and in religion, the sixteenth century was among the most creative centuries of the millennium.

Superstition and the Sixteenth-Century Worldview

Jean de Bourdigne

Though the sixteenth century was a time of rebirth of scientific knowledge and rational thinking, the era was in many ways no different from the superstitious medieval period that preceded it. The 1500s were a time of omens and portents. Unusual weather patterns were widely assumed to be signs from the heavens. Unusual events of any kind—the birth of strange animals, erratic harvests, the coming of strangers to a town—presaged good or poor fortune, God's pleasure or displeasure. Commoners and nobles, priests and monks—with few exceptions, people viewed the world as a great mystery from which a few answers could be divined if you knew where to look and how to interpret signs.

This passage, from the 1529 *Chronicle of Anjou* by Jean de Bourdigne, tells of a series of disasters striking parts of France in 1521. De Bourdigne not only argues that virtually every event was somehow foreshadowed, but also believed that some of the disasters were the supernatural consequences of the immoral acts of individual people. Over time, ideas such as these would diminish. Early in the sixteenth century, however, de Bourdigne was far from alone in these superstitious beliefs; he represented the prevailing European worldview.

All the country parishes in Anjou were constrained to raise men-at-arms commonly called *francs-archers*, which was a grievous

Excerpted from *Chronicle of Anjou*, by Jean de Bourdigne, 1529.

burden; for each parish furnished one man whom they had to fit out with cap, plumes, doublet, leather collar, hosen and shoes, with such harness and staff as the captain should command. . . . Albeit they were raised, fed, clothed and armed at so great a cost, yet they were unprofitable both to prince and to people; for they began to rise up against the common folk, desiring to live at ease without further labouring at their wonted trades, and to pillage in the fields as they would have done in an enemy's country; wherefore several of them were taken and given into the hands of the provost-marshals, ending their lives on the gibbet [gallows] which they had so well deserved.

This year also the country of Anjou was infested by exceeding grievous rains that did much harm to the fruit: moreover the earth quaked sore, wherefrom many had but evil forebodings. And certainly men heard daily reports of follies and barbarities committed by these francs-archers, to the great scandal of the Faith and detriment of the people. For about this season, after that the aforesaid miscreants had scoured and rifled the province of Maine, beating and grieving the people sore, then they feared not to do a most detestable deed; for, by instigation of the Devil, they took a calf and set it upon the holy font ordained for the giving of baptism to christian folk; and there one of them, taking the church ornaments and holy water, made a form and pretence of baptizing him and giving him such a name as one would give to a christian, all in scorn and disdain of the holy sacrament of baptism, which was a strange thing to christian folk.

Again, in the village called St-Côme de Ver, in the said country of Maine, as the francs-archers aforesaid had (according to their wont) done several insolences and derisions against the holy relics in that church, and against the sacraments and ceremonies of the Church, finally one of them came behind the said church of St-Côme, hard by the glass window which giveth it light, where the said franc-archer found an apple-tree laden with fruit, which apples he plucked one by one, and threw them for his pleasure against the painted window of the church. And, having thrown several without being able to strike or break the glass, then it befel that, cursing and blaspheming, he cast one wherewith he smote the crown on a pictured St Cosmo that was in the window; which apple stuck there amidst the glass for a whole year's space, in the sight of all people, without decay or corruption; yet on the other hand all the other apples that hung on the tree fell to the ground from that day forward, and rotted in the twinkling of an eye, as though poisoned and infected by the touch of that wretch who had laid hands on the tree; who nevertheless escaped not our Lord's judgment and vengeance. For, in that night following, the arm wherewith he had cast the said

apples was stricken with palsy, not without grievous pain and torment; whereof he was nevertheless afterwards cured to his own confusion; for, having done some deed that brought him into the hands
of justice, he was hanged and strangled by the provost-marshal. Yet
this shameful death of his amended not his fellows, but that they
wrought many crimes and barbarities unwonted and unheard-of before this time; for they pillaged in their own country as in a foreign
land, forced women and maidens, beat priests and men of all estates,
and took horses or mares from the fields and meadows wheresoever
they found them, to bear themselves and the raiment which they
gathered by their robberies throughout the country; feeding their
horses and mares on pure wheat which they took from the poor folk,
and giving them wine to drink. And it befel in one place of Anjou
that, after these miscreants had drunken outrageously of the best
wine that was in the house wherein they lodged, then they began to
cast the rest away; and as the master of that house, a man of holy
church far advanced in age, gently reproved them, showing how it
was a sin to waste the good things which God giveth for our sustenance, then these evil folk waxed wroth and constrained him to set
a caldron on the fire, and fill it with wine, wherewith, when it was
warmed he must needs wash their feet. . . .

Other Signs

In the month of November of this year it rained in so great abundance that men thought the deluge [that is, another Noah's Flood]
had come (for some had foolishly foretold this the year before);
whereof many men of light faith were sore afraid, both in Anjou and
in Touraine. The river Loire swelled into so great a flood that it did
much harm throughout the land; for in many places it brake the dikes
and wrought piteous havoc in the lowlands; wherein some houses
were overthrown by the violence of the waters, and much sown corn
was lost, and many beasts drowned; so that the country folk were in
sore poverty for many years after. And this same year, on the twelfth
day of December, in the city of Freiburg in Germany, a cow brought
forth a monstrous birth shaped like a man, yet hideous and deformed, bearing on his head a sort of tonsure, both broad and white,
his body and tail shaped like a swine, and the whole colour as
though he had been smoked. Moreover the skin round his neck was
doubled and folded like a monk's cowl; and the shape thereof was
soon afterwards brought into Anjou, wherefrom many drew manifold interpretations; and, among others, they attributed the form of
this monster to the Lutheran doctrine, seeing that there was then in
Germany a Friar, Martin Luther by name, who preached and dog-
matized many articles and propositions which since by the Roman
Church and the Sorbonne at Paris have been declared false and er-

roneous. Wherefore many folk named this misbegotten creature the Lutherick Monster, in mockery and derision of that same Luther and those of his damnable sect. . . .

Moreover in the month of March, the moon being in opposition, it was seen striped in many colours, to wit white and yellow and black and red, whereat folk marvelled sore. And soon afterwards came certain news of the enterprise which that unhappy enemy to the Christian Faith, Sultan Solyman called the Great Turk, had wrought upon the knights of Rhodes [in Greece], whom we call Hospitallers, taking from them their most mighty and well-fortified city of Rhodes together with the whole island, and banishing them from those parts, to the great shame, confusion, and scandal of christian princes and prelates, and to the irrecoverable loss of all christendom. Whereof the knights of that same Order were much blamed; for the common rumour ran that (seeing how long warning they had received of that which the Turk meditated [that is, intended]) they had very ill furnished their said town, both in victuals and in soldiers, artillery, powder, and other munitions of war; and thus they had done but little good for the great revenues which they gather wellnigh daily throughout all christian kingdoms, which revenues (as we may well believe) were given only to set the knights forward as the bulwark and defence of christenedom, and especially of the said city of Rhodes.

Renaissance City Life

E.R. Chamberlin

European cities of the sixteenth century were small and crowded by current standards. Though even the largest of them rarely had more than one hundred thousand inhabitants, city dwellers were packed into areas almost unimaginably tiny. Disease spread quickly, and fire and crime were always a fear; moreover, city populations suffered sooner and more intensely from famines than did people living in the countryside. Yet cities also provided economic opportunity for a good many Europeans, and were full of excitement and activity. Despite the drawbacks, an increasing number of rural Europeans moved to the cities during the sixteenth century.

In this excerpt from his book *Everyday Life in Renaissance Times*, historian E.R. Chamberlin describes the cities of the Renaissance. He explains how and why they grew, the extent to which they were planned, and how they protected themselves from attack. The excerpt also discusses the often rocky relationship between the cities and the surrounding countryside.

[B]y the sixteenth century] the city consisted of a group of men who, after generations of conflict among themselves, had evolved a workable system of self-government. That system varied from city to city; in any one of them the proportion of men who could claim full citizenship was always small, the great mass of people still little more than serfs, exerting their rights only through the medium of fierce rebellions against the upper classes. Yet throughout Europe, in Italy, Germany, and the Low Countries in particular there had been a common agreement as to the ends if not the means of government— a society in which most of the rulers were chosen by some of the ruled. Out of the civic concept arose endless and bloody wars; the price the citizens paid for their freedom was measured precisely by their willingness to bear arms in defence of their city against its rivals.

The true voice of the city was the great bell, of town hall or cathedral, which bellowed the alarm on the approach of armed citizens of an enemy city, summoning all able men to walls and gates. The Italians, indeed, took the bell and made of it a moving shrine, a kind of civic Ark which led the armies to battle. Battles against neighbouring cities for the possession of a scrap of farmland; battles against the Emperor or the king for civic rights; battles against hordes of wandering soldiery; during all these, the economic life of the city came to a standstill, for all fit men, without exception, from the age of 15 to 70 were taken from their normal activities to fight. So, at length, for the sake of economic survival, professionals were hired to fight the wars, while at the same time civic power began to fall into the hands of a prominent citizen. Controlling money and arms as he did, the citizen evolved into the prince in the once free cities. In those countries which acknowledged a central monarchy, city and throne made peace through exhaustion; some cities, such as London, retained much of their autonomy; others were absorbed totally into the framework of monarchy. Nevertheless, throughout the Renaissance, cities continued still as living units, discharging for themselves most of the functions which in modern society fall to the jurisdiction of the central authority. They were not the dormitories or industrial centres or pleasure gardens that so many were to become, but seemingly organic structures of flesh and brick with their own, identifiable, rhythm of life.

Population and Expansion

The cities which studded Europe like jewels were already ancient, coming down through the centuries curiously regular in shape and constant in size. Only in England was the sense of symmetry absent, for the English cities, with a few exceptions, had not been planned as such but grew up from humble beginnings and remained amorphous [vaguely shaped] as building was haphazardly added to building. The continental tendency had been to found new cities rather than to expand the old to unmanageable proportions; in Germany alone, 2,400 had been founded over some 400 years. In terms of population, they would today be called towns or even large villages. Orange in France numbered only 6,000 souls until well into the nineteenth century. A city of a quarter of a million inhabitants was a giant and there were few of those. Milan, the capital of a dukedom, held 200,000, twice the size of its great rival, Florence, for size was not necessarily an indication of power. Rheims, the place of coronation and a great commercial city, numbered 100,000, Paris perhaps 250,000. A figure ranging between 10,000 and 50,000 would apply to most European cities. Even the ravages created by the plague had no long-term effect upon the static nature of population. The totals of plague deaths were always exaggerated but, nevertheless, perhaps a quarter of the population would be carried off within a few months; yet, within a generation, the city would return to its original level. Overspill population found their way into the new cities. The Italian pattern, followed in greater or lesser degree throughout Europe, was that of a number of cities, linked by conquest or commercial federation, around a single giant. Systems of government and local customs peculiar to each city in the federation were jealously preserved but taxation and defence were controlled from the centre.

A city expanded as a tree does, retaining its shape but increasing its size, the city walls, like tree rings, marking growth. It was the poorer classes who lived immediately outside the walls, beggars, outcasts, men with humble trades, who would build hovels against the city wall, forming a vile ring of squalid streets outside the city. Occasionally they would be the target of an energetic municipality but usually they would be allowed to remain until some pattern became evident. The well-to-do lived in an outer ring of villas in large grounds, protected by their own walls. When at length civic pride or economic necessity required an expansion of the city, a new circuit of walls would be traced outside the old, encompassing the new growth and leaving space for more. The old walls would remain, possibly for centuries afterwards, or were cannibalised to make new buildings. Cities tended to renew their form, not their material, so that the same piece of brick or squared stone might have a life of a thousand years or more in half a dozen different buildings. The sites of those walls which have disappeared can still be traced, for they later provided valuable, ready-made ring-roads or, less often, public gardens.

Walls and Gates

The city wall was the factor which governed shape and size. During the Middle Ages they had been the ultimate in defence for a city well supplied with water and food. A general contemplating a siege would have to be prepared to spend months waiting for the enemy's supplies to run out. The walls were maintained at the public expense; whatever else was allowed to fall into ruin, they took priority in the allocation of funds. A collapsed wall was an indication of a collapsing city, and the first task of a victorious general was to raze the walls if he did not intend to occupy the city. The gradual decline in the importance of walls was reflected in the changing methods of portraying a city [in art or in maps]. The plan view came in extensively during the sixteenth century;

it was a method which enhanced the importance of the streets, communication triumphing over insulation. The streets were shown lined with houses, the prominent buildings still appeared but gradually all was flattened, formalised as the plan became more accurate—and less visually interesting. But before the plan view, the custom had been to show the city as a traveller might view it from a distant road so that it appeared in art as it was in reality, a single unit with walls, towers, churches blending together as though it were one great castle. Such cities exist still and those such as Verona, that lie on a hillside, show very clearly the form which their builders gave them. In the south, particularly in Italy, a dominant feature was the great towered houses which gave to some cities the appearance of a petrified forest. These houses were relics of a more violent age, when faction and family feuds rent the cities so that those who could built ever higher and higher to achieve advantage over their neighbour. Successive city governments had managed to reduce their number, but many still towered, a threat to internal security, robbing the narrow streets of air and light.

The gates which pierced the walls played a double role, for not only were they part of the defences but they contributed to the city's revenue. Officers were stationed at them to levy tax on everything entering the city. Sometimes the goods might be the produce of fields and gardens of the nearby country; sometimes they were exotic spices come from thousands of miles away but all yielded up tax at the gate. On one occasion when Florentine revenues were running dangerously low, an official suggested that the number of gates should be doubled, thereby doubling the revenue. He was laughed out of the council chamber but his unthinking suggestion arose out of the prevailing idea that the city was an independent entity. The country people loathed the taxes, for they received little more from them than the dubious promise of military protection. They went to extreme lengths to avoid paying, and [a] story of the farmer who concealed eggs in his baggy trousers with intent to defraud has the ring of truth. The guards at the gate, who had been informed by his enemy, courteously insisted that he should be seated while they examined his baggage.

In cities controlled by a lord, the gates acted as ears and eyes. They were the only point of contact with the outside world; it was from the outside world that his main threat came and the guards at the gates kept him closely informed of the comings and goings of foreigners. In free cities, the closing of the gate was both a symbol and a means of independence. The belated traveller, arriving after sunset, had no choice but to camp outside—whence arose the custom of building inns just outside the main gates. These gates appeared as small fortresses, housing the garrison of the city and, indeed, the great castles which dominated the medieval cities were usually merely extensions of the main gate-houses.

City Planning

The lack of plan in late medieval cities was more apparent than real. True, the streets seem to wander without object, to curl and coil back upon themselves or even peter out in a backyard, but they were intended less to provide access from one point to another of the city than to provide a setting for communal life. A stranger passing through a gate would find his way without difficulty to the heart of the city, for the main roads radiated from the central square. *Piazza, place, platz*— whatever it might be called in the native language—it was the descendant of the Roman *forum*, the place where men rallied in times of war or lingered in times of peace. Again, only in England was this meeting place absent, the English usually preferring to widen their high street for the market; it served the same purpose but lacked the sense of unity and, when traffic increased, lost its value as a central meeting place. But on the Continent this echo of Rome continued. It could be humble—an unpaved area shaded by trees, perhaps, and lined with a ragged row of buildings. It could be stupendous, as the great square of Siena or Venice, planned as a unit so that it seems like a vast, roofless hall. But whatever its appearance, it was the city made visible, the place of congregation, and flanking it would be the vital organs of the city, the centres of government and justice. Elsewhere in the city there would be another great natural centre: the cathedral with its ancillary buildings, frequently set in a smaller square. From city-gate to square, to cathedral the road would run wide enough and clean enough and straight enough. But away from the centres the streets would be local veins serving local needs. They were made deliberately narrow, as much to provide shelter from sun or rain as to conserve space, and sometimes the upper storeys of houses would be a bare few feet apart. The narrowness of the streets acted as a military defence for the citizens; the first act of an occupying power would be to gallop through them before barricades could be erected. It was virtually impossible for a military force to keep any semblance of order while marching through them and, under these conditions, a hostile crowd armed only with cobblestones could keep a professional force at bay. The paving of streets had begun in Italy as early as the thirteenth century, and by the sixteenth the main streets, at least, of most European cities were paved. No distinction was made between street and pavement, for the only traffic was pedestrian or horse. Carriages began to appear in the sixteenth century, and gradually, as wheeled traffic grew in volume, streets were straightened to accommodate it and provision made for pedestrians, making even clearer the distinction between rich and poor.

The hygiene of cities was even more neglected than the hygiene of persons. Travellers reported with monotonous regularity the disgusting conditions which they met, conditions which were no worse than those of their own cities but were seen with a fresh eye. The gradually increasing prohibition on keeping livestock within the city-walls probably increased the level of filth; the pig, that universal scavenger kept by most poor families, had been allowed to wander at will to find his own food. Excluded from the city, the task of street cleaning was left to dogs, rather more choosy in their diet. The streets were a dumping ground for every form of rubbish; only the fact that it was organic and sooner or later became a sludge saved the streets from becoming impassable. In the process of breaking down, it turned into a thick, oily, blue-black liquid which saturated the ground, stained walls all along their base and provided a fruitful breeding ground for disease. The practice of burying the dead within the city did nothing to lower the threshold of disease. The height of a cemetery would increase fourfold and more over the centuries; it would be located near the parish church—and so would the common well. The gradual percolation of tainted water would find its way into the drinking supply with inevitable results. The fires which frequently swept through cities were the most efficient prophylactic [means of prevention] known; without them, the crowded quarters of rich and poor alike would have become untenable [unlivable].

Pre-Shakespearean Drama

Author unknown

The theater of the early sixteenth century was quite different from drama as presented today. There were few actual theaters. Those that existed were often open to the air; their stages slanted toward the audience, and they lacked all but the most rudimentary sets and lights. Indeed, plays were most often presented in village squares by groups of players who traveled from town to town. The plays usually were designed to carry a moral, often expressly religious, though secular plays were becoming more popular during this period than they had been during earlier medieval times.

This excerpt from the popular drama *The Summoning of Everyman* is an excellent example of early-sixteenth-century theater. The main character is Everyman, who stands for all humanity. The events of the play are meant to be taken allegorically; what happens to Everyman is to be interpreted as the fate of all humans, rather than specific to a particular character. Though the play is of anonymous authorship, it has had an enormous influence on literature: The term "Everyman" has come to mean an entire literary genre in which a character stands for all people.

Everyman also expresses some common themes in sixteenth-century religious thought. Not nearly as complex or as finely crafted as the works of later dramatists such as Shakespeare, this play offers obvious morals stated several times by various characters: We all must die; life is fleeting; do not sin; wordly goods and relationships are not the path to a righteous life. God opens the play by bemoaning Everyman's obsession with things on earth and lack of attention to God Himself and Heaven, and sends for Death to teach Everyman a lesson.

Excerpted from *The Summoning of Everyman*, author unknown.

Death: Almighty God I am here at your will,
   Your commandment to fulfill.

God: Go thou to *Everyman*
   And shew him, in my name,
   A pilgrimage he must on him take,
   Which he in no wise may escape;
   And that he bring with him a sure reckoning
   Without delay or any tarrying.

Death: Lord, I will in the world go run over all,
   And cruelly outsearch both great and small.
   Every man will I beset that liveth beastly
   Out of God's laws and dreadeth not folly.
   He that loveth riches I will strike with my dart,
   His sight to blind, and from Heaven to depart—
   Except that alms [charity] be his good friend—
   In Hell for to dwell, world without end.

(*Exit* God. Death *moves to stage of the World*).

   Lo, yonder I see *Everyman* walking.
   Full little he thinketh on my coming;
   His mind is on fleshly lusts, and his treasure;
   And great pain it shall cause him to endure
   Before the Lord, Heaven's king.

(Everyman *enters with a company of men and woman. They break
   into a dance*. Death *watches awhile*).

   Everyman, stand still! Whither art thou going
   Thus gaily? Hast thou thy Maker forgot?

Everyman (*still dancing*): Why askest thou?
   Wouldest thou wit [know]?

Death: Yea, sir; I will shew you:
   In great haste I am sent to thee
   From God out of his Majesty.

Everyman (*faltering*): What, sent to me?

Death: Yea, certainly.
   Though thou have forgot him here,
   He thinketh on thee in the heavenly sphere,
   As, or we depart, thou shalt know.

Everyman: What desireth God of me?

Death: That shall I shew thee.
   A reckoning [that is, an accounting of
   good and bad deeds] he will needs have

Without any longer respite.

Everyman: To give a reckoning longer leisure I crave.
  This blind matter troubleth my wit.

Death: On thee thou must take a long journey.
    Therefore thy book of count with thee thou bring,
    For turn again thou cannot by no way!
    And look thou be sure of thy reckoning
    For before God thou shalt answer and shew
    Thy many bad deeds and good but a few,
    How thou hast spent thy life, and in what wise,
    Before the chief Lord of Paradise.
    Have a do that we were in that way,
    For wete [know] thou well thou shalt make none thy attornay.

Everyman: Full unready I am such reckoning to give.
  I know thee not. What messenger art thou?

Death: I am *Death* that no man dreadeth.
    Every man I arrest and no man spareth;
    For it is God's commandment
    That all to me should be obedient.

(*The dance peters out and the guests leave*).

Everyman: O *Death*, thou comest when I had ye least in mind!
    In thy power it lyeth me to save;
    Yet of my goods will I give ye, if thou will be kind;
    Yea, a thousand pound shalt thou have
    And thou defer this matter till another day.

Death: *Everyman*, it may not be, by no way!
    I set not by gold, silver, nor riches,
    Ne [nor] by Pope, Emperor, King, Duke, ne princes;
    For and I would receive gifts great,
    All the world I might get.
    But my custom is clean contrary.
    I give thee no respite. Come hence, and not tarry!

Everyman: Alas, shall I have no longer respite?
    I may say *Death* giveth no warning!
    To think on thee it maketh my heart sick,
    For all unready is my book of reckoning.
    But twelve year and I might have abiding,
    My counting book I would make so clear
    That my reckoning I should not need to fear.
    Wherefore, *Death*, I pray thee, for God's mercy,
    Spare me till I be provided of remedy!

Death: Thee availeth not [that is, it does not
    help you] to cry, weep, and pray,
    But haste thee lightly that thou wert gone that journay!
    And prove thy friends, if thou can.
    For wete thou well the tide abideth no man;
    And in the world each living creature
    For Adam's sin must die of nature.

Everyman: *Death*, if I should this pilgrimage take,
    And my reckoning surely make,
    Shew me for Saint Charity,
    Should I not come again shortly?

Death: No, *Everyman;* and thou be once there,
    Thou may'st never more come here,
    Trust me verily.

Everyman: O gracious God in the high seat celestial,
    Have mercy on me in this most need!
    Shall I have no company from this vale terrestrial
    Of my acquaintance that way me to lead?

Death: Yea, if any be so hardy
    That would go with thee and bear thee company.
    Hi thee that thou wert gone to God's magnificence,
    Thy reckoning to give before his presence.
    What, weenest thou [do you imagine] thy life is given thee
    And thy worldly goods also?

Everyman: I had weened so, verily.

Death: Nay, nay, they were but lent thee;
    For as soon as thou art gone
    Another awhile shall have it, and then go therefrom
    Even as thou hast done.
    Everyman, thou art mad! Thou hast thy wits five
    And here on earth will not amend thy life;
    For suddenly I do come.

Everyman: O wretched caitiff [despicable one], whither shall I flee
    That I might 'scape this endless sorrow!
    Now, gentle *Death*, spare me till tomorrow,
    That I may amend me
    With good advisement.

Death: Nay, thereto I will not consent,
    Nor no man will I respite;
    But to the heart suddenly I shall smite
    Without any advisement.

And now out of thy sight I will me hie.
See thou make thee ready shortly
For thou mayest say this is the day
That no man living may scape away.

(Death *goes*).

Everyman: Alas, I may well weep with sighs deep!
Now have I no manner of company
To help me in my journey and me to keep;
And also my writing is full unready.
How shall I do now for to excuse me?
I would to God I had never been got!
To my soul a full great profit it had been,
For now I fear pains huge and great.

(*A distant clock strikes*)

The time passeth. Lord, help, that all wrought [created]!
For though I mourn it availeth nought;
The day passeth and is almost agone.
I wot not well what for to do.
To whom were I best my complaint to make?
What and [if] I to *Fellowship* thereof spake,
And shewed him of this sudden chance?
For in him is all mine affiance [all my trust].
We have in the world so many a day
Been good friends in sport and play.
I see him yonder certainly.
I trust that he will bear me company,
Therefore to him will I speak to ease my sorrow.
Well met, good *Fellowship!* and good morrow!

(Fellowship *has entered during the above*).

Fellowship: *Everyman*, good morrow, by this day!
Sir, why lookest thou so piteously?
If anything be amiss, I pray thee me say,
That I may help to remedy.

Everyman: Yea, good *Fellowship,* yea,
I am in great jeopardy.

Fellowship: My true friend, show to me your mind,
I will not forsake thee to my life's end
In the way of good company.

Everyman: That was well spoken and lovingly.

Fellowship: Sir, I must needs know your heaviness;

I have pity to see you in any distress.
If any have you wronged, ye shall revenged be,
Though I on the ground be slain for thee,
Though that I know before that I should die.

Everyman: Verily, *Fellowship*, gramercy [great thanks].

Fellowship: Tush, by thy thanks I set not a straw!
    Shew me your grief and say no more.

Everyman: If I my heart should to you break
    And then you to turn your mind from me
    And would not me comfort when ye hear me speak,
    Then should I ten times sorrier be.

Fellowship: Sir, I say as I will do indeed.

Everyman: Then be you a good friend at need.
    I have found you true here before.

Fellowship: And so ye shall evermore;
    For, in faith, and [if] thou go to hell
    I will not forsake thee by the way.

Everyman: Ye speak like a good friend. I believe you well.
    I shall deserve it and I may.

Fellowship: I speak of no deserving, by this day!
    For he that will say and nothing do
    Is not worthy with good company to go.
    Therefore show me the grief of your mind,
    As to your friend most loving and kind.

Everyman: I shall shew you how it is.
    Commanded I am to go a journey—
    A long way, hard and dangerous—
    And give a straight count, without delay,
    Before the high judge, Adonay [a Hebrew name for God].
    Wherefore I pray you, bear me company,
    As ye have promised, in this journay.

Fellowship: This is matter indeed! Promise is duty.
    But and I should take such a voyage on me,
    I know it well it should be to my pain.
    Also it make me afeard, certain.
    But let us take counsel here, as well as we can,
    For your words would fear [that is, terrify] a strong man.

Everyman: Why ye said if I had need
    Ye would me never forsake, quick nor dead,
    Though it were to hell truly.

Fellowship: So I said certainly.
  But such pleasures be set aside, the sooth to say.
  And also if we took such a journay,
  When should we come again?

Everyman: Nay never again till the day of doom!

Fellowship: In faith, then will I not come there!
  Who hath you these tidings brought?

Everyman: Indeed, *Death* was with me here.

Fellowship (*backing away in fear*): Now, by God,
    that all hath bought,
  If *Death* were the messenger,
  For no man that is living today
  I will not go that loath journay—
  Not for the father that begat me!

Everyman: Ye promised otherwise, pardee.

Fellowship: I wot well I said so, truly.
  And yet if thou wilt eat and drink and make good cheer,
  Or haunt to women the lusty company,
  I would not forsake you while the day is clear,
  Trust me, verily.

Everyman: Yea, thereto ye would be ready!
  To go to mirth, solace, and play
  Your mind will sooner apply,
  Than to bear me company in my long journay.

Fellowship: Nay in good faith I will not that way.
  But an [if] thou wilt murder, or any man kill,
  In that I will help thee with a good will.

Everyman: O that is a simple advice indeed.
  Gentle *Fellow*, help me in my necessity!
  We have loved long and now I need;
  And now, gentle *Fellowship*, remember me.

Fellowship: Whether ye have loved me or no,
  By Saint John I will not with thee go!

Everyman: Yet, I pray thee, take ye labour and do so much for me
  To bring me forward, for Saint Charity,
  And comfort me till I come without [that is, outside] the town.

Fellowship: Nay, and [if] thou would give me a new gown
  I will not a foot with thee go.
  But an thou had tarried I would not have left thee so.

And as now God speed thee in thy journay!
For from thee I will depart as fast as I may.

Everyman: Whither away, *Fellowship?* Will ye forsake me?

Fellowship: Yea, by my faith! To God I betake [commit] thee.

Everyman: Farewell, good *Fellowship!* For ye my heart is sore.
Adieu for ever. I shall see thee no more.

Fellowship: In faith, *Everyman*, fare well now at the end!
For you I will remember that parting is mourning.

(Fellowship *hurries away*).

Everyman: Alack! Shall we thus depart indeed—
Ah, Lady, help!—without any more comfort?
Lo, *Fellowship* forsaketh me in my most need.
For help in this world whither shall I resort?
Fellowship here before with me would merry make,
And now little sorrow for me doth he take.
It is said, "In prosperity men friends may find
Which in adversity be full unkind."
Now whither for succour shall I flee,
Sith that [because] *Fellowship* hath forsaken me?
To my kinsmen I will, truly,
Praying them to help me in my necessity.
I believe that they will do so,
For "kind will creep where it may not go".
I will go assay [try], for yonder I see them go.
Where be ye now, my friends and kinsmen?

(*Enter* Kindred, Cousin *and her* Maid).

Kindred (*making a reverence*): Here be we now at your commandment.
Cousin, I pray you show us your intent
In any wise and do not spare.

Cousin: Yea, *Everyman*, and to us declare
If ye be disposed to go any whither;
For wete you well we will live and die together.

Kindred: In wealth and woe we will with you hold,
For over his kin a man may be bold.

Everyman: Gramercy, my friends and kinsmen kind.
Now shall I show you the grief of my mind.
I was commanded by a messenger
That is a high king's chief officer.
He bad me go a pilgrimage to my pain,
And I know well I shall never come again.

Also I must give a reckoning straight,
For I have a great enemy that for me doth wait,
Which intendeth me for to hinder.

Kindred (*alarmed*): What account is that which ye must render?
That would I know.

Everyman: Of all my works I must show
How I have lived and my days spent;
Also of ill deeds that I have used
In my time sith [since] life was me lent,
And of all virtues that I have refused.
Therefore I pray you go thither with me
To help to make mine account, for Saint Charity.

Cousin: What? To go thither? Is that the matter?
Nay, *Everyman*, I had liefer [rather] fast [upon] bread and water
All this five year and more.

Everyman: Alas that ever I was born!
For now shall I never be merry
If that you forsake me.

Kindred: Ah, sir, what? Ye be a merry man!
Take good heart to you and make no moan.
But one thing I warn you, by Saint Anne—
As for me ye shall go alone.

Everyman: My *Cousin*, will you not with me go?

Cousin: No, by Our Lady! I have the cramp in my toe.
Trust not to me; for, so God me speed,
I will deceive you in your most need.

Kindred: It availeth not us to tyse [bargain].
Ye shall have my maid with all my heart;
She loveth to go to feasts, there to be nice,
And to dance, and abroad to start.
I will give her leave to help you in that journay,
If that you and she may agree.

Everyman: Now show me the very effect of your mind;
Will you go with me or abide behind?

Kindred: Abide behind? yea, that will I and I may!
Therefore farewell till another day!

(Kindred *goes*).

Everyman: How should I be merry or glad?
For fair promises men to me make,

But when I have most need they me forsake.
I am deceived: that maketh me sad.

Cousin: Cousin *Everyman*, farewell now;
   For verily I will not go with you.
   Also of mine own life an unready reckoning
   I have to account; therefore I make tarrying.
   Now God keep thee, for now I go.

   (Cousin *goes, followed by the* Maid).

Apparel and Attire

William Harrison

William Harrison was a minister in a rural English church and an amateur historian. He was the author of a chronology of the world that included events from the biblical Creation to his own time. This book was never published, however, and he is best remembered today for a volume that he completed in 1577 (it was revised ten years later) and which is known today as *The Description of England*. In it Harrison set to paper everything he knew about the England of the late sixteenth century. The work is a wealth of facts and figures as well as interpretation: Harrison includes chapters on universities, "savage beasts and vermin," and "palaces belonging to the Prince," among many, many other topics.

This excerpt from *The Description of England* deals with the fashions of the day and Harrison's opinion of them. As Harrison makes clear, tastes in fashion during the 1500s were every bit as fleeting as they are today. The Elizabethan era was certainly a time of fancy costuming, complete with ruffled collars, bright colors, and high hats of velvet or silk; some travelers of the time found the English more ostentatious dressers than any other European people. As a rule, Harrison thinks little of the English interest in finery. While he describes some costume in detail, he is more concerned with what he sees as an overemphasis on dress and a lack of focus on other, more important parts of life.

A n Englishman, endeavoring sometime to write of our attire, made sundry platforms [sketches] for his purpose, supposing by some of them to find out one steadfast ground whereon to build the sum of his discourse. But in the end (like an orator long without exercise), when he saw what a difficult piece of work he had taken in hand, he gave over his travail and only drew the picture of a naked man, unto whom he gave a pair of shears in the one hand and a piece of cloth in the other, to the end he should shape his apparel after such fashion as himself liked, sith [since] he could find no kind of garment that could please him any while together; and this he called an Englishman. Certes [certainly] this writer (otherwise being a lewd popish hypocrite and ungracious priest) showed himself herein not to be altogether void of judgment, sith the fantastical folly of our nation, even from the courtier to the carter, is such that no form of apparel liketh us longer than the first garment is in the wearing, if it continue so long and be not laid aside to receive some other trinket newly devised by the fickle-headed tailors, who covet to have several tricks in cutting, thereby to draw fond customers to more expense of money.

For my part, I can tell better how to inveigh against [complain about] this enormity than describe any certainty of our attire; sithence [since] such is our mutability that today there is none to [better than] the Spanish guise, tomorrow the French toys are most fine and delectable, ere long no such apparel as that which is after the High Almain [German] fashion, by and by the Turkish manner is generally best liked of, otherwise the Morisco [Moorish] gowns, the Barbarian sleeves, the mandilion [cape with sleeves] worn to Collyweston-ward [sideways], and the short French breeches make such a comely vesture that, except [that is, unless] it were a dog in a doublet, you shall not see any so disguised as are my countrymen of England. And as these fashions are diverse, so likewise it is a world to see the costliness and the curiosity, the excess and the vanity, the pomp and the bravery, the change and the variety, and finally, the fickleness and the folly that is in all degrees, insomuch that nothing is more constant in England than inconstancy of attire. Oh, how much cost is bestowed nowadays upon our bodies and how little upon our souls! How many suits of apparel hath the one, and how little furniture hath the other! How long time is asked in decking up of the first, and how little space left wherein to feed the latter! How curious, how nice also, are a number of men and women, and how hardly can the tailor please them in making it fit for their bodies! How many times must it be sent back again to him that made it! What chafing, what fretting, what reproachful language doth the poor workman bear away! And many times when he doth nothing to it at all, yet when it is brought home again, it is very fit and handsome; then must we put it on, then must the long seams of our hose be set by a plumb line, then we puff, then we blow, and finally, sweat till we drop that our clothes may stand well upon us.

Hair and Beards

I will say nothing of our heads, which sometimes are polled, sometimes curled or suffered to grow at length like woman's locks, many times cut off above or under the ears round, as by a wooden dish. Neither will I meddle with our variety of beards, of which some are shaven from the chin like those of Turks, not a few cut short . . . some made round like a rubbing brush, . . . or now and then suffered to grow long, the barbers being grown to be so cunning in this behalf as the tailors. And therefore, if a man have a lean and strait face, a Marquis Otto's cut [that is, a short beard] will make it broad and large; if it be platter-like, a long slender beard will make it seem the narrower; if he be weasel-becked [-beaked], then much hair left on the cheeks will make the owner look big, like a bowdled [ruffled] hen, and so grim as a goose, . . . many old men do wear no beards at all. Some lusty courtiers also and gentlemen of courage do wear either rings of gold, stones, or pearl in their ears, whereby they imagine the workmanship of God not to be a little amended. But herein they rather disgrace than adorn their persons, as by their niceness in apparel, for which I say most nations do, not unjustly, deride us, as also for that we do seem to imitate all nations round about us, wherein we be like to the *polypus* [octopus] or chameleon; and thereunto bestow most cost upon our arses, and much more than upon all the rest of our bodies, as women do likewise upon their heads and shoulders.

Women

In women also it is most to be lamented that they do now far exceed the lightness of our men (who nevertheless are transformed from the cap even to the very shoe), and such staring attire as in time past was supposed meet for none but light housewives [hussies] only is now become an habit for chaste and sober matrons. What should I say of their doublets with pendant codpieces on the breast, full of jags and cuts, and sleeves of sundry colors? their galligaskins [leggings] to bear out their bums and make their attire to fit plum-round (as they term it) about them? their farthingales [petticoats] and diversely colored netherstocks [stockings] of silk, jersey, and suchlike, whereby their bodies are rather deformed than commended? I have met with some of these trulls in London so disguised that it hath passed my skill to discern whether they were men or women.

Thus it is now come to pass that women are become men and men transformed into monsters; and those good gifts which Almighty God hath given unto us to relieve our necessities withal . . . not otherwise bestowed than in all excess, as if we wist not otherwise how to consume and waste them. I pray God that in this behalf our sin be not like unto that of Sodom and Gomorrah, whose errors were pride, excess of diet, and abuse of God's benefits abundantly bestowed upon them, beside want of charity toward the poor and certain other points which the prophet shutteth up in silence. Certes the commonwealth

cannot be said to flourish where these abuses reign but is rather op-
pressed by unreasonable exactions made upon rich farmers and of
poor tenants, wherewith to maintain the same. Neither was it ever
merrier with England than when an Englishman was known abroad
by his own cloth and contented himself at home with his fine kersey
hosen and a mean slop [breeches], his coat, gown, and cloak . . . with
some pretty furniture of velvet or fur, and a doublet of sad tawny
[orange brown] or black velvet or other comely silk, without such
cuts and garish colors as are worn in these days and never brought
in but by the consent of the French, who think themselves the gayest
men when they have most diversities of jags and change of colors
about them.

Certes of all estates our merchants do least alter their attire and
therefore are most to be commended, for albeit that which they wear
be very fine and costly, yet in form and color it representeth a great
piece of the ancient gravity appertaining to citizens and burgesses,
albeit the younger sort of their wives, both in attire and costly house-
keeping, cannot tell when and how to make an end, as being women
indeed in whom all kind of curiosity is to be found and seen, and in
far greater measure than in women of higher calling. I might here
name a sort of hues devised for the nonce wherewith to please fantastical heads, as gooseturd green, pease-porridge tawny, popinjay
blue, lusty gallant, the-devil-in-the-head (I should say "the hedge"),
and suchlike; but I pass them over, thinking it sufficient to have said
thus much of apparel generally, when nothing can particularly be
spoken of any constancy thereof.

The Gregorian Calendar

Stephen Jay Gould

One of the great scientific advances of the sixteenth century was the development of the Gregorian calendar, which remains in use today. Putting the calendar together required an extensive understanding of astronomy and mathematics. Putting it into practice, however, also involved a certain amount of political will. Europeans had known for centuries that the solar year does not divide neatly into an even number of days. They had therefore established the idea of leap year, which assumed that the year was exactly 365 and one-quarter days long; adding a leap year every four years allowed the calendar and the celestial year to keep in pace with each other. However, that assumption turned out not to be entirely correct, with significant problems resulting from that miscalculation by the sixteenth century.

   In this excerpt, science writer Stephen Jay Gould explains the development of the calendar with particular reference to the events of the 1500s. The author of many books on scientific topics, Gould is a professor of zoology and geology at Harvard University. He is also a museum curator and a well-known authority on evolution.

The first modern reform of the Western calendar, introduced by Julius Caesar himself in 45 B.C., didn't recognize the additional irregularity of 365-and-a-teeny-little-bit-less-than-a-quarter-of-a-day (365.242199 . . . to be precise) and used exactly 365-and-a-quarter instead. Can we possibly need to worry about such a minor rounding-off that overestimates the true solar year by a mere eleven minutes and change? Thus, the Julian calendar operated in a maximally simple manner (given the undeniable reality of that fractional day after the full 365). That is, the Julian calendar makes one correction, and one correction only—and this correction follows an invariable rule. On every fourth or "leap" year, the calendar adds an extra day to make a year of 366 days. Since we cannot abide fractional days in a rational calendar, an endlessly repeating sequence of 365, 365, 365, and 366 will serve as a good whole-day version of a solar year that actually runs for 365 and a quarter days.

Except for the inconvenient additional complexity that the solar year doesn't quite reach 365 and a quarter days. The year falls short of this fractional regularity by those pesky eleven minutes and change. The minor overestimate of the Julian calendar will not matter much at first, but those eleven extra minutes do begin to add up after a while, and Caesar did live a rather long time ago. Eventually, the calendar will start to accumulate noticeable extra days (seven every thousand years, in fact), and the process must continue indefinitely, forcing the Julian calendar more and more out of whack with the true solar year. That is, if we want the vernal equinox to fall on about the same day, March 21 or so, every year (an enormous convenience for all manner of people, from priests to farmers, and a pressing necessity, as we shall see, for the crucial determination of Easter), then the Julian calendar gets progressively worse as the centuries roll. The vernal equinox (and any other fixed date) begins to creep farther and farther up the calendar. And this blot on Caesar's reputation, rather than Brutus's wound, may turn out to be the most unkindest cut of all.

Clavius and Gregory

Pope Gregory XIII therefore made a kind and rational cut instead. By the sixteenth century, this inexorable overestimate, ticking along at eleven minutes and fourteen seconds per year, had accumulated ten extra days. This sloppiness had begun to generate some serious consequences, particularly for priests and astronomers charged with the solemn and sacred duty of determining the date for Easter. So Gregory followed a strategy favored from time immemorial—he convened a committee and appointed a very smart chairman, the eminent Jesuit mathematician Christopher Clavius. This committee, beginning its work in 1578, came up with one of those lovely, practical solutions that has absolutely no mandate in elegant or highfalutin theory but possesses the cardinal virtue of working pretty damned well. Pope Gregory proclaimed the new rules in a papal bull issued on February 24, 1582. We call his correction the Gregorian reform, and the improved calendar—the one we still use today—the Gregorian calendar.

Clavius's committee faced two separate problems and solved them in different ways. First of all, the old Julian calendar was now running ten days ahead and had to be brought back into alignment with the solar year (so that equinoxes and solstices would fall at their traditional times—and stay put). This problem could only be solved by old-fashioned damage control—of a fairly radical sort, but what else could they do? Clavius recommended that ten days be dropped into oblivion by official proclamation, and Pope Gregory did so—just like that, and by fiat! In 1582, October 5 through 14 simply disappeared and never occurred at all! The date following October 4 became October 15, and the calendar came back into sync.

This solution strikes many people as bizarre, if not monstrous— an affront both to nature and to human dignity. How can any arbitrary earthly power make days disappear at a whim? Now I don't deny that Gregory's solution imposed some problems (salaries, bank interest—if such a concept existed—ages, birthdays, and so on). . . .

Mathematical Reasoning

In fact, Gregory's solution of dropping days was not monstrous in the slightest but eminently wise and practical. The day records a true astronomical cycle, but the date that we affix to each day is only a human convention. October 5–14 were always part of an invented human system, not a natural reality. If we need to excise these dates in order to bring our artificial system into conformity with a natural cycle of equinoxes and solstices, then we may do so at will, and without guilt.

Second, Clavius and company had to devise a new calendrical rule that would avoid the creeping inaccuracy of the Julian system. They accomplished this goal by devising a year of 365.2422 days, much closer to astronomical reality than the calculationally simpler Julian solution of 365.25. To institute this new year, they made a second-order correction to the old rule of leap years—thus setting a more complex rule that we still use today. The Julian calendar had included too many leap years, so Clavius devised a neat little way to drop an occasional leap year in a regular manner that would give the entire system an appearance of wisdom and principle (thus hiding the purely practical problem that only required a workable and arbitrary solution). Clavius suggested that we drop the leap year at century boundaries, every hundred years. . . .

Simple rules rarely work, and the decision to drop leap years at century boundaries required yet another correction—third-order this time, with the Julian leap year as a first-order correction for the fractionality of days, the century drop as a second-order correction for the Julian overestimate, and this final rule as a third-order correction to the century drop.

Clavius recognized that if the Julian solution added too much, the century-dropping correction took away too much—requiring that something be put back every once in a while. Clavius therefore suggested that the leap year be restored every fourth century. He then expressed this procedure as a rule: Remove leap years at century boundaries, but put them back at century boundaries divisible by 400. (As I said, this may sound like a principled decision, but really represents no more than a codified rule of thumb.)

This third-order correction isn't perfect either, but it does bring the Gregorian calendar—that is, our calendar—into pretty fair sync with the solar year. In fact, the Gregorian year now departs from the solar year by only 25.96 seconds—accurate enough to require a correction of one day only once every 2,800 years or so. Finally, the discrepancy has become small enough not to matter in any practical way. (Or will these become famous last words as our technological society becomes ever more needful of precision?)

Reaction

In summary, the Gregorian reform of 1582 revised the Julian calendar by dropping those "extra" ten days, and then promulgating a new rule of leap years to prevent any substantial future inaccuracy: Proclaim a leap year every four years, except for three out of four century boundaries; institute this rule by retaining the leap year at century boundaries divisible by 400. This Gregorian rule has an interesting consequence for the . . . millennial year 2000. What a special time, and what a privilege for all of us! Not only [did] we get to witness a millennial transition, but we also [got] to live in that rare year that comes only once in four hundred—a century boundary with a February 29. Yes, 2000 [was] a leap year—and our lives [included] the special bonus of an extra day that comes only once every four hundred years. . . .

So much for astronomy, but we also have to deal with the foibles of human history and human xenophobia. The truly improved Gregorian calendar was quickly accepted throughout the Roman Catholic world. But in England, the whole brouhaha sounded like a Popish plot, and the Brits would be damned if they would go along. Thus, England kept the Julian calendar until 1752, when they finally succumbed to reason and practicality—by which time yet another "extra" day had accumulated in the Julian reckoning, so Parliament had to drop eleven days (September 3-13, 1752) in order to institute the belated Gregorian reform.

Effect of the Gregorian Calendar

When you know this history, some puzzling little footnotes in our common chronology gain an easy explanation (trivial in one sense, to be sure, but ever so frustratingly annoying if you don't know the reason). George Washington's birthday, for example, is sometimes given, particularly by contemporary sources in colonial America, as February 11, 1731—rather than the February 22, 1732, that we used to celebrate on time, before all our public holidays moved to convenient Mondays and we decided to split the difference between Lincoln and Washington with a common Presidents' Day. As an English colony, America still used the Julian calendar at Washington's birth. The eleven days had not yet been dropped (so Gregorian February 22 still counted as Julian February 11 in the British world). Moreover, the Julian year began in March (at least in England), so Washington was born a year early as well.

Similarly, many people used to puzzle every year at the Soviet celebration of the "October Revolution" in November. . . . Russia did not adopt the Gregorian calendar until 1918, when the secularists ousted the orthodoxy. So the Julian October revolution had actually occurred in Gregorian November—those extra days again! Finally, since the enemy within is always more dangerous than the enemy without, the Eastern Orthodox church has still not accepted the Gregorian calendar.

The Copernican Revolution

Thomas S. Kuhn

If there was one certainty in medieval Europe, it was this: The earth was stationary, and the sun and the rest of the heavens revolved around it. The Greek astronomer Ptolemy had said so, and had seemingly proved it scientifically in his treatise *Almagest*. Over the years, it was true that Ptolemy's tables had had to be continually revised, and by the sixteenth century the Ptolemaic model of the heavens was strikingly complex. Nevertheless, until the sixteenth century no European scientist seriously questioned the basic assumption that the earth stood at the center of the universe.

That changed in 1543, when Polish astronomer Nicolaus Copernicus published his *De Revolutionibus*. However, as historian of science Thomas S. Kuhn points out in this excerpt from his book *The Copernican Revolution*, Copernicus's conclusions were far from quickly or easily accepted. For what Copernicus proposed was more than a simple shift in scientific thinking. Instead, the notion of a sun-centered solar system and an earth that moved upset the standard view of religion, of the nature of knowledge, and of the importance of humankind. Though slow to catch on, Copernicanism was indeed a revolution.

A professor for many years, Thomas S. Kuhn is the author of many works on science and science history. He is perhaps best known for his book *The Structure of Scientific Revolutions*.

Copernicus died in 1543, the year in which the *De Revolutionibus* was published, and tradition tells us that he received the first

Excerpted from *The Copernican Revolution: Planetary Astronomy in the Development of Western Thought* (Cambridge, MA: Harvard University Press, 1957) by Thomas S. Kuhn. Copyright © 1957 by the President and Fellows of Harvard College, 1985 by Thomas Kuhn. Reprinted with permission from Harvard University Press.

printed copy of his life's work on his deathbed. The book had to fight its battles without further help from its author. But for those battles Copernicus had constructed an almost ideal weapon. He had made the book unreadable to all but the erudite [learned] astronomers of his day. Outside of the astronomical world the *De Revolutionibus* created initially very little stir. By the time large-scale lay and clerical opposition developed, most of the best European astronomers, to whom the book was directed, had found one or another of Copernicus' mathematical techniques indispensable. It was then impossible to suppress the work completely, particularly because it was in a printed book and not, like [earlier scientists] Oresme's work or Buridan's, in a manuscript. Whether intentionally or not, the final victory of the *De Revolutionibus* was achieved by infiltration [that is, slowly and stealthily].

For two decades before the publication of his principal work Copernicus had been widely recognized as one of Europe's leading astronomers. Reports about his research, including his new hypothesis, had circulated since about 1515. The publication of the *De Revolutionibus* was eagerly awaited. When it appeared, Copernicus' contemporaries may have been skeptical of its main hypothesis and disappointed in the complexity of its astronomical theory, but they were nevertheless forced to recognize Copernicus' book as the first European astronomical text that could rival the *Almagest* in depth and completeness. Many advanced astronomical texts written during the fifty years after Copernicus' death referred to him as a "second Ptolemy" or "the outstanding artificer of our age"; increasingly these books borrowed data, computations, and diagrams from the *De Revolutionibus*, at least from parts of it independent of the motion of the earth. During the second half of the sixteenth century the book became a standard reference for all those concerned with advanced problems of astronomical research.

But the success of the *De Revolutionibus* does not imply the success of its central thesis. The faith of most astronomers in the earth's stability was at first unshaken. Authors who applauded Copernicus' erudition, borrowed his diagrams, or quoted his determination of the distance from the earth to the moon, usually either ignored the earth's motion or dismissed it as absurd. Even the rare text that mentioned Copernicus' hypothesis with respect rarely defended or used it. With a few notable exceptions, the most favorable of the early reactions to the Copernican innovation are typified by the remark of the English astronomer Thomas Blundeville, who wrote: "Copernicus . . . affirmeth that the earth turneth about and that the sun standeth still in the midst of the heavens, by help of which false supposition he hath made truer demonstrations of the motions and revolutions of the celestial spheres, than ever were made before." Blundeville's remark appeared in 1594 in an elementary book on the heavens that took the earth's stability for granted. Yet the tenor of Blundeville's rejection must have sent his more alert and proficient readers straight to the *De Revolutionibus,* a book which, in any case, no proficient astronomer could ignore. From the start the *De Revolutionibus* was widely read, but it was read in spite of, rather than because of, its strange cosmological hypothesis.

Debate and Disagreement

Nevertheless, the book's large audience ensured it a small but increasing number of readers equipped to discover Copernicus' harmonies and willing to admit them as evidence. There were a few converts, and their work helped in varied ways to spread knowledge of Copernicus' system. The *Narratio Prima* or *First Account* by Copernicus' earliest disciple, George Joachim Rheticus (1514–1576), remained the best brief technical description of the new astronomical methods for many years after its first publication in 1540. The popular elementary defense of Copernicanism published in 1576 by the English astronomer Thomas Digges (1546–1595) did much to spread the concept of the earth's motion beyond the narrow circle of astronomers. And the teaching and research of Michael Maestlin (1550–1631), professor of astronomy at the University of Tübingen, gained a few converts, including [well-known astrophysicist Johann] Kepler, for the new astronomy. Through the teaching, writing, and research of men like these, Copernicanism inevitably gained ground, though the astronomers who avowed their adherence to the conception of a moving earth remained a small minority.

But the size of the group of avowed Copernicans is not an adequate index of the success of Copernicus' innovation. Many astronomers found it possible to exploit Conernicus' mathematical system and to contribute to the success of the new astronomy while denying or remaining silent about the motion of the earth. Hellenistic [Greek] astronomy provided their precedent. Ptolemy himself had never pretended that all of the circles used in the *Almagest* to compute planetary position were physically real; they were useful mathematical devices and they did not have to be any more than that. Similarly, Renaissance astronomers were at liberty to treat the circle representing the earth's orbit as a mathematical fiction, useful for computations alone; they could and occasionally did compute planetary position *as if* the earth moved without committing themselves to the physical reality of that motion. Andreas Osiander, the Lutheran theologian who saw Copernicus' manuscript through the press, had actually urged this alternative upon readers in an anonymous preface attached to the *De Revolutionibus* without Copernicus' permission. The spurious preface probably did not fool many astronomers, but a number of them nevertheless took advantage of the alternative that it suggested. Using Copernicus' mathematical system without advocating the physical motion of the earth provided a convenient escape from the dilemma posed by the contrasting celestial harmonies and terrestrial discord of the *De Revolutionibus*. It also gradually tempered the astronomer's initial conviction that the earth's motion was absurd.

Erasmus Reinhold (1511–1553) was the first astronomer to do important service for the Copernicans without declaring himself in favor of the earth's motion. In 1551, only eight years after the publication of the *De Revolutionibus*, he issued a complete new set of astronomical tables, computed by the mathematical methods developed by Copernicus, and these soon became indispensable to astronomers and astrologers, whatever their beliefs about the position and motion of the earth. Reinhold's *Prutenic Tables*, named for his patron, the Duke of Prussia, were the first complete tables prepared in Europe for three centuries, and the old tables, which had included some errors from the start, were now badly out of date—the clock had run too long. Reinhold's supremely careful work, based on somewhat more and better data than had been available to the men who computed the thirteenth-century tables, produced a set of tables which, for most applications, were measurably superior to the old. They were not, of course, completely accurate; Copernicus' mathematical system was intrinsically no more accurate than Ptolemy's; errors of a day in the prediction of lunar eclipses were common, and the length of the year determined from the *Prutenic Tables* was actually slightly less accurate than that determined from the older tables. But most comparisons displayed the superiority of Reinhold's work, and his tables became increasingly an astronomical requisite. Since the tables were known to derive from the astronomical theory of the *De Revolutionibus*, Copernicus' prestige inevitably gained. Every man who used the *Prutenic Tables* was at least acquiescing in an implicit Copernicanism.

Gaining Ground?

During the second half of the sixteenth century astronomers could dispense with neither the *De Revolutionibus* nor the tables based upon it. Copernicus' proposal gained ground slowly but apparently inexorably. Successive generations of astronomers, decreasingly predisposed by experience and training to take the earth's stability for granted, found the new harmonies a more and more forceful argument for its motion. Besides, by the end of the century the first converts had begun to uncover new evidence. Therefore if the decision between the Copernican and the traditional universe had concerned only astronomers, Copernicus' proposal would almost certainly have achieved a quiet and gradual victory. But the decision was not exclusively, or even primarily, a matter for astronomers, and as the debate spread from astronomical circles it became tumultuous in the extreme. To most of those who were not concerned with the detailed study of celestial motions, Copernicus' innovation seemed absurd and impious. Even when understood, the vaunted harmonies seemed no evidence at all. The resulting clamor was widespread, vocal, and bitter.

But the clamor was slow in starting. Initially, few nonastronomers knew of Copernicus' innovation or recognized it as more than a passing individual aberration like many that had come and gone before. Most of the elementary astronomy texts and manuals used during the second half of the sixteenth century had been prepared long before Copernicus' lifetime—John of Holywood's thirteenth-century primer was still a leader

Copernicus

in elementary training—and the new handbooks prepared after the publication of the *De Revolutionibus* usually did not mention Copernicus or dismissed his innovation in a sentence or two. The popular cosmological books that described the universe to laymen remained even more exclusively Aristotelian in tone and substance; Copernicus was either unknown to their authors or, if known, he was usually ignored. Except, perhaps, in a few centers of Protestant learning, Copernicanism does not seem to have been a cosmological issue during the first few decades after Copernicus' death. Outside of astronomical circles it seldom became a major issue until the beginning of the seventeenth century.

There were a few sixteenth-century reactions from nonastronomers, and they provide a foretaste of the immense debate to follow, for they were usually unequivocally negative. Copernicus and his few followers were ridiculed for the absurdity of their concept of a moving earth, though without the bitterness or the elaborate dialectic which developed when it became apparent that Copernicanism was to be a stubborn and dangerous opponent. One long cosmological poem [by writer G. Du Bartas], first published in France in 1578 and immensely popular there and in England during the next century and a quarter, provides the following typical description of the Copernicans as

Those clerks who think (think how absurd a jest)
That neither heav'ns nor stars do turn at all,
Nor dance, about this great round earthly ball;
But th'earth itself, this massy globe of ours,
Turns round-about once every twice-twelve hours:
And we resemble land-bred novices
New brought aboard to venture on the seas;

Who, at first launching from the shore, suppose
The ship stands still, and that the ground it goes.

. . . Uncritical offhand condemnations of Copernicus and his followers were not restricted to conservative and unoriginal populariz-
ers. Jean Bodin, famous as one of the most advanced and creative political philosophers of the sixteenth century, discards Copernicus' innovation in almost identical terms:

> No one in his senses, or imbued with the slightest knowledge of physics,
> will ever think that the earth, heavy and unwieldy from its own weight
> and mass, staggers up and down around its own center and that of the
> sun; for at the slightest jar of the earth, we would see cities and
> fortresses, towns and mountains thrown down.

. . . Bodin was quite willing to break with tradition, but that was not
enough to make a man a Copernican. It was almost invariably also
necessary to understand astronomy and to take its problems immensely seriously. Except to those with an astronomical bias, the
earth's motion seemed very nearly as absurd in the years after Copernicus' death as it had before.

Biblical Objections

The anti-Copernican arguments suggested by Du Bartas and Bodin . . .
appear again and again during the first half of the seventeenth century
when the debate about the earth's motion became bitter and intense.
The earth's motion, it was said, violates the first dictate of common
sense; it conflicts with long-established laws of motion; it has been
suggested merely "to save better of the stars th'appearance," a ridicu-
lously minuscule incentive for revolution. These are forceful arguments, quite sufficient to convince most people. But they are not the
most forceful weapons in the anti-Copernican battery, and they are not
the ones that generated the most heat. Those weapons were religious
and, particularly, scriptural.

Citation of Scripture against Copernicus began even before the publication of the *De Revolutionibus*. In one of his "Table Talks," held in
1539, Martin Luther is quoted as saying:

> People gave ear to an upstart astrologer who strove to show that the earth
> revolves, not the heavens or the firmament, the sun and the moon. . . .
> This fool wishes to reverse the entire science of astronomy; but sacred
> Scripture tells us [Joshua 10:13] that Joshua commanded the sun to stand
> still, and not the earth.

Luther's principal lieutenant, Melanchthon, soon joined in the increasing Protestant clamor against Copernicus. Six years after Copernicus' death he wrote:

> The eyes are witnesses that the heavens revolve in the space of twenty-
> four hours. But certain men, either from the love of novelty, or to make

a display of ingenuity, have concluded that the earth moves; and they maintain that neither the eighth sphere nor the sun revolves.

Melanchthon then proceeded to assemble a number of anti-Copernican Biblical passages, emphasizing the famous verses, Ecclesiastes 1:4–5, which state "the earth abideth forever" and that "The sun also ariseth, and the sun goeth down, and hasteth to his place where he arose." Finally he suggests that severe measures be taken to restrain the impiety of the Copernicans.

Other Protestant leaders soon joined in the rejection of Copernicus. Calvin, in his *Commentary on Genesis*, cited the opening verse of the Ninety-third Psalm—"the earth also is stablished, that it cannot be moved"—and he demanded, "Who will venture to place the authority of Copernicus above that of the Holy Spirit?" Increasingly, Biblical citation became a favored source of anti-Copernican argument. By the first decades of the seventeenth century clergymen of many persuasions were to be found searching the Bible line by line for a new passage that would confound the adherents of the earth's motion. With growing frequency Copernicans were labeled "infidel" and "atheist," and when, after about 1610, the Catholic Church officially joined the battle against Copernicanism, the charge became formal heresy. In 1616 the *De Revolutionibus* and all other writings that affirmed the earth's motion were put upon the Index. Catholics were forbidden to teach or even to read Copernican doctrines, except in versions emended to omit all reference to the moving earth and central sun.

A Larger Issue

The preceding sketch displays the most popular and forceful weapons in the arsenal arrayed against Copernicus and his followers, but it scarcely indicates what the war was really about. Most of the men quoted above are so ready to reject the earth's motion as absurd or as conflicting with authority that they fail to show, and may not at first have realized fully, that Copernicanism was potentially destructive of an entire fabric of thought. Their very dogmatism disguises their motives. But it does not eliminate them. More than a picture of the universe and more than a few lines of Scripture were at stake. The drama of Christian life and the morality that had been made dependent upon it would not readily adapt to a universe in which the earth was just one of a number of planets. Cosmology, morality, and theology had long been interwoven in the traditional fabric of Christian thought described by Dante at the beginning of the fourteenth century. The vigor and venom displayed at the height of the Copernican controversy, three centuries later, testifies to the strength and vitality of the tradition.

When it was taken seriously, Copernicus' proposal raised many gigantic problems for the believing Christian. If, for example, the earth were merely one of six planets [known at the time], how were the stories of the Fall and of the Salvation, with their immense bearing on Christian life, to be preserved? If there were other bodies essentially like the earth, God's goodness would surely necessitate that they, too, be inhabited. But if there were men on other planets, how could they be descendants of Adam and Eve, and how could they have inherited the original sin, which explains man's otherwise incomprehensible travail on an earth made for him by a good and omnipotent deity? Again, how could men on other planets know of the Saviour who opened to them the possibility of eternal life? Or, if the earth is a planet and therefore a celestial body located away from the center of the universe, what becomes of man's intermediate but focal position between the devils and the angels? If the earth, as a planet, participates in the nature of celestial bodies, it cannot be a sink of iniquity from which man will long to escape to the divine purity of the heavens. Nor can the heavens be a suitable abode for God if they participate in the evils and imperfection so clearly visible on a planetary earth. Worst of all, if the universe is infinite, as many of the later Copernicans thought, where can God's Throne be located? In an infinite universe, how is man to find God or God man?

These questions have answers. But the answers were not easily achieved; they were not inconsequential; and they helped to alter the religious experience of the common man. Copernicanism required a transformation in man's view of his relation to God and of the bases of his morality. Such a transformation could not be worked out overnight, and it was scarcely even begun while the evidence for Copernicanism remained as indecisive as it had been in the *De Revolutionibus*. Until that transformation was achieved, sensitive observers might well find traditional values incompatible with the new cosmology, and the frequency with which the charge of atheism was hurled at the Copernicans is evidence of the threat to the established order posed to many observers by the concept of a planetary earth.

Shakespeare

Robert Payne

Probably no other literary figure has attained the stature of William Shakespeare. Poet, playwright, actor, and stage manager, Shakespeare is still considered the greatest writer in the English language even several centuries after his death. We know a great deal about his plays but we know surprisingly little about the man himself. In this excerpt, from the introduction of Robert Payne's biography *By Me, William Shakespeare,* Payne summarizes the research into Shakespeare's life. He begins with a description and analysis of Shakespeare's signature on the last page of his will.

On the last page of his will, written shortly before his death, Shakespeare wrote the clearest of all the signatures that have come down to us. In an astonishingly firm hand he wrote: "By me William Shakespeare," employing his pen vigorously until just before the end, when, writing the last syllable of his name, his strength begins to fail, the pen quivers, and the letters melt and fuse into one another. It was as though every ounce of his energy had been directed toward composing the words precisely and elegantly, and suddenly, when he had almost completed it, there was a failure of nervous energy, and he found himself incapable of doing it properly. One imagines an enormous willpower which collapsed in the midst of writing his name for the last time.

What is chiefly moving about the document is not the failure but the achievement. The letters are beautifully formed and possess great dignity. It is not the secretary hand favored by the officials and educated men of his time, but an older English script akin to modern German with a Gothic *B* and *S* and a decorative *W*, where a dot, which may be the dot over the first *i* of William, is enclosed within the final loop of the *W*. This *W* has a long descender and gives an effect of grace and a certain imperiousness. The *B* is as monumental as a Chinese ideogram and is well-balanced by the *y* with a sweeping tail. Everything about the handwriting suggests refinement and studied ease, as of a man who took care with his handwriting and enjoyed his skill in forming letters, until we come to the letter *k*, where there occurs the first sign of disintegration. Thereafter there is little more than a scratchy blur, although he is still attempting with a failing hand to form the remaining letters of his name.

There are some other things which should be noted in this signature. Quite evidently Shakespeare had intended to write the four words clearly and neatly. He maintained a steady rhythm throughout the writing of the first three words. The rhythm is broken when he comes to "Shakespeare," for the *S*, although grandly conceived in the Gothic manner, lacks the clear definition of the W: there is already a hint of the catastrophe to come. Usually when a man's handwriting weakens, it tends to droop, to go downhill. Shakespeare's handwriting moves upward as he still doggedly attempts to form the name which is the most important part of his signature.

One can make too much of handwriting, but these four words have a special significance. They are the only four words written by him in his most careful handwriting that have survived. There are five other authentic signatures, and all of them have been written quickly, carelessly, and impatiently; there are two in the will, one on a deposition, another on a conveyance, and still another on a mortgage. In addition, there are the pages of his handwriting in the uncompleted play *Sir Thomas More*, which he wrote in collaboration with at least four other playwrights, but these pages were written hurriedly, with no concern for penmanship, as the inspiration took hold of him. It is only on the last page of the will that we see him taking his own time to write legibly, knowing that his words will be examined by those who come after him.

Today the will lies in a glass case in the museum of the Public Record Office in Chancery Lane, London. It is crumpled with age and bears the marks of many folds and many stains. It is one of the most venerated documents in England, and people come to it to see if they can find, amid the tangle of a law clerk's handwriting streaming across the whole page, the famous bequest of the second-best bed [left to his wife]. In the dimly lit room, which looks as though it was once a dungeon, the words stand out, "By me William Shakespeare," dark and luminous, possessing a hallucinatory quality. Suddenly we feel that we are in his presence.

Gentleness and Ferocity

What do they tell us about Shakespeare? They tell us, I believe, of his sense of style, his fortitude, his imperiousness and authority. It is the handwriting of a man completely in charge of whatever he undertakes, who gives orders and expects them to be obeyed. In his own time he was known as "gentle Shakespeare," but there is nothing gentle in the handwriting. Gentle he may have been among his friends, but I suspect that his gentleness concealed an angelic ruthlessness. He was a man without diffidence who asserted himself whenever it suited him. I detect a certain fierceness and inner violence, a man capable of lashing out in fury as ghosts and enemies, vivid and alert even when he was dying. He possessed the Tudor ferocity, which tends to have been forgotten by scholars, and he would have looked at a hanging, disemboweling, and quartering at Tyburn without flinching.

William Shakespeare

He towers over English literature, so mountainous and craggy that we are all in awe of him, as he may have been in awe of his own gifts. In New York's Central Park his statue fittingly confronts the statue of Columbus: they were both discoverers of new worlds. We are still exploring those worlds and he is therefore our contemporary. Since he is the friendliest of guides, there are some advantages in knowing the living man.

Shakespeare reveals himself continually. . . . While every character in every play is a disguise worn by him, the disguise is palpably transparent. The plays are the records of his spiritual adventures written in a manner wonderfully suited to display the spirit's trajectories, the landscapes of his dreams, abysses and avalanches and lonely journeys into unknown territories. He is surefooted and always knows when to step back at the cliff's edge.

We know the outward man almost as well as we know any man of the Elizabethan age. . . . The auburn hair, the hazel eyes, the heavy lids, the flush of excitement on the cheeks, the moustache trimmed cunningly, the huge domed forehead bald as an apple—we know him well and would recognize him if he entered the room. He has the soaring forehead of a man who thinks too much for his own comfort, but the sensual nose and chin show that he had many remedies against the oppressive weight of thought. We have only to look at the Droeshout portrait [a famous surviving picture of Shakespeare] to know that he has fine manners and is fastidious to a fault. He is a natural aristocrat fully aware of his responsibilities. He met kings and queens, and was at ease with them, and he was on terms of intimacy with many members of the nobility and felt equal to them. Knowing that he was himself descended from ancient Saxon kings, he felt no need to humble himself before anyone.

Character

We know a good deal about his daily habits, his likes and dislikes, his hatreds, his loves, and his fears. We know, for example, that he talked quickly with a Warwickshire accent which he retained throughout his life, that he suffered from insomnia, that in his later years he suffered from sciatica [back pain]. We know that he detested the dogs that often crowded round an Elizabethan table. He had never been a soldier; he knew no more about seafaring than a man might learn by sailing in a ship down the Thames to Gravesend. He knew brawls, and his excitement is present whenever he describes them. He liked bowling, which is a suitable pastime for a meditative man who enjoys having company around him, and detested fishing, which is a solitary occupation. He was happily married to Anne Hathaway, who bore his children; we can be certain that if the marriage had been unhappy some gossipmonger would have recorded that she was a shrew. He adored his two daughters; and his grief over the death of his only son haunted him through all the remaining years of his life. He was obsessively afraid of death by drowning, and some of his greatest poetry is an attempt to exorcise his fear. He attended church regularly, but in his works there is scarcely a trace anywhere of Christian sentiment. He believed in the fall of the sparrow. He believed even more strongly in the need to explore the boundaries of the human spirit, and to do this single-handedly, nakedly, at whatever cost to his reason and his spiritual health. He would have agreed with Dostoyevsky, who wrote: "Man is a mystery. This mystery must be solved, and even if you pass your entire life solving it, do not say you have wasted your time. I occupy myself with this mystery, because I want to be a man."

He was not well read, and it is likely that there were very few books in his library. . . .

Above all he was a producer, stage manager, and actor. To a quite extraordinary degree he possessed a sense of the stage. He knew stage space, entrances and exits, the way to achieve dramatic focus, confrontation following swiftly on confrontation in order to maintain theatrical excitement. There are few stage directions; the poetry includes them. The stage, for him, was like a lake, mirroring whatever colors the playwright poured into it, changing its shape according to his fancy, so fluid that he should shape it at will and so solid that it took on the appearance of woodlands, rocks, palaces, and battlements.

Everything in the plays suggests that he was a player who enjoyed acting and was at ease on the boards. We think of him as a poet and dramatist first and an actor second, but it is much more likely that he spent more time acting than he ever spent writing at his desk. He acted often and played many roles, not only the Ghost in *Hamlet*.

The miracle is that he could be all the things he was—poet, playwright, actor, stage manager, producer, landowner, buyer of houses, occasional moneylender, friend of noblemen, family man, and all these simultaneously, and for so short a time. He died at fifty-two, with a quarter of a century of work still in front of him. *The Tempest* [often considered his last work] was not his farewell to the stage, for he wrote at least two plays subsequently.

I have written this book because I wanted to know what manner of man he was. It was necessary to stretch him, to shake him out, to break him up and then put the pieces together again in order to see him afresh. I found him more violent and more authoritarian than I had expected, and closer to intrigues and conspiracies than I had thought possible. . . .

Ben Jonson spoke of his "rage and influence," and those three words haunted me through the writing of the book. Violent, imperious, wonderfully learned in the ways of the world and determined to penetrate the heavenly mysteries, he comes to us like a blaze of pure intellectual energy and human sympathy, and we can still warm ourselves beside his fire.

The Renaissance

PREFACE

The word *Renaissance* literally means "rebirth," and the flowering of arts and sciences that took root in Italy shortly before the sixteenth century was in some ways just that. The works produced by the great sculptors and painters of the time were indeed reminiscent of the works of classical Greece and Rome. More to the point, the emphasis the Renaissance placed on learning and culture as part of a well-rounded life also hearkened back many centuries to the days of the ancients. The Renaissance was a time when kings and princes collected Greek artifacts, when scholars studied Roman architecture and even dug up a few of the ruins, and when artists drew inspiration from the mythology and the literature of the ancient world.

But the term *Renaissance* is somewhat misleading, for it can suggest that Europeans of the period did nothing more than slavishly recreate the old ways. The Renaissance, in truth, was much more than simply a rebirth of ancient ways and ideas. Although artists of the time undeniably looked to Rome and Greece for models, the period produced new and exciting ways of viewing the world and gave rise to styles undreamed-of in earlier centuries. The great names of Renaissance art created works that are distinctive in time and place. No one would mistake Leonardo da Vinci's *Mona Lisa* or Michelangelo's statue of David for works by artists from ancient Rome or Greece.

The great men of the Renaissance also developed an artistic ethos that was entirely new. No longer was art considered a subject off on its own, isolated from the rest of the world. The great painters and sculptors of the Renaissance were keenly aware of recent events in science, literature, and other realms of knowledge. The latest scientific discoveries were incorporated into their artwork. Perhaps more importantly, the ideas behind these discoveries inspired these artists and affected their view of themselves and their work. Each in their own way, they saw themselves not just as artists but also as researchers, scientists, experimenters, and advocates for lives that would be filled with art; as the phrase has it, they were true "Renaissance men," at home in a variety of styles, subjects, and fields.

Placing the Renaissance in time is somewhat complicated. The period spanned parts of two centuries. By the 1500s the Renaissance was well under way in Italy and in parts of northern Europe; however, it was by no means over. The sixteenth century saw the great-

est period of artistic development in the northern part of the continent, and much of the greatest production in Italy occurred during
the early years of the sixteenth century, too. Indeed, the late fifteenth
century is often referred to as the Early Renaissance, leaving the title of High Renaissance to the sixteenth. Whatever the title, Renaissance ideas and art greatly influenced the course of the sixteenth
century.

Michelangelo

Charles Avery

The Italian Renaissance was a golden age of sculpture. The flowering of artistic expression during the time led to the creation of many well-known and well-loved statues and other works. Among the greatest of the sculptors was Michelangelo Buonarroti. Though perhaps best remembered today for his painting of the ceiling of the Sistine Chapel in Rome, Michelangelo saw himself first and foremost as a sculptor. This excerpt, from Charles Avery's *Florentine Renaissance Sculpture*, discusses some of Michelangelo's work in the early part of the sixteenth century. While Avery's analysis deals most specifically with Michelangelo, the insights expressed also apply to other Renaissance sculptors and their work. Avery is an art historian with a particular interest in the sculpture of the Italian Renaissance and the Baroque period.

Editor's Note: Avery takes up the narrative with Michelangelo's return to Florence from a first trip to Rome, where he had been asked to carve a series of statues for a cathedral altar. The work involved many specifications and restrictions, and Michelangelo chafed at the loss of creative control. This would be a running theme in Michelangelo's career. In 1503, for instance, as Avery explains, Michelangelo left Rome angry after having been assigned to construct a monumental tomb. Taking time away from what he felt was an impossible assignment, he returned to Florence and resumed work instead on a statue of St. Matthew for the local cathedral.

Returning to Florence in 1501, [Michelangelo] was soon [given an] attractive proposition, a colossal statue of David, as a symbol of the Republican government. The carving took three years and the

Excerpted from *Florentine Renaissance Sculpture* (New York: Harper & Row, 1970) by Charles Avery. Reprinted with permission from John Murray, agent for the author.

statue that resulted established Michelangelo's reputation not only in Florence but all over Italy and even further afield. To this day it has remained his most celebrated work. Unlike the earlier statues of David by [Italian sculptors] Donatello and Verrocchio, Michelangelo's marble giant was so conceived that it conveyed an eternal image of spiritual courage and physical energy without the need for a symbolic weapon such as the sword, and even the sling is nearly obscured from the front. A comparison with his earlier figure of St Proclus [carved in 1494] shows how rapidly he had perfected his means of expression: the nude body, its pose and gestures, and facial expression. The fierce glare of David has infinitely greater nobility than the caricatured anger of St Proclus, copied from Verrocchio's Colleoni; his hands have become far larger in proportion and correspondingly more expressive; and his measured stance is more secure than the uncertain half step of the saint. Though tense and alert, the David was conceived as momentarily standing still, and not as a moving figure like the earlier Bacchus [another statue]. This solution was forced on Michelangelo both by the comparative shallowness of the actual block of marble and by the vain efforts of several earlier sculptors who had made false starts on carving. The lack of depth demanded a frontal figure without much projection into space. Fortunately, his method of carving was ideally suited to overcoming the difficulties inherent in the shape of the block.

When faced with carving a statue in the round, Michelangelo would begin by cutting into the face of the block, gradually removing layer after layer of marble round the edge of his figure, as though it were simply a relief. He does not seem to have cut into the block from all sides, which was the normal method. This meant that he had scope for continual alterations and revisions of the contours, and even the positions, of all the parts of his projected figure that lay further back within the remainder of the untouched block. The forms nearest the surface would be worked up to the stage of claw-chiselling, while those lying behind were as yet only roughly blocked out. By this continuous process of blocking out the broad masses of marble and then refining the most prominent details, the creation of the figure was constantly in flux and needed the complete attention of the artist at every stage. . . .

As the figure was revealed from the front by cutting back into the depth of the block, so side views would automatically begin to emerge. Only at this stage would Michelangelo begin to work up the statue from these angles too. . . . The existence of so many statues that were left by sheer coincidence at different stages of completion enables us to plot every point in the process of creating an individual work; while sculptures that were finished, or nearly so, permit us to guess the intended appearance of those which were abandoned. The unfinished statues are always more colossal than the finished ones, as several extraneous layers of marble remain to be cut away to reveal the final forms. These layers of course alter the proportions of the figure, particularly of the limbs, where an additional thickness of marble appears greater than on the torso. . . .

In 1505 he [Michelangelo] was summoned peremptorily to Rome by Pope Julius II, who ordered him to design a monumental tomb which was to be housed in St Peter's. This project, calling initially for over forty statues of life size or above, was impossibly ambitious and caused the artist much distress throughout his career, owing to the importunity [excessive persistence] of his patrons. Things began badly when he found himself short of

Michelangelo's statue of Moses

funds within a few months of starting work, owing to the Pope's decision to channel most of the available resources into Bramante's reconstruction of St Peter's itself. After futile protests, Michelangelo fled back to Florence in April 1506, out of sheer frustration, and began furiously to carve the St Matthew.

We are surely justified in reading into the fiercely angular and distorted shapes of the Apostle some of the deep disappointment and violent resentment that the sculptor felt. The composition with its bold muscular torsions reflects the impression made on him by the Hellenistic [Greek] marble group of Laocoön [a figure in Greek mythology], which had just been excavated in Rome, but Michelangelo made it the vehicle of his own strong emotions. His sculptures were such urgent and personal creations that his own states of mind were inevitably imparted to them, particularly in times of stress, even when they were not logically applicable to the particular subject he was treating. This aspect of his statues, even when unfinished, as extensions of his personality and tangible manifestations of his emotions gives them the profound appeal that they have exerted on all who have seen them, from the sixteenth century until the present day.

Michelangelo's main opportunity to explore the expressive possibilities of movement came not in sculpture, however, but in the more immediate and flexible medium of fresco painting. For between 1508 and 1512 he was totally occupied with the ceiling of the Sistine

Chapel, imposed on him as a form of discipline by the Pope. Although be resented this distraction from his favourite art, Michelangelo was able to explore more freely in paint than would have been possible in marble the expressive effects that he could convey through ideal human bodies in movement. The experience provided a catalyst for the release of his full powers in his chosen medium.

The Pope's Tomb

It was not until after the completion of the ceiling and the subsequent death of the Pope (1513) that Michelangelo was free to start carving some of the many figures required for Julius' Tomb. A revised contract was signed with Julius' heirs in May 1513, which stated that the tomb was to have one end abutting a wall. It was therefore no longer completely free-standing as in the initial project and the total number of sculptures was reduced. At this stage Michelangelo carved the three most finished figures: the Moses, unhappily ensconced in the monument as it was ultimately erected, and the two Slaves, now in the Louvre. All three demonstrate his new-found range of expression. The Dying Slave has a spiral movement, reminiscent of the Bacchus, but infinitely more refined. His supremely graceful, languid posture and sensuous expression suggest an entirely different mood. Our impression is that the mind of this ideal being must be suspended on the borders of consciousness either because of some deep emotional suffering or through the effort to awake from a deep slumber. These contradictory interpretations have both found support among Michelangelo's early biographers and later critics.

An unfinished ape behind the Slave seems to justify an interpretation of these ideal nudes as allegories [representations] of the visual arts (the ape symbolizing the imitative aspect of art), but whether they are meant to be dying, with the Pope, or to be freeing themselves from symbolic bonds in token of his enlightened patronage while alive seems to be an open question. . . . The various levels of meaning possibly reflect the development of Michelangelo's own thinking during the lengthy process of executing the monument.

The other Slave (called Rebellious from his pose) and the Moses are less relief-like than the Dying Slave, because they were designed as corner figures and had to offer two satisfactory views, from the front and from the side. In the Rebellious Slave, this is achieved by a violent *contrapposto*, giving him a spiral movement, while in the Moses, the seated position is opened out to the side by the withdrawal of one leg and the turn of the head. His present setting in the central niche at ground level in the wall-monument at San Pietro in Vincoli fails to take account of this directional bias and drastically reduces the effectiveness of a figure originally designed as one of the climaxes of a mass of intimately related sculpture.

Work on the tomb was next interrupted by a project for a permanent façade for San Lorenzo, instigated by the Medici Pope Leo X, as a result of his ceremonial entry into Florence in 1515. The question of cooperating with Jacopo Sansovino arose, but Michelangelo refused to work with a man whom he felt belonged to the camp of his great rivals, Raphael and Bramante. The project was terminated in 1519 after some four years' work, owing to the Pope's decision to give precedence to a funereal chapel annexed to the transept of San Lorenzo to commemorate four members of his family, two of whom had died not long before. During this busy period, Michelangelo seems to have carved the four unfinished Slaves, all still in Florence, for a third, still further reduced version of the Julius tomb. They are appreciably larger than the earlier pair, for which two appear to be replacements. All four now give the impression of supporting something above their heads, and the sculptor may have intended them for the role of caryatids, to be integrated into the architecture of the tomb. This alteration in their function is typical of his creative process and is reflected in carefully revised compositions. Their movements are given a common motivation which lends a greater unity to the series.

Renaissance Painting

Hermann Voss

In the following excerpt, art historian Hermann Voss describes some of the characteristics of Renaissance painting. His focus is on Italy and specifically on two great Italian cities, Florence and Rome, where the arts flourished spectacularly. As Voss explains, the term "painting" to sixteenth-century artists did not necessarily imply easels and canvases.

"The finest and noblest task for a painter of the first rank is the decoration of a stately and well-proportioned church"—with these words [sixteenth-century commentator on art Giovanni Battista] Armenini expresses the overwhelming conviction of his contemporaries, at least those in Rome and Florence. In what manner was this great task solved in the sixteenth century? The building as a whole, with its numerous larger and smaller components, was seen as a body with many parts—all its different organs were brought to life by painterly means in the most varied manner, according to their specific character or function. The subjects to be painted were from the Old and New Testaments, whose most important events were to be executed in such a powerful style that worshippers would to some extent be "overwhelmed and moved" by them.

The choir and the dome are the most difficult parts of a church interior for the painter; they have a large number of irregularly shaped, in some cases spherical architectural spaces, whose decoration requires the painter to possess a complete mastery of the laws of perspective. Armenini recognized two types of solution, which we may call the Roman and the northern Italian methods. Though he describes these somewhat unclearly, we may interpret his explanations roughly as follows. The architectural element was foremost in the Roman style. Following the various architectural elements, it divided the vaulting of the choir, the dome, etc. into fields with relatively closed geometrical limits, which are defined by sculptural stucco work borders with fruit garlands, genii, etc. The northern Italians, on the other hand, favored painting the largest possible surfaces in an illusionistic manner, so that the walls and ceiling appeared to be broken through and the architecture was dissolved by painterly means. The principal examples of this are [Antonio] Correggio's dome frescoes in the Cathedral and in S. [San, or Saint] Giovanni Evangelista [church] in Parma. Armenini includes only one important example from central Italy: the painting by [Giorgio] Vasari and Zuccari of the dome of Florence Cathedral, although this possesses very little illusionistic force—its overall design is very much a geometrical one. Only in the early Baroque period [following the Renaissance] did the style created north of the Apennines [that is, north of peninsular Italy] triumph in central Italy too. Here again it was the Carracci [an Italian family of artists] who played the pivotal role, by making numerous copies after Correggio's frescoes in Parma. It was furthermore a Parma artist, Giovanni Lanfranco, who as a pupil of the Carracci brought illusionistic dome painting to Rome and developed it to its peak.

The late Renaissance in Rome and Florence also took the given architectural structure as its criterion with regard to the painting of nave ceilings. Because these structures differed greatly—from barrel vaulting to Gothic cross vaulting to simple raftered ceilings—they offered a wide range of possibilities to the painter. The most important example in Rome was universally conceded to be Michelangelo's ceiling for the Sistine Chapel, where the illusionistic effect was restrained by the rigor with which the architectural structure was simulated. However, almost no painted church ceilings on a grand scale from the immediately succeeding period have come down to us intact. Emphatically illusionistic attempts can be cited towards the end of the century in the works of the brothers Alberti who in S. Silvestro al Quirinale and elsewhere already anticipated in part the style of later ceiling frescoes. The defining of architectural subdivisions by means of stucco (mostly monochrome, with sparing use of gold) prevailed in Rome. Florence, where raftered ceilings were the general rule (mostly without any painted decoration) offers little of note.

On the other hand, the Cinquecento [sixteenth century] offers an extraordinarily rich panorama in terms of the pictorial decoration of chapels. In Rome this practice enjoyed particular popularity. Beginning with the Chigi Chapel in S. Maria del Popolo and continuing on to the two enormous chapels of Sixtus V and Paul V in S. Maria Maggiore, there are a considerable number of self-contained, centrally planned chapels with prominent domes. Florence also possesses an important example of this type, the Cappella Salviati in S. Marco, In addition, there are the usual chapels surrounding the nave and choir of churches; their number is of course legion. . . . Again, architectural structure is the criterion, by means of stucco framing, occasionally replaced by illusionistic painted frames. Armenini mentions one such painted effort by Daniele da Volterra, noting that in relatively small chapels the problem of sculptured, projecting frames overlapping the frescoes was avoided by the use of this technique.

The altarpiece, perhaps the painter's most important task in a church interior, remains to be discussed. Its transformation and elevation to the level of an architectural element in the sixteenth century was also Raphael's achievement, one of the most significant contributions of his rich career. It naturally follows from such an architectural conception that a painting intended for an altar, whether as a free-standing tabernacle serving to decorate the high altar, or conceived as the centerpiece of a chapel, should itself be given an architectural function. Accordingly it would have to be painted with keen awareness of its assigned location. Armenini was not alone in emphasizing the necessity of such a concern; so too did the Milanese painter and theoretician [Giovanni Paolo] Lomazzo who spent an extended period in Rome and Florence soon after the mid-century point. He expressly included among the decisive compositional factors of a painting its *collocazione*, in other words its formal and contextual adaptation to its setting. What is meant above all by this is explained in Armenini's brief remarks concerning the frequently inadequate light conditions in churches, which often worked very much to the detriment of paintings that are good in themselves, but not suited to their location. The height at which the altarpiece is mounted must also be precisely taken into account; it is of crucial importance in determining the size of the figures in a painting as well as the perspectival construction of the entire work.

Houses, Easels, and Portraits

It might appear that in contrast to the restrictions involved in church painting, the decoration of palaces and private houses would permit the artist the widest latitude for his imagination. Freedom in this area was indeed considerably greater, but the artist nevertheless had to pay close attention to his patrons. Whether they were great lords and princes, or high churchmen, civil officials or authorities, or simply private persons, scholars or merchants—their individual character, social rank and habits had to be taken into consideration, and no less so of course the kind of building and the particular rooms that were to be decorated. A grand palace on one of the principal streets of the city (for example the Via Giulia in sixteenth century Rome) required a different treatment from a more modest private house or a villa outside the city gates; a formal reception room or salon naturally required a more elevated style than lesser chambers, studies, *loggie* [open galleries with roofs], and the like.

The most significant task was the painting of entire extensive apartments in which the individual rooms, gradated according to their size and function, had to be unified by means of an overall "program." The series of stanze in the Vatican are of this type and, in an even more comprehensive sense, so is the arrangement and artistic adornment of the Palazzo Vecchio by Vasari, or again the vast suite of chambers in the Palace of Caprarola. The highlight of such grand designs was always the salon which dominated the entire suite; its decoration at times extended to effects of great splendor (the principal example is the Salone dei Cinquecento in the Palazzo Vecchio). Here the grand style of glorifying history painting was the rule, while simpler themes were deemed adequate for the adjoining rooms. Frieze paintings depicting either decorative figures or smaller narratives (*"historiette"*) were particularly popular in Rome. The Tuscans, on the other hand, generally preferred a flat timbered ceiling with pictures of various shapes (square, oblong, octagonal, etc.) set into them. Their framing elements were frequently decorated with painted *grotteschi* [caricatures and other designs verging on the absurd].

The *loggie* comprise a separate category, as does the *galleria* [roofed walkway], whose origins are not entirely understood. Here the painted decoration of the pilasters and ceilings tends to dominate in an ornamental, playful manner. The principal elements here were *grotteschi*— it was Raphael, again, who in the Vatican *loggie* provided the first important and most often imitated examples of their use. In the vaulting, purely ornamental motifs alternate with *historiette*, a scheme that is still fairly strictly adhered to in Raphael's work, but which was later often treated with greater freedom and individual discretion (for example in the great Galleria Geographica in the Vatican). . . .

In surveying the rich variety of functions assigned to Roman and Florentine painting in the Cinquecento, one understands why the concept of a picture in the absolute sense, as a free creation of the imagination, was of necessity alien to the period. Many of the criticisms addressed to the works of this period are thus without foundation, because they pass judgment on the specific pictorial representation without considering the framework which enclosed it and in part determined its style. In order to attain a real understanding and artistic sympathy with the art of this period, however, it is necessary to view each work as belonging to an architecturally determined type. . . .

Easel painting as such in sixteenth century Rome and Florence, whether a small image of the Madonna or a saint, a Biblical or mythological scene, an allegorical figure or a portrait, is hardly to be seen as something autonomous, but rather as an echo of the more monumental genres. Such a relationship of dependence exists even with respect to the composition of portraits. The life-like depiction of an individual figure was evidently held in little regard in Rome at that time. Types rather than individuals were considered so much more meaningful that little pleasure could be found in the accurate reproduction of an individual, including all his specific peculiarities and flaws. It is indicative of the low esteem in which portraiture was then held that in Armenini's view far greater knowledge, skill, and intelligence would be required to paint one or more naked figures in such a manner that they seemed to appear palpably before the viewer with all their musculature and potentiality for movement, in color and chiaroscuro [arrangement of light and dark] than to acquire the few items of knowledge required in order to paint a portrait. One could even go so far as to assert that the more an artist understood about drawing, the less capable he was of painting portraits. The great masters, to be sure, surpassed all others in this specialty, too, insofar as artistic finish and style are concerned, but they were in fact in most cases inferior to lesser painters in achieving exact likenesses.

Today one can of course only speculate about the degree of actual likeness in Cinquecento portraits. In general, one has the impression that the achievement of typical form was of even greater concern in Rome than in Florence, where a more personalized depiction of the individual was appreciated at least to a certain extent. It is true that even in the portraits of [Angelo] Bronzino the architectural structuring and stylizing element is very clearly visible alongside the individual element. He quite intentionally assigned such a significant role in his pictures to the architecture of the background, and no less consciously gave them that sculpturally polished quality which distinguishes them so sharply from all north Italian portraiture. Even in their general appearance these portraits in no way conflict with the monumental surroundings which they were intended to decorate so outstandingly; occasionally the person depicted is even elevated to an almost superhuman grandeur or rigidity. Not to be forgotten in this connection, finally, is the particular sort of monumentality given to Roman and Florentine portraits by their massive ornamental frames. In the Cinquecento, in particular, the frame is an important architectural element which is definitely part of the work's total effect. By means of the frame the picture was connected to its environment, whose elevated character necessitated an analogous elevation of the picture's subject matter.

Art and Thought in Renaissance Italy

Nothing characterizes more clearly the late Renaissance way of thinking in its final phases than the powerful influence it exerted on the supposedly free categories of painting. It is hardly excessive to claim that the concept of a painting as the completely uninhibited expression of an individual artistic vision had not yet been discovered. There were panel and easel paintings of course, and these were in fact used to a certain extent as a means of more freely expressing personal experience and emotion; here too, however, the parameters of the artist's vision were still limited by a set of fixed categories.

There is a conception of artistic production—something which tends to be instinctively rooted in the modern consciousness—that wants to perceive in an artist's individual creation the precipitation of a unique artistic experience, unaffected by any external considerations. Such a strongly subjective viewpoint can achieve very little understanding of the art of the Italian Cinquecento, especially that of Rome and Florence. It has rather more application to northern European painting of the period. A picture by [German artists] Hans Baldung, [Lucas] Cranach, or [Albrecht] Altdorfer has indeed an incomparably greater element of personal experience; it expresses, in a way we feel a kinship with today, an autonomous individuality as opposed to the collective consciousness which governs Italian art of this and subsequent periods. This is all the more true of those most intensely personal creations of inner vision with which we are familiar from [Albrecht] Dürer's engravings and woodcuts. The graphic arts in any case tend to escape every form of external influence, every consideration of conventional realities. When it is independent of its surroundings, the individual work of art becomes the outpouring of a highly personal inner struggle with the world. Artistic expression is transformed into human confession; in works such as Dürer's *Melancolia* it seeks to make itself heard directly, beyond any time-specific limits.

Nothing could be further removed from this subjective creative process than the Italian way of thinking about art in the sixteenth century. Even the most personal creations of Michelangelo do not sever the bonds of that idealizing communal feeling which bound the pictorial arts of Italy so tightly to one another. It is true that the personal element asserts itself more strongly in the case of a genius than with his more ordinary contemporaries, but as an artist Michelangelo, too, strove toward the typical and the rule—governed. His forceful inner vision was accompanied by a creative power of unparalleled intensity, capable of integrating the most intense human experience within a very wide-ranging and rational system of laws.

It is a paradox of historical development that the same characteristic which constituted the strength of the Italian Renaissance—namely, the fact that all the branches of its artistic activity were equally saturated with the same spirit—also contained the seeds of its disintegration. The close connection of architecture and decoration with painting certainly had a fruitful effect in some respects, but nevertheless limited its opportunities for autonomous development. This was true not only for the purely stylistic aspects of the craft of painting but even more so for its intellectual orientation. Given that the architectonic sensibility of the Cinquecento strove for the elevation of human conduct toward absolute perfection, and thereby of necessity led to a general levelling and devaluation of the individual, then painting necessarily concerned itself only with the human ideal. The entire rich course of human development from childhood to old age was certainly reflected, but only within a scheme which assigned every nuance its specific, universally valid content. Each element, as Armenini formulated it, must in its type be of the greatest beauty and perfection. So while the painter's task may vary greatly according to the individual case, the final goal, the formation of the ideal type, always remains the same.

The aestheticians of the sixteenth century wrote in great detail about how to achieve this final and highest goal, and the works of the artists of the period confirm the guiding principles of these theoretical discussions. For example, it was expected that the elderly should be depicted with an expression of *gravità* [seriousness], youths should be fiery and alert in bearing and physiognomy, children full of natural charm and lively movement, and so on. Similarly, soldiers must look brave and daring, women graceful, while in young maidens the ideal of radiant beauty must be combined with a modest and chaste demeanor. The depiction of emotional states and bodily movements were couched in similar typifying formulas. A fairly comprehensive scale of human emotions was available; indeed, there was a preference for the dramatic and spiritually rousing, but here too, typical elements predominated, that is to say those passions and movements which served to raise the individual to an elevated level.

It is clear that a style of painting so one-sidedly oriented to the ideal, however magnificent and almost unnaturally perfect its results sometimes were, must gradually poison free artistic creativity at its source, namely an open receptiveness to nature. Stylistically as well as intellectually under the spell of this monumental grandeur, which was expressed so powerfully in the architecture of the period, painting lost more and more of its directness and human warmth; in form it deteriorated into a superficial decorative conventionality and virtuosity. Under such circumstances a renewal of vitality could only come from northern Italy, where painting had maintained its independence and closeness to nature to a much greater extent. The valuable heritage of central Italy, the internal and external unity of the arts, could not be allowed to be lost, however. While [Michelangelo de] Caravaggio, with north Italian single-mindedness, concentrated exclusively on the purely sensual, optical fundamentals of artistic vision, the Bolognese painters [in and around Bologna in northern Italy] sought to reconcile the new conception of painting with the Roman monumental tradition. In this way they placed collaboration between the arts on an infinitely broader footing than the sixteenth century had been able to achieve. A rejuvenation and broadening of outlook similar to that in painting was also the aspiration of the architects, sculptors, and decorative artists of the period; indeed the entire intellectual and artistic tendency at the end of the century was pushing in this direction. It was from the unification of all these forces that the successor to the exhausted Renaissance ideal arose, the last great expression of the Italian artistic sensibility: the Baroque style.

Science, Art, and the Renaissance

Otto Benesch

The word renaissance literally translates as "rebirth." The period of the Renaissance is best known in the popular mind today for its great art, but in fact the time was a reawakening of interest in science and other disciplines as well. The Renaissance led to great discoveries in biology, astronomy, and physics and was also a time when scientists began pursuing questions that had been ignored for many centuries.

Many commentators consider the scientific progress of the Renaissance separately from the artistic works of the time. This excerpt, by art historian Otto Benesch, considers scientific and artistic achievement together. Indeed, Benesch sees the two disciplines as connected. Without the scientific advances, he argues, much of the great art of the period could not have been produced. The art, music, and architecture, in his view, reflects the science and the scientific worldview that was beginning to flower during the sixteenth century.

Although Copernicus removed the earth from its central position and built the cosmos around the sun as centre, he did not change the ruling idea of the cosmic space itself. This idea regarded cosmic space as a series of seven concentric spheres of solid crystal-clear substance. Each sphere contains one of the great planets firmly anchored in its perfect round. The outermost spheric husk is studded with the multitude of the fixed stars. According to this notion, the universe is something perfectly spheric in shape, yet limited. We find this notion of the limited universe visualized in a drawing of the *Last Judgement*

Excerpted from *The Art of the Renaissance in Northern Europe* (London: Phaidon Press) by Otto Benesch. Copyright © 1965 by Phaidon Press.

done in 1555 by the Westphalian painter Hermann tom Ring. It is a dramatic work, filled with Michelangelesque nudes in wild motion, representing the struggle between the resurrected and the demons. The universe is shown as the interior of a tremendous solid dome. Its vault is cut by a circular opening; the lid sinks down and hangs freely in the air carrying Mary, St. John, and the angels who announce the Last Day. Christ floats on the globe as a separate little sphere. Above Him hovers a ring with angels who hold the instruments of the Passion, rotating around the dove of the Holy Ghost. Beyond the inner circle with the figures of the apostles extends an amphitheatre of blessed souls. This building of concrete supplants [replaces] the usual ranges of clouds. It is supplemented by a spiral staircase on which the blessed souls mount to heaven.

This drawing is an instructive example of the way in which art and science in history are linked with each other. *The creative mind at a given historical moment thinks in certain forms which are the same in arts and sciences.*

We meet this notion of the universe as a concrete cosmic building in an earlier painting by Hieronymus Bosch representing the *Assumption of the Blessed Souls to Paradise*. In it a long dark tunnel breaks through the husk of the cosmic sphere and opens into a magic realm of light beyond.

Thinking in terms of mathematically defined space increased in arts and sciences in the second half of the sixteenth century. After the medieval complexity, the Copernican system had brought . . . a great simplification which answered the aesthetic striving of High Renaissance art for balance and harmony. On the other hand, it rooted up the geocentric anchor hold of man and threw him out into the space of the universe. The ground yielded, and man hovered in bottomless space. We can well understand that a firmly established Church, whether Catholic or Protestant, would violently oppose the new theory as something threatening all divine stability. This feeling is conveyed by a composition of Jacopo Tintoretto, painted in 1548, five years after the publication of Copernicus' book, which represents the miraculous rescue of a Christian slave by St. Mark. The main figure falls upside down into the picture space like a messenger from another celestial body with opposite gravity. Everything seems to totter. The figures are poised in contrasting diagonals and no longer have the firm hold on the earthly ground which they had in the High Renaissance compositions.

To shape *space* is one of the foremost artistic problems. From static space it becomes increasingly curved, dynamic, potential space. We can follow this development in [Flemish painter Pieter] Bruegel's dealing with the subject of the *Tower of Babel*. In 1563 he painted the picture now in the Museum of Vienna. The tower grows out of natural rock, and is already reaching into the clouds, throwing a gigantic shadow over land and sea. One storey is superimposed upon the other in solid balance. Where the building is incomplete, its inner structure becomes visible, seemingly inspired by the Colosseum, which the painter had seen in Rome. The tower which we observe from a hill seems to incline to fall out of space towards us. This inclination increases the feeling of space as much as it impairs the stability. In a later version, Bruegel diminished the stability still more. Without any foothold, we hover over the scenery. This tower is taller and more slender in proportions, and screws itself up into the clouds in a dynamic spiral. We saw a similar spiral form in Hermann tom Ring's *Last Judgement.* This later version found so many repetitions in Manneristic paintings of the late sixteenth century that it must have appealed more to the ruling taste than the earlier one. It proves that the High Renaissance stability was replaced in the second half of the century by more complicated kinetics [motions]. We shall see something similar in science. . . .

None of the professional scientists conceived so daring and prophetic an idea of the universe as did the greatest philosopher of science in the second half of the century, Giordano Bruno. Bruno was a fervent advocate of the Copernican system, but he eliminated the idea of the universe as a limited sphere and established it as the unlimited space filled with countless celestial bodies, with fiery suns and cold watery moons which receive their light from the suns, with fixed stars and planets whose movements we cannot observe because of their remoteness. He developed this idea with artistic intuition mainly in the *Dialogues on the Infinite, Universe and Worlds* and in the satirical dialogue the *Ash-Wednesday Feast.* We read in the latter the following sentences: 'We comprehend that there is only *one* sky, *one* infinite ether in which those resplendent lumina [that is, stars and planets] keep their lawful distances in order to participate in the eternal life. Those flaming celestial bodies are the ambassadors who glorify the sublimity and majesty of God.'

Three years after these words were written, the aged [Italian artist known as Il] Tintoretto began to paint the *Paradise* in the Sala del Gran Consiglio of the Ducal Palace in Venice. According to the order of the Litany, the Angels, Saints, and Blessed in increasingly larger circles range themselves around the Virgin who is praying before the Saviour as the centre. They are freely hovering and revolving celestial bodies, . . . The space of the universe is filled with countless figures. A passage from the *Dialogues on the Infinite, Universe and Worlds* says: . . . 'For the reception of those countless celestial bodies, an infinite space is required.' Here, without any doubt, painting and scientific thought have expressed the same profound idea. We do not need to assume a direct mutual influence which is rather unlikely, but *these great problems and ideas impregnated the spiritual atmosphere of the time, and found their expression in arts and sciences independently.*

The Venetian master's [that is, Tintoretto's] huge, multifold compositions seem to be ruled by a mechanical regularity and mathematical exactness. The figures of the *Resurrection of the Dead* which Tintoretto painted in 1560 for his own burial church S. Maria dell' Orto rush up and down, driven by an inner dynamism like the automatic figures of an immense clock. Automatons and clockworks were favoured in the era of Mannerism, but not as a mere pastime and amusement. . . . This fashion had a deeper spiritual reason: *the automatons mirrored the mechanism of the universe.* We notice here in Tintoretto's art a remarkable similarity to that of Bruegel, a similarity which is dictated by the spirit of the time, and not caused by outer influences.

One can recognize in Tintoretto's paintings certain recurring types of figures in movement, only seen in different aspects. They are not individuals, only embodiments of abstract spiritual motions. They change their significance according to their varying placement like the motifs in a musical canon or fugue, which remain the same and change their meaning only by altering their position.

At this time, in Venice and to the north of the Alps, a revival of the polyphony [multivoice musical texture] of the Late Middle Ages took place in music as much as in the visual arts. Andrea and Giovanni Gabrieli of Venice and the great organ master Claudio Merulo are representatives of this new polyphony which cultivated especially the musical form of the motet [an unaccompanied song sung in parts]. The fugues of the vocal compositions of Mannerism tower up to the altitude of sixteen and twenty voices like the tremendous pictorial inventions of Tintoretto. The Netherlanders, who during the fifteenth century had dominated in the musical field as much as in painting, again played a leading part in this revival of medieval polyphony. The greatest composer of the time was Roland de Lattre of Mons, who Italianized his name to Orlando di Lasso. He was active at the court of the Duke of Bavaria at Munich, a centre of Manneristic art. He handled the style of the worldly madrigal and the spiritual motet with equal virtuosity, making both types of musical composition benefit from each other. He gave a new harmonic meaning to the polyphonic structure, achieving new and surprising effects. He provided the single voices with vigorous accents according to the words of the text, increased their rhythmical articulation and the width of their tonal strides. He made abundant use of chromatics [that is, moving in half steps], as we see the painters of the time cultivate iridescent [glittery] shiftings of colours. . . .

In the field of architectural ornament, the style of Cornelis Floris of Antwerp was dominant. In the interlacement of his designs, we find mathematical exactitude combined with irrational fantasy. This style found a tremendous following in Germany, where arts and crafts were attracted by its irrational character. Masonry and décor, furniture and jewellery eagerly absorbed this international style. It is a complicated, brittle, spiny, thorny world of forms which threatens to hurt one wherever one touches it. Here belong the works of the great goldsmith Wenzel Jamnitzer of Nuremberg.

In science we notice a similar tendency towards renewed complexity and refinement. Astronomy became the leading science because it is the science not only of abstract intellectual motions but also of the basic realities in the universe. After the grandiose spatial simplicity of Copernicus' system, Tycho Brahe, the foremost astronomer in the last decades of the century, brought about a new complication. In his book *De Mundi Aetherii Recentioribus Phaenomenis* (1588), he returned to the medieval concept of the earth as the unmoved centre of the universe, but he made all the other planets revolve around the sun. The sun on its part revolved like the moon and the sphere of the fixed stars around the earth as the centre. The great concentric harmony of Copernicus was again replaced by a new objective eccentricity. . . . This is a scientific parallel to the medieval revival in the fine arts.

Leonardo da Vinci

Robert N. Linscott

One of the most influential and intriguing figures of the Renaissance was the Italian Leonardo da Vinci. The term "Renaissance man," meaning a person versed in many different fields, might have been coined to describe him. Artist, scientist, engineer, sculptor, and more, Leonardo cast a very long shadow over a variety of disciplines. Though the artist died in 1519, much of his most brilliant work belongs to the 1500s. This excerpt, drawn from Robert N. Linscott's introduction to Leonardo's notebooks, describes Leonardo's life and points out some of the puzzling contradictions that make Leonardo an enigmatic figure today.

Leonardo da Vinci was born near Florence, Italy, in 1452, and died in France in 1519. During these sixty-seven years he painted a few superb pictures and modeled one colossal statue, but by far the greater part of his time and energy was spent in observing the world around him, and in filling some twenty notebooks with the results of his observations.

Most men see much but comprehend little. Leonardo burned with desire to observe, to deduce and to understand. If he lifted a finger he had to analyze the mechanism of the movement even though it meant the dissection of a human body. If he noticed that a swallow held its tail in a certain way at the instant of alighting, then he must check the flight of hundreds of other birds in order to establish a principle of landing techniques and the laws that govern them. An eddy in running water was an invitation to study the nature of the flow and the contours of banks and bottom for an explanation of why the water was whirled clockwise or counterclockwise. To him a landscape was not only a thing of beauty but a problem in optics: how could its image

Excerpted from *The Notebooks of Leonardo da Vinci* (New York: The Modern Library, 1957) translated by Edward MacCurdy. Copyright © 1957 by Random House, Inc. Reprinted with permission from Edward MacCurdy.

enter the eye and be recorded by the brain? And always, when he had observed, analyzed and drawn his conclusions, down would go the results haphazard in his notebooks.

These notebooks, then, are the testament of a man who sought knowledge as a mystic seeks God; the record of a lifetime of observation and speculation, set down in five thousand manuscript pages, illustrated with hundreds of sketches, and containing some of the most brilliant and far-ranging deductions that the mind of man has ever conceived.

The price Leonardo paid for his curiosity was high. To gratify it he sacrificed the full flower of his career as painter and sculptor, perhaps the greatest the world has ever known. There is on record a letter to the Marchioness Isabella d'Este from an emissary she had sent to Florence to persuade Leonardo to paint a picture for her (in vain, as it turned out). The letter says, "He is working hard at geometry and is very impatient of painting. . . . In short his mathematical experiments have so estranged him from painting that he cannot bear to take up a brush." And this is typical, for Leonardo's career is one long record of commissions refused; of paintings unfinished.

Why did Leonardo thus sacrifice his greatest talent? To answer this question one turns first to the notebooks for whatever light they may throw on this most enigmatic of all great men. But Leonardo's thirst was for knowledge of things and forces; never of people and events. In the whole vast manuscript there is virtually no mention of his outward life or the world in which he lived; of friends, of women, of fellow artists, or of the men for and with whom he worked. In short, these are laboratory notes set down with a minimum of comment by a genius with a complex for secrecy, and whatever light they throw on his life and times is incidental and inferential. Moreover, to appraise even this fitful illumination it will be necessary to review first the known facts of Leonardo's career.

Leonardo's Life

He was born out of wedlock, the son of a peasant girl and a prosperous lawyer. His earliest years were spent with his mother; then his father adopted him and he was brought up by a kindly and childless stepmother, the first of his father's four wives. . . .

Having as a child shown a natural talent for drawing, Leonardo was apprenticed to a painter at the age of eighteen and soon achieved a reputation for his skill in uniting precision of line with rhythm of movement, and for his technical innovations in the representation of light and shade. Already his passion for knowledge had begun to curtail his artistic career as he immersed himself more and more in scientific studies and experiments. During these early years he was designing buildings, machines and canals, devising engines for moving earth and drawing water, and studying botany and astronomy. In a city and a period glittering with the vitality of the high Renaissance, he was outstanding, not only for his manifold talents, but no less for his beauty, his charm, his strength, and for the brilliance of his conversation.

At the age of thirty, Leonardo left Florence for Milan, then ruled by Lodovico Sforza, who was attempting to secure more firmly the throne his family had usurped, by subsidizing poets and artists to celebrate his magnificence.

As usual with Leonardo, the reason for his change of scene can only be conjectured. Vasari, in his *Lives of the Italian Painters*, written about thirty years after Leonardo's death, says: "He was invited with great honor to Milan by the Duke who delighted in the music of the lute, to the end that the master might play before him; Leonardo, therefore, took with him a certain instrument which he himself had constructed almost wholly of silver and in the shape of a horse's head. Here Leonardo surpassed all the musicians . . . and the Duke was so charmed by his varied gifts, that he delighted beyond measure in his society." And now, as an example of the inconsistencies that baffle the biographer . . . compare Vasari's romantic statement with the curious and childishly boastful letter in which Leonardo attempts to sell his services to the Duke, not primarily as an artist, and certainly not as a musician, but as a military engineer and inventor of engines of destruction.

In Milan, Leonardo was employed by Sforza to devise and carry out elaborate pageants with ingenious mechanical accompaniments. He also made studies for completing the cathedral and modernizing the city, designed improvements and decorations for the palace, planned canals and irrigation projects, modeled a huge equestrian statue of Sforza's father and completed his *Cenacolo* or *Last Supper* in which he brought the art of painting to a point never before and scarcely since achieved.

Four years were spent on this magnificent picture, and the only authentic glimpse we have of Leonardo at work was given by Bandello, a contemporary novelist, who wrote: "It was his habit often, and I have frequently seen him, to go early in the morning and mount upon the scaffolding as the *Cenacolo* is some distance from the ground; it was his habit, I say, from sunrise until dusk never to lay down his brush, but, forgetful alike of eating and drinking, to paint without intermission. At other times two, three or four days would pass without his touching the fresco, but he would remain before it for an hour or two at a time merely looking at it, considering, examining the figures. I have also seen him, as the caprice or whim took him, set out at midday from the Corte Vecchia, where he was at work on the clay model of the great horse, and go straight to the Grazie and there mount on the scaffolding and take up the brush and give one or two touches to one of the figures and suddenly give up and go away again."

Characteristically, the statue was so large that it was never cast, and the painting began almost at once to flake from the wall, due to Leonardo's insistence on experimenting with new techniques.

To this period also is attributed the exquisite *Virgin of the Rocks*, with its glittering technique and romantic background of rocks and water.

The Sixteenth Century

Sforza was eventually involved in war and appointed Leonardo his chief military engineer. When Milan was captured by the French, Leonardo fled to Venice and then to Florence, where he drew up plans for the control of the river Arno, and sketched (but never completed) his famous *Virgin and St. Anne*. Next he served for two years as engineer for Cesare Borgia, most ruthless of the Renaissance princelings, returning to Florence in 1502 at the age of fifty. Here we find him at work on a flying machine, and painting a battle scene to adorn the new council chamber. The flying machine failed to fly; the painting created an immense sensation but was never transferred to the wall.

One painting of this period which he did finish (though not, it is reported, to his own satisfaction) was the world's most famous portrait, *Mona Lisa*, or *La Gioconda*. This he loitered over, as Vasari says, for four years, taking the precaution, meanwhile, "of keeping someone constantly near her to sing, or play on instruments, or to jest and otherwise amuse her, to the end that she might continue cheerful." The celebrated and mysterious smile that plays upon the lips, not only of Mona Lisa, but of other women whom Leonardo painted, was, in Freud's opinion, a memory of his peasant mother.

In 1506, Leonardo was again in Milan and serving under the French. Six years later he moved to Rome, but there the younger generation in the persons of Raphael and Michelangelo dominated the world of art, and after two years he left Rome, struck up a friendship with the new French king, Francis I, and accepted his offer of a generous pension and the use of his castle of Cloux in France. There he died two and a half years later at the age of sixty-seven. His epitaph was pronounced by the king, who said that "he did not believe there had ever been another man born into the world who had known as much as Leonardo, and this not only in matters concerning sculpture, painting and architecture, but because he was a great philosopher.". . .

These are the outward facts of a life that would seem to have been a miracle of inconsistency. Two questions are especially perplexing: first, why a man uniquely gifted as an artist and with a reputation that made him sought after by kings and princes should have spent the greater part of his life in study and have written down his findings in code and without organization so that succeeding generations had no opportunity to profit from his discoveries; second, why a man who hated war (he called it bestial madness) and loved liberty (he would buy caged birds in order to set them free) should have served the tyrants of the period and expended such ingenuity in devising more lethal weapons of destruction. Vasari says he kept many servants and horses, but moneymaking could not have interested him or he would never have spent so many years in abstract studies. One might imagine that he passed through life as in a trance, following his fancies, and unaware of, or indifferent to, the forces of good and evil, if it were not for the high moral tone of the philosophic maxims that are scattered through his manuscripts.

And the questions raised by the notebooks are no less baffling. Consider, first of all, that the whole vast manuscript was written backward; i.e., from right to left. One would infer from this and from the occasional use of rebuses and anagrams (Amor, for example, instead of Roma) that Leonardo had a passion for concealment, but the labor of writing backward would surely have been out of all proportion to the secrecy value, since the script could be read by anyone with a mirror. Consider also the extraordinary and extraneous material which he copied into his notebooks. This includes an apparently meaningless list of nearly eight thousand words; parts of a Latin grammar; a large collection of popular superstitions about animals, some taken from [Roman writer] Pliny and some from medieval bestiaries; hundreds of quotations or paraphrases from other writers, unmarked and with no clue to their origin, so that in reading his aphorisms one never knows whether to pay tribute to Leonardo as a thinker or as an appropriator; and finally a section of excessively dull jokes. Are the letters that purport to describe events in Asia Minor evidence that he actually traveled in the East as some commentators believe, or are they the beginnings of an attempt at fiction?

One can answer these questions only by affirming that Leonardo was unique, conforming to no pattern, and can be comprehended only in the context of his time, as an intermediary between the Middle Ages and the modern world. Harvey had yet to discover the circulation of the blood; Newton the law of gravitation; Galileo the movements of the heavenly bodies. Leonardo half anticipated these discoveries but lacked the accumulated knowledge to define his surmises. If, now and then, his conclusions seem childlike or absurd, it must be remembered that he was still partly in the medieval night of the mind, attempting by faulty reasoning based on erroneous premises to understand phenomena dependent on principles beyond the comprehension of the age in which he lived.

The Reformation

The Protestant Reformation was a pivotal moment of the sixteenth century. Indeed, where the sweep of religious history is concerned, it was arguably one of the most important events of all time. Initiated by a young German monk named Martin Luther, the movement started out as a single-handed protest against a particular policy of the Catholic Church, but it soon mushroomed. By the middle of the 1500s the Catholic Church's near-monopoly on the western Christian faith was irretrievably gone. Across much of northern Europe and some of the central parts of the continent as well, the population had rejected Catholicism in favor of a new and different form of Christianity. Politically and religiously, Europe would never again be the same.

Much of Luther's quarrel with the church—though by no means all of it—involved theological matters. Over time his reformist views led him to argue that the entire foundation of Catholicism was wrong. Catholic theologians had traditionally stressed good works as a means of salvation. A person who led a good life on Earth—who helped feed the poor, who sinned infrequently and repented promptly, who resisted temptation—would, according to these Catholic thinkers, eventually earn a spot in heaven.

To Luther and his fellow Protestants, this line of reasoning was anathema. No one "earned" admission to heaven, Luther preached; no amount of good works, however great, could by themselves save a person's eternal soul from damnation. Only the gift of grace, freely given by God, could accomplish that. Humans were inveterate sinners, but God's goodwill could forgive all sins—and would, too, for those who truly believed. Later Protestant thinkers refined Luther's ideas on this score, but they also came down on the same general side of the debate. Whereas Catholics tended to rely on works, Protestants preached an abiding faith.

Lutheranism had other theological arguments with Catholicism. One wide-reaching example involved the role of priests and the importance of the Bible. To Protestants, the Bible was the unchanging word of God. It belonged at the center of worship, and its authority was not to be usurped. In Luther's view, the Catholic system reduced the Bible to a supporting role, even hid it behind several other layers of authority. Priests interposed themselves between the Bible and the congregation by interpreting it for them; popes and bishops behaved in ways that seemed to ignore biblical mandates or directly contradicted them; even the Latin translations of the Bible used throughout the Catholic realm made it impossible for people to experience the Bible directly. Thus, a major tenet of the Protestant faith was a reliance on the Bible and a diminution of the authority of the clergy. Even today, no Protestant sect has anyone whose power and position matches that of the Catholic pope.

Of course, the two theologies were not nearly so widely separated as their adherents came to believe during the 1500s. Like Protestants, Catholics placed great value on faith in God, even though faith was not their main criterion for salvation. Nor was the notion of God's grace a new one for Luther's supporters: It was a part of Catholic theology as well, if not the central theme. Similarly, Lutherans accepted the importance of good works, although they tended to believe that works flowed naturally from a heart that was full of faith. Today, the differences are smaller still. Catholics hear the words of the Bible in their native language; in turn, Protestant ministers play roles not much different from those of their counterparts in the Catholic churches. Whatever the similarities today may be, however, there is no denying the reality that Luther's movement tore European religion apart during the sixteenth century.

The Church in 1500

E. Harris Harbison

The Protestant Reformation did not occur in a vacuum. Rather, it was sparked in part by significant problems in the Catholic Church of the early sixteenth century. In this excerpt from his book *The Age of Reformation*, historian E. Harris Harbison explores corruption in the church at the time and the ways the church lost its moral and political authority. In particular, interest in secular gain often seemed to outweigh the church's interest in spiritual issues.

A bove all towns and cities, all counties and duchies, all monarchies and even the empire itself, yet reaching down to touch the life of the humblest peasant, was the Roman Catholic Church. It was the one institution common to all of Europe up to the frontiers of Eastern Orthodox Christianity in the East and of Islam in the South. It was the largest and wealthiest institution in Europe, almost impossible to describe in terms of twentieth-century experience.

"Thou art Peter," Jesus had said to the chief of his disciples, "and on this rock [*petros* in Greek] will I found my church." The church was the visible historical institution founded by Christ himself upon Peter and his confession of his Lord's divinity. Peter was reputed to have died in Rome, and succeeding bishops of Rome were taken to be his successors, the vicars of Christ on earth.

The church, then, was a divine, not a human, institution. Yet it was composed of human material—certain human beings set aside from all others to act as ministers of the sacraments and mediators between

God and man. These clerics, or "men chosen," were of two kinds: the secular clergy, or priests and bishops, who acted as pastors or shepherds of the flock of Christian laymen; and the regular clergy, or monks and mendicant friars, who lived by a special rule of life which released them from all worldly ties and freed them either for a life of prayer or for a sort of wandering ministry. The paradox of the church from the beginning was that it was a divinely founded institution with the highest purpose—that of mediating God's grace to man through the sacraments and bringing man to salvation in God—and yet an organization inevitably composed of human beings and deeply involved in worldly affairs. This is simply to say that there never was a time when the church was not "corrupt," unworthy of its high purpose and in need of "reform," if judged by religious standards.

Troubles in the Church

This was particularly true in the early sixteenth century. Not that the abuses were any worse than they had been for a century or two. There are evidences that they were not, that conditions were improving to some extent. Nor was it that the Christian religion was on the wane. The later fifteenth century was, if anything, a period of religious revival. Rather, familiar abuses, such as clerical immorality and the sale of church offices, were now more conspicuous, more talked about, and more resented than they had been. The economic and political changes we have described were having their effect on the church, and new ways of looking at things were encouraging men to regard long-standing abuses in a new light. The church was certainly not in a healthy state. It had lost unity and influence steadily since the height of its prestige in the twelfth and thirteenth centuries. But this was not simply the result of the sins of the priests and monks who composed it. It was not even the result of evil practices and questionable doctrines which had crept into the ecclesiastical organization, though there seemed to be much of this. It was rather the result of a long and slow shifting of social conditions and human values to which the church was not responding readily enough. The sheer inertia of an enormous and complex organization, the drag of powerful vested interests, the helplessness of individuals with intelligent schemes of reform—this is what strikes the historian in studying the church of the later Middle Ages. The church as a human institution had apparently lost its ability to adapt and change and grow.

The main evidence of this was that the church had lost the administrative efficiency and centralization which it had had three centuries earlier. The three key powers of thirteenth-century popes—those of appointment, taxation, and jurisdiction—had been steadily circumscribed in the fifteenth century by the rising national monarchs. Whenever a monarch had pretensions to real sovereignty in his realm, he claimed the right to control the appointment of bishops (whom he often used as his own civil servants in important positions), to limit the amount of money the church could take out of his dominions, and to curtail the appeal of ecclesiastical cases to Rome.

[Spanish rulers] Ferdinand and Isabella went furthest along these lines. By the early sixteenth century they had set up a kind of national church in which the powers of appointment, of taxation, and of ecclesiastical jurisdiction in Castile and Aragon were in effect theirs. In 1516 Francis I of France made a famous and important deal, known as the Concordat of Bologna, with the Medici pope Leo X. This gave the French king almost the same powers that the Catholic kings of Spain had gained, particularly in appointment of the higher clergy, in return for renouncing the doctrine, dear to French hearts for a century, that a church council is superior to the pope. In England much the same limitations of papal power had been on the parliamentary statute books since the fourteenth century, but the kings were sometimes inclined to wink at the law and allow the pope somewhat more influence over appointments, somewhat more revenue and jurisdiction, than he was allowed in Spain or France. Between 1515 and 1529 Cardinal Wolsey was able to build up a kind of dictatorship over the English Church with the blessing of both the pope and King Henry VIII. This centralized ecclesiastical power might of course have served to establish full Roman control over the English Church, but it was more likely to serve (as in the end it did) as a model for complete royal control. Strict royal control over national churches was no invention of the sixteenth century. By 1517 the pope's power to appoint, to tax, and to judge had been stringently limited in several nations which (like Spain) were otherwise zealously Catholic.

Concerns in Germany

Significantly there was no such limitation in Germany because there was no secular power strong enough to stand up to the pope. The great bishops in Germany were prince-bishops, ruling wealthy ecclesiastical principalities which were practically independent. The papacy drew a relatively enormous revenue from Germany, in spite of continual and futile complaints from the Imperial Diet [council] or Reichstag about abuses and the burden of ecclesiastical taxation. Unlike the western monarchs, the emperor generally divided the spoil with the pope instead of attempting to stop the flow of gold to Rome. The rising national resentment of the papal powers of appointment, taxation, and jurisdiction in the empire made Germany potentially the most likely scene of revolt against the church in all of Christendom.

There were other limitations on the hierarchical centralization and administrative efficiency of the church beside the pretensions of secular rulers. Many bishops no longer had control either of the monks or of the parish priests within their dioceses. Monastic orders were largely exempt from episcopal jurisdiction [the rule of the bishop], and the appointment of priests was often in the hands of others than the bishop. Most bishops were nobles, with little interest in anything but the revenues and prestige of their position. The gift of a bishopric was a good way for a great lord to provide for a younger son or for a king to support a clever administrator—or his bastard children. Too many bishops held more than one bishopric; many never bothered even to visit their dioceses. The parish clergy—generally poor, ignorant, often indistinguishable from their lay parishioners in mind and morals—were left largely to themselves to administer the sacraments and care for their flock as best they could. The state of the monastic orders varied greatly from order to order and from country to country. But in spite of the genuine zeal and strict discipline of some like the Carthusians, the general trend of monastic piety and morals was downward throughout a good deal of Europe. Even if a reforming bishop or abbot appeared—and there were a few shining examples—he found almost insuperable difficulties in his way because of the general decentralization within the church and the strength of vested interests all down the line.

If reform was to come at all, apparently it could come only from the top, from the papacy itself. But the papacy of the Renaissance was a most unlikely source of reform. In 1500 the worst of all the popes was on the papal throne, Alexander VI, indulgent father of the notorious Cesare Borgia and benefactor of hordes of rapacious relatives from Spain. Under Alexander the immorality, the venality, and the conspicuous spending which had already made the papal court a by-word among those who knew Rome reached their height. Typically, the contributions which flowed in from the faithful all over Europe during the jubilee year of 1500 went mostly to help Cesare carve out a principality for himself in central Italy. There were reformers at the Vatican, but they were helpless because any real reform which was proposed had the effect of cutting down the papal revenues, and this promptly sent panic through the host of officials and hangers-on who made up the cumbrous machinery of papal government.

Indulgences and Finance

This brings us to the heart of the problem of the condition of the church. The papacy of the early sixteenth century was only one step ahead of bankruptcy a good deal of the time. The necessity of defending the papal states (and the desire to enlarge them), the burden of supporting an elaborate administrative organization (and a luxurious court), the obligation to support anti-Turkish crusades (and perhaps also wars against papal enemies closer to home in France, Germany, or Italy)—all this cost money. This money was squeezed out of the higher clergy in various ways, particularly by what was called simony, or the sale of spiritual offices. But the clergy had in the end to squeeze the money out of the producing classes in society, the peasants and artisans, the merchants and professional people. Rents were raised on the enormous holdings of church lands, and fees were increased for spiritual services performed by the clergy. In the end the squeeze imposed by the papacy on the higher clergy was passed on to the laity in the form of higher charges by the parish clergy for everything from burials and the probate of wills to administration of the sacraments themselves.

The practice of issuing indulgences in return for "contributions" from the faithful is the best illustration of how a hard-pressed papacy was tempted to trade spiritual benefits for hard cash. An indulgence was originally a remission of the "penance," or temporal penalty for sin, imposed by the priest in the sacrament of penance. Indulgences were granted by papal dispensation to crusaders, to pilgrims, and finally to any who contributed to some such cause as building a church. Indulgences were very lucrative. The revenue which they brought into the papal treasury was greatly increased in the fifteenth century by the popular belief that an indulgence could not only assure divine forgiveness of sins with a minimum of contrition, but also release the souls of the dead from Purgatory. The best teaching of the church insisted upon the necessity of full contrition and was very cautious about asserting the pope's power over Purgatory. But extravagant claims were made for the papal power by some. During the fifteenth century it became official dogma that there was a treasury of superfluous merits accumulated by Christ and the saints, and that the church could dispense these merits to the buyers of indulgences. In this as in so many other contemporary practices—including the veneration of saints and relics, pilgrimages, and the administration of the sacraments themselves—the line between the spiritual and the material became blurred in the eyes of many ordinary believers. The church was trading upon its monopoly of the means of salvation in order to raise money for largely secular purposes, or so it seemed to increasing numbers of laymen and conscientious clergymen. The sacred and the secular were inextricably confused in innumerable ways and at every level in ecclesiastical practice.

Many Catholic writers put the whole blame for this general situation on the "greed, thirst for power, and lusts of the flesh" of secular rulers who sabotaged every attempt at reform. Many Protestant writers tend to blame the same faults in clergymen, from the pope down. Clearly one must look deeper for the underlying causes—in the economic expansion, the growing need for political consolidation, and the increasing worldliness of taste and thought both within and outside the clergy. The impulse to be a Christian was probably as strong in as many people then as it had been three centuries earlier, but disturbing and half-formulated questions were occurring to many people. What was it to be a Christian? To buy an indulgence? To become a monk? Or to read the Bible and live a good life? Was a great supranational organization centered in Rome a necessary part of Christianity? Was a mediating priesthood necessary to represent the divine power on earth, and were the sacraments the only channels of God's grace to man? Not one of these questions was new, but unless reform could be accomplished, they would grow in urgency and poignancy.

Justification by Faith: Early Lutheran Thought

George L. Mosse

Martin Luther was bothered both by political issues in the Roman
Catholic Church such as the sale of indulgences, and by more strictly
spiritual issues such as the roles of the individual and the pope. The specific political event that triggered Luther's ire was the indulgence of
1517. The new archbishop of Mainz in Germany had paid twenty-four
thousand ducats for his position. To recoup some of the money, the pope
had suggested that the archbishop sell indulgences, which he did through
his assistant Johann Tetzel. Luther had long disapproved of the sale of
indulgences. In his opinion, it was neither appropriate nor effective for
the church to offer forgiveness for sin, especially not in exchange for
money. Remitting sin was a matter for God. Angry and disappointed,
Luther lashed out at the church hierarchy.

However, as professor George L. Mosse explains, Luther's theological
journey had already taken him to a place from which a break from the
church was perhaps inevitable. Catholic theology of the time focused on
atoning for sins by doing good; Luther, in contrast, determined that salvation—or justification, in his term—was to be obtained strictly through faith
and through God's ultimate grace. In Luther's belief system, good works
all by themselves could not lead to salvation, no matter how good they were
or how many were carried out. Together, the political and theological conflicts made it impossible for Luther to reconcile with the church.

Excerpted from *The Reformation*, by George L. Mosse. Copyright © 1963 by Holt, Rinehart, and
Winston, renewed 1991 by George L. Mosse. Reprinted with permission from Harcourt, Inc.

Martin Luther was the son of Thuringian peasants who had attained modest middle class wealth. Reared against a background of popular piety, young Martin was determined to become a monk and to devote his life to the service of God. . . . He first came into close contact with orthodox theology at the University of Erfurt. . . . The theology taught at Erfurt was the theology of the Englishman William of Occam, which had found acceptance by the Church. Occam stressed the absolutism of God, who could save or condemn by His will alone. Yet Occam admitted the *possibility* that man, through his own force of will, could prepare the ground for salvation. What this theology meant to a sensitive and pious soul like Luther's was a growing uncertainty, a feeling of being buffeted between God's absolutism and man's possibility of preparing for salvation through his own power. Where, in this theology, was certainty to be found? Luther's struggle of the spirit and his frequent depressions were centered around the problem of how man can be certain of that salvation for which his soul searches.

These spiritual struggles did not end when Luther fulfilled his life's goal by entering the Augustinian priory at Erfurt (1505). They were further enhanced by his glimpse of life at the papal court during his one visit to Rome (1510). Pomp and splendor proved no solution for a hungry soul in the quest of salvation. Before he had journeyed to Rome, Luther had been transferred to the Augustinian priory at Wittenberg (1508); and here, where he was to make his home for the rest of his life, he faced the spiritual crisis which was to transform his own life and the lives of his fellow men.

It was von Staupitz, the vicar of the priory, who first tried to lighten the load which seemed to rest on the troubled spirit of this young monk. Staupitz's mild mysticism attracted Luther. He thought that this heightening of popular piety by the attempt to fuse one's soul with God might solve the quest for certainty. Yet Luther never became a disciple of the mystics; he was unable to quiet his soul by immersing it in the Creator. To him the mystical experience was a momentary one, and did not lead to permanent peace of the soul. Staupitz decided to try another medicine. He gave Luther a teaching position at the University. His subject matter was the Bible. He commenced by teaching the Psalms and by 1515 he was teaching the Epistles of St. Paul. It was while performing his daily task of teaching that Luther resolved the great conflict between the mercy and the wrath of God, and it was St. Paul who was his inspiration, just as the Apostle had inspired Lefévre to a belief in the primacy of faith.

The Apostle Paul

The connection between St. Paul and the reform movement is not difficult to trace. The Apostle had criticized the early Christian Church, just as these men were criticizing the Church of their day, and for much the same reasons. For St. Paul, too, there had been the danger of substituting the Church for the Scriptures and the church hierarchy for God's faith. If for St. Paul many members of the Church were confining the grace of God within the limitations of the Jewish Torah, so for Luther that grace was imprisoned within the walls of theological orthodoxy. In this way, the Epistles of St. Paul played a very real part in the Reformation, and seemed especially relevant to the problems of the late medieval Church as Martin Luther saw them.

"Night and day I pondered until I saw the connection between the justice of God and the statement, 'The righteous shall live by his faith.' Then I grasped that the justice of God is that righteousness by which through grace and sheer mercy God justifies us through faith. Thereupon I felt myself to be reborn and to have gone through open doors into Paradise." Thus Martin Luther arrived at salvation through faith alone; his quest for spiritual certainty had been solved. Faith is not an achievement; it is a gift which comes to man through the hearing and the study of the Word. Luther had studied the Bible for his lectures, and had come to see the solution to his spiritual problems. Faith justifies man before God, and it is part of that faith to trust God, to believe that he is, through Christ, constantly striving to save mankind. This insight was to be the motivating force of Luther's life and work. All else was but a commentary upon it.

It was after he had reached this central conclusion that Luther encountered the Indulgence of 1517. Here was an action directly opposed to his new-found certainty and conviction, a substitution of works for faith. Already, prior to 1517, Luther had begun to preach against the growing number of indulgences which were being sold throughout Germany. But the numbers in which the citizens of Wittenberg went to acquire Tetzel's indulgences, and then demanded that on their presentation they be absolved from sin, brought matters to a head. Luther was shocked by the fact that the archbishop of Mainz could be a party to such practices, and was naively sure that the pope would disapprove. As he wrote to the archbishop, his theses were meant not to create strife, but to prevent it. He did not broadcast his views throughout the land, but posted them on the bulletin board of the university at the castle church. These ninety-five theses were a call to theological disputation as well as an appeal to the conscience of the archbishop. The first of these theses shows how the whole practice of indulgences ran counter to Luther's conviction of salvation by faith: "If Christ, our Lord and Master says, 'Do penance,' he wants the entire life of the pious to be one penance." Penance was the humility of faith, and had nothing to do with atonement through works or through the payment of money. October 31, 1517, was meant by Luther to mark the starting point in rectifying an obvious abuse which did damage to the Church. Instead, this date marks the beginning of his break with Rome.

Argument

"He has touched the crown of the pope and the stomachs of the monks." Erasmus' evaluation of the importance of Luther's action proved correct. The financial interests of the papacy were attacked, and the echo which Luther's action aroused among the people imperiled the whole success of the Indulgence. . . . The Dominicans pressed for action against Luther. But now they overplayed their hand, for it was the disputations, in which Luther had to defend his faith against orthodox theologians, that gained him nation-wide attention. Already after his first public defense at Augsburg (1518) before the kindly papal legate Cajetan, it was said that Luther was the most famous man in Germany. The most crucial of these disputations took place at Leipzig (1519) with the able and violently orthodox Johannes Eck. Through his cogent argumentation as Luther's adversary, Eck pushed Luther into questioning the divine appointment of the papacy and, worse, into admitting a sympathy with some of the ideas of both [fourteenth-century English reformer John]

Martin Luther

Wycliffe and [fifteenth-century Czech reformer Jan] Hus. The customary public disputation of theological points had led Luther into a heretical position, for he was forced to argue out the consequences of his central belief in "justification by faith," and to approach ever nearer the idea of the primacy of all believers over any church organization. This was the core of that religious individualism to which Lutheranism inevitably led. Why should the Church have a pope if Christ was her head? Every believer was a priest insofar as he had found faith and had been justified by God through his faith. At Leipzig these consequences of his belief were as yet to be sought underneath Luther's guarded language, though Eck correctly divined them. But one year later, the papacy itself acted. Luther was condemned as a heretic in the bull *Exsurge* (1520). He had to retract or stand in danger of becoming a revolutionary. Owing to the certainty of his convictions, Luther had no choice. Before the assembled students of the University of Wittenberg, the professor of Bible committed to the flames of the bull which placed him outside the Church.

The University of Wittenberg was in sympathy with the gesture of its professor, and from this University a whole series of disciples were to go out among their fellow men to educate them in the Lutheran faith. Luther had by now gained attention far beyond the confines of the Saxon town. He had won the ear of the nation, and he now used this popular appeal to further his cause through the printed word. It was fortunate for Luther that the printing press had been developed by the time of the Reformation (1450), and he made full use of this new invention. All the reformers were to rely heavily on the printed word in spreading their message, drawing ever wider circles into the controversies of the age. In a real sense this was the first use of books as propaganda weapons, and here, too, Luther pioneered. His scurrilous language, which has shocked subsequent ages, was meant to bring home the truth of the gospel to people untouched by intellectual refinements—people for whom the elegant satires of the Christian Humanists were too subtle and not forceful enough to drive home the point. The year 1521 saw Luther's ideas spelled out for all the world to read.

The Tracts of 1520–1521

The three great tracts of 1520–1521 clarify Luther's principal religious ideas. In the *Babylonish Captivity of the Church*, he used the force of his language to castigate the abuses of the Church, while going beyond the abuses themselves by advocating actual change in liturgy. Because the *Babylonish Captivity* abolished several central rites of the Church, it was thought by contemporaries to be his most radical tract and confirmed his irrevocable breach with the papacy. His keynote was the perversion of the sacraments by the Church, and he reduced them to two in number; the Lord's Supper and Baptism alone remained, for only these two seemed to Luther to have been directly instituted by Christ. His belief in the supremacy of faith dictated the abolition of priestly absolution from sin as a vital part of penance, because man cannot anticipate the decision of God. The denying of ordination for priests dealt a severe blow to the clergy as a special caste, and put them on an equal footing with the rest of the believers. To Luther all Christians were priests. Abolition of Ordination as a sacrament had another consequence. It reduced the Catholic Mass to a celebration of communion or the Lord's Supper. No longer was the priest alone endowed with the power to perform the miracle of the bread and wine. No longer, therefore, was the Church the sole custodian of the body of Christ. Instead, the religious service became the concern of the whole congregation of the faithful, a communal action in which the entire priesthood of believers participated.

The symbol for this full participation in the religious service was the hymn. The Gregorian chants of the Church had been so technical that they were sung by special choirs or by priests. Luther adapted the

German folk song to religious poetry and thus made it possible for all the faithful to participate fully in every part of the service. He composed at least thirty-seven of these hymns, and in 1524 published the first evangelical hymnbook. Thus the transformation of the liturgy as put forward in the *Babylonish Captivity* eventually meant the beginning of the great age of Protestant church music, which found its climax over a hundred years later in the chorals of Johann Sebastian Bach (1685–1750).

In adapting German folk music for his hymns, Luther showed again his close affinity with the spirit of his own people. That same spirit is evidenced in his *Appeal to the Christian Nobility of the German Nation*. . . . If the *Babylonish Captivity* dealt with liturgy, the *Appeal* was directed toward the problem of church organization.

Luther advised the German ruling classes that by God's command it was the duty of the magistrates [secular authorities] to punish evildoers, and called upon them to repulse the pretensions of the Roman Church. But Luther went beyond this; the magistrates were called upon to reform the Church, to strip it of worldly power and wealth which disguised and smothered true faith. Thus he began to endow the rulers with ecclesiastical functions, for were they not baptized and Christians like anybody else? If the worldly power of the clergy had to vanish in the name of a reinvigorated faith, then someone else had to assure that there was "order" in the affairs of the Church, and that must be the magistrate who was set by God over men, and who shared in the priesthood of all believers. It was not to curry favor with the princes that Luther gave them authority over church organization, but as a natural consequence of the equality of all believers.

Political Consequences

To Luther, the external order of the Church was of secondary importance. For this reason, in his *German Mass* (1525), he disclaimed any intention of making his order of service a law for his church. Salvation by faith was, after all, an individual matter. For all that, Luther did not intend unbridled individualism. St. Paul teaches us that we must see to it that we have the same ideals; are we not all born in the same way? Baptized in the same way? Do we not have the same sacraments? God has not given special dispensation to anyone. In this way, princes or city councils could regulate the Church, asserting that they were seeing to it that "due order" was observed.

Luther tried to follow a moderate course, but the outcome of his ideas on church organization was the alliance between altar and throne which was to make Lutheranism a state church, thus strengthening the hand of the government against dissent. . . . If this absolutism was to be facilitated as a consequence of Luther's church organization, what, then, did he mean by Christian liberty? This is the theme of his third great tract, *Concerning the Liberty of a Christian Man*.

The liberty with which Luther dealt was not outward political or social freedom, but the inward liberty which comes from a faith found. The liberty of justification before God has good works as a natural consequence, but good works themselves have nothing to do with this liberty. "Good works do not make a man good, but a good man does good works." God has given great riches to the world and the man worthy of them through faith will do all to please God. He will give himself to his neighbor, as Christ gave Himself to mankind. However, the Christian must not reject such happy hours as God confers upon him, and the good doctor himself spent many happy hours over his glass of beer, or over a game of cards. It is important to remember, however, that Christians were not authorized to break through the bonds of class and social distinctions, or even to reach for political power. It was not that Luther was indifferent to the downtrodden, but to him, for whom inner freedom and certainty were the only concerns, worldly rebellion was a sign of insufficient attention to the real business of life, which lay in the attainment of faith and not in the gathering of riches.

With the year 1521, Luther's views were fully revealed and elaborated upon. Typically enough, he still dedicated *The Liberty of a Christian Man* to Pope Leo X, in the faint hope of a reconciliation. But even if the idea of Christian liberty might prove acceptable, Luther had burned his bridges behind him in the other tracts. He now faced the world not as a reformer, but as a heretic. Not only the Church was taking notice of the Wittenberg professor, but the worldly authorities had to take a stand also.

Luther and the Diet of Worms

John M. Todd

By 1520, civil and religious leaders' patience with Martin Luther had come to an end. His teachings, officials were sure, constituted heresy: that is, his ideas were outside the teachings of the church. However, Luther had an increasingly large following within Germany. Catholic leaders and the German emperor Charles V decided to fight back. The church excommunicated him—that is, forbade him to take part in church rituals—and Charles, in turn, declared that all of Luther's writings were to be banned.

In 1521, Luther was summoned to give a full accounting of himself to religious and civil authorities before the Diet of Worms, a formal council in Worms, Germany. What happened at Worms changed few minds and included no compromises. Luther arrived branded as a heretic and he left the same way. In the meantime, however, Luther had an opportunity to explain his ideas in a public forum, and the authorities had an opportunity to respond; the proceedings helped establish the philosophical and political differences separating the two sides. This excerpt, from John M. Todd's *Luther: A Life*, describes Luther's testimony against the political and theological background of the council's proceedings.

L uther, in his normal Augustinian habit, tonsure recently shaven, thick-set, a little gaunt for his thirty-seven years, made obeisance to the Emperor and the Emperor's representative, the Archbishop of Trier. The Archbishop's Chancellor, Johann von Eck . . . then addressed Luther, pointed to a pile of books and asked Luther very briefly whether they were his and whether he wished to retract any of them. This blunt approach surprised Luther. His lawyer [Jerome Schurf] jumped in immediately and requested that the titles of the books be read out. It was a motley collection of Luther's German and Latin works, but it included both the German *Appeal to the Nobility* and the Latin *Prelude to the Babylonian Captivity*. While they were being read out, Luther and Schurf had a quick word together. Luther then replied, speaking first in German then in Latin. He asked for time to consider his answer, 'because this is a question of faith and the salvation of souls'. It was at first sight an odd reply, apparently unexpected by the Emperor and his advisers who went into a huddle to decide what to do about it. But Schurf had given Luther the obvious advice. Only now had they learnt for certain the mood of the Emperor— Luther, it was clear, had been summoned solely to recant. It was best, then, to take time over preparing his exact reply.

They were told that Luther could have twenty-four hours, though that should be regarded as a special kindness since he should have come prepared to answer. He was abjured not to come with a written statement but be ready, at the same time tomorrow, to answer verbally.

The next day the hearing was resumed in another, bigger room, which soon became overcrowded and too hot. The Electors, the Estates [civil authorities], and many others were there as well as the Emperor and his advisers. It was six o'clock before they started and by then Luther was feeling ill and was in a great sweat. However, as soon as proceedings began the adrenalin flowed and he was able to speak to the brief which he and Schurf had worked out. It took about a quarter of an hour in German and nearly the same in Latin, and was recorded in writing by both friends and enemies; part of Luther's own script has survived.

Luther's Response

It was a prepared speech which Luther had more or less learnt off by heart:

> Most serene Emperor, most illustrious princes, most clement lords . . . deign to listen graciously to this my cause—which is, as I hope, a cause of justice and of truth. If through my inexperience I have either not given the proper titles to some, or have offended in some manner against customs and court etiquette, I ask you kindly to pardon me, as a man accustomed not to courts but to the cells of monks. I can say nothing about myself but that I have taught and written up to this time with simplicity of heart, as I had in view only the glory of God and the sound instruction of Christ's faithful.

The quiet, persuasive, intellectual voice flowed gently and deliberately on, emotion held only partially in check, visible in the changing expressions on his face—'frivolous' expressions, said one Spanish reporter.

Addressing himself to the two questions, he said that there was not much doubt about the first one. Obviously his books were his books, unless someone had slipped in some of someone else's.

The second question was more difficult, because he had written three kinds of books. 1. Simple gospel works—if he were to renounce these he would 'condemn the very truth upon which friends and enemies equally agree' [that is, the validity of the Bible]. 2. Books against the papacy and the concerns of the papists. He asked what was wrong with such works, when everyone knew that the papal tyranny did so much harm to the Christian world and especially to 'this illustrious nation of Germany'. 3. 'I have written a third sort of books against some private and (as they say) distinguished individuals—those, namely, who strive to preserve the Roman tyranny and to destroy the godliness which I teach.'

Against these latter people, he confessed he had been more violent than his religion or his profession demanded—but then he did not set himself up as a saint, nor was he disputing about his life, but about the teaching of Christ. His books against such people could not be renounced without renouncing the battle against the tyranny of anti-Christ. Finally, he repeated that he was always ready to be shown that his doctrines were wrong.

The Need for Reform

Then, although the substance of the reply was complete, Luther added a more personal kind of comment. They could see, he said, that he had thought long and hard about these things. If disturbance and dissension arose because of his teachings, that was a case for rejoicing, because Christ did indeed say 'I have come to bring not peace but a sword'—Christianity was no easy option. . . . He ended: 'I do not say these things because there is a need of either my teachings or my warnings for such leaders as you, but because I must not withhold the allegiance which I owe to Germany. With these words I commend myself to your most serene majesty and to your lordships, humbly asking that I should not be allowed to become hateful to you because of the scheming of my enemies. I have finished.' Luther, although sometimes naive, and exercising poor judgement politically, was never careless of political fact. Man's task always involved attention to immediate responsibilities and loyalties, and the use of appropriate and reasonable policies. So, the effect of his actions was not something which could be left aside, nor 'the allegiance which I owe to Germany'. He was well aware . . . of the genuine danger of violent social disruption. It was true that nothing would tend towards the prevention of this more than a movement of genuine reform. Reform was precisely what was required, reform of institutions so deeply involved in the injustices and so deeply implicated as causes of the sheer poverty and misery, the re-

sentment and the envy which were the boiling origins of a likely social revolution.

The Chancellor of Trier then answered Luther in a speech which
kept to the high level of debate and rhetoric set by Luther himself. It
was an effective reply from the orthodox papal position. The Emperor,
he said, would be willing to consider making a distinction between the
harmless and the harmful, of Luther's writings, but Luther was only
doing what every heretic always did, the Waldensians, the Beghards,
the Poor Men of Lyons, etc.; they all turned to Scripture, and they all
wished it to be interpreted in their sense. He mocked a little: 'Do not,
I entreat you, Martin, do not claim for yourself that you are the one and
only man who has knowledge of the Bible, who has true understanding. . . . Do not place your judgement ahead of so many distinguished
men . . . as wiser than others.' Then he became more confident still,
and finally threatening: 'What the doctors have discussed as doctrine
the Church has defined as its judgement, the faith in which our fathers
and ancestors confidently died and as a legacy have transmitted to us.
We are forbidden to argue about this faith by the law of both pontiff
and emperor . . . both are going to judge those who with headlong rash-
ness refuse to submit to the decisions of the Church. Punishments have
been provided and published.' He then told Martin to answer clearly
and simply and not with a 'horned'(*cornutum*) reply.

"Here I Stand"

The two poles were far apart. The Chancellor, as its obedient and
humble, believing servant, was defending an organisation which
claimed to act from 1500 years of tradition on its own authority as the
vicegerent [deputy] of God. The friar, speaking from his own struggles with the meaning of the Word of the Gospel, listened to in his inner being, worshipped daily in the liturgy in his own local church,
himself a product precisely of the same 1500 years, was convinced
that the authorities in the organisation had made great errors and that
they must be brought back to what he felt he now knew to be the evident Christian faith.

> Since then Your Serene Majesty and Your Lordships seek a simple answer,
> I will give it in this manner, neither horned nor toothed. Unless I am con-
> vinced by the testimony of the Scriptures or by clear reason (for I do not
> trust either in the Pope or in councils alone, since it is well known that they
> have often erred and contradicted themselves), I am bound by the Scrip-
> tures I have quoted and my conscience is captive to the Word of God. I
> cannot and I will not retract anything since it is neither safe nor right to go
> against conscience. Here I stand, may God help me, Amen.

The hour was late, the light poor, the air foul, and the moment of
truth occurred in an atmosphere of bathos, which turned speedily to
some confusion. The Emperor was rising to leave. The crowd began

to chatter and to move to the door—clearly there was no more to be said. The irritated Chancellor wanted the last word. He shouted that Martin must put his conscience aside and that he could never prove Councils had erred. Martin shouted that he could; he and his party began to move to the door, Martin in a state of enormous relief at having given the witness clearly and without hesitation. As he turned to his friends, he raised his two arms in the gesture of a victorious medieval knight. As they left, a clique of Spanish courtiers jeered and gestured. Luther retired, exhausted, to supper and to some malmsey wine, a great crowd of supporters accompanying him noisily through the streets.

Charles's Response

Late that evening or early the following morning, young Habsburg [that is, Charles] took his pen and wrote in French his own response, a famous paragraph, redolent of 'imperial Christianity'. Von Eck and the Emperor were in close consultation about the Luther case, and there were items of similarity between Eck's speech at the hearing of Luther and the Emperor's piece—but the Emperor's words had the clear stamp of personal conviction, with an authoritarian, slightly impatient note about them. He lost no time. The statement was written out, dated in 19 April, signed and addressed to the meeting of the Diet on that day immediately following the day of Luther's hearing:

> You know that I am descended from the most Christian emperors of the German nation, from the Catholic kings of Spain, the Archdukes of Austria and the dukes of Burgundy. . . . After death they left us by natural right and heritage these holy Catholic observances, to live according to them and to die according to their example. . . . I am determined to support everything that these predecessors and I myself have kept. . . . It is certain that a single friar errs in his opinion which is against all of Christendom and according to which all of Christianity will be and will always have been in error both in the past thousand years and even more in the present . . . I am absolutely determined to stake on this cause my kingdoms and seignories, my friends, my body and blood, my life and soul. It would be a great shame to me and to you, the noble and renowned German nation . . . if heresy or decrease of the Christian religion should through our negligence dwell after us in the hearts of men. . . . I regret having delayed so long to proceed against this Luther and his false doctrine . . . he is to be taken back, keeping the tenor of his safe-conduct. . . . I am determined to proceed against him as a notorious heretic, requesting of you that you conduct yourselves in this matter as good Christians as you have promised it to me, and are held to do it. Given by my hand this nineteenth day of April 1521. Signed *Carolus.*

John Calvin: The Philosophy of Protestanism

John Calvin

John Calvin was a leading theologian of the Protestant Reformation. Though his ideas differed from Martin Luther's in degree, emphasis, and detail, the two men were fundamentally in agreement. Calvin wrote voluminously on religion. However, this excerpt, from his "A Comparison of the False and True Church," is at least as much a political as theological document. Calvin upholds certain doctrines basic to Protestantism—the importance of looking less to the authority of priests and more to the authority of Jesus Christ and the Bible, for example. At the same time he scathingly attacks Catholicism as a "mass of superstitions." The excerpt sheds light on the theology of reforms, while demonstrating the anger and hysteria with which they often viewed the established church.

1. *The basic distinction*

It has already been explained how much we ought to value the ministry of the Word and sacraments, and how far our reverence for it should go, that it may be to us a perpetual token by which to distinguish the church. That is, wherever the ministry remains whole and uncorrupted, no moral faults or diseases prevent it from bearing the name "church." Secondly, it is not so weakened by trivial errors as not to be esteemed lawful. We have, moreover, shown that the errors which

Excerpted from *Institutes of the Christian Religion* (Library of Christian Classics) by John Calvin, edited by John T. McNeill. Reprinted with permission from Westminster John Knox Press.

ought to be pardoned are those which do not harm the chief doctrine of religion, which do not destroy the articles of religion on which all believers ought to agree; and with regard to the sacraments, those which do not abolish or throw down the lawful institution of the Author. But, as soon as falsehood breaks into the citadel of religion and the sum of necessary doctrine is overturned and the use of the sacraments is destroyed, surely the death of the church follows—just as a man's life is ended when his throat is pierced or his heart mortally wounded. And that is clearly evident from Paul's words when he teaches that the church is founded upon the teaching of the apostles and prophets, with Christ himself the chief cornerstone. If the foundation of the church is the teaching of the prophets and apostles, which bids believers entrust their salvation to Christ alone—then take away that teaching, and how will the building continue to stand? Therefore, the church must tumble down when that sum of religion dies which alone can sustain it. Again, if the true church is the pillar and foundation of truth, it is certain that no church can exist where lying and falsehood have gained sway.

2. *The Roman Church and its claim*

Since conditions are such under popery, one can understand how much of the church remains there. Instead of the ministry of the Word, a perverse government compounded of lies rules there, which partly extinguishes the pure light, partly chokes it. The foulest sacrilege has been introduced in place of the Lord's Supper. The worship of God has been deformed by a diverse and unbearable mass of superstitions. Doctrine (apart from which Christianity cannot stand) has been entirely buried and driven out. Public assemblies have become schools of idolatry and ungodliness. In withdrawing from deadly participation in so many misdeeds, there is accordingly no danger that we be snatched away from the church of Christ. The communion of the church was not established on the condition that it should serve to snare us in idolatry, ungodliness, ignorance of God, and other sorts of evils, but rather to hold us in the fear of God and obedience to truth.

They indeed gloriously extol their church to us to make it seem that there is no other in the world. Thereupon, as if the matter were settled, they conclude that all who dare withdraw from the obedience with which they adorn the church are schismatics [those who separate from an existing church]; that all who dare mutter against its doctrine are heretics. But what are their reasons to prove that they have the true church? From ancient chronicles they allege what once took place in Italy, France, and Spain. They claim to take their origin from those holy men who with sound doctrine founded and raised up churches, and by their blood established the very doctrine and upbuilding of the church. Moreover, they say that the church was so consecrated both by spiritual gifts and by the blood of martyrs among them, and preserved by an unending succession of bishops, in order that it should not perish. They recall how much Irenaeus, Tertullian, Origen, Augustine, and others made of this succession.

But I shall easily enable those willing to consider these claims for a moment with me to understand how trifling and plainly ludicrous they are. Indeed, I would urge them also to give serious attention to this, if I were confident that I could benefit them by so teaching. But since their one purpose is to defend their own cause in any way they can without regard for truth, I shall say only a few things by which good men and those zealous for truth can extricate themselves from their deceits.

First, I ask them why they do not mention Africa, Egypt, and all Asia. The reason is that in all these districts this sacred succession of bishops, by virtue of which they boast that the churches have been maintained, has ceased to be. They therefore revert to the point that they have the true church because from its beginning it has not been destitute of bishops, for one has followed another in unbroken succession. But what if I confront them with Greece? I therefore ask them once more why they say that the church perished among the Greeks, among whom the succession of bishops (in their opinion the sole custodian and preserver of the church) has never been interrupted. They make the Greeks schismatics; with what right? Because in withdrawing from the apostolic see [that is, the unbroken succession of bishops], they lost their privilege. What? Would not they who fall away from Christ deserve to lose it much more? It therefore follows that this pretense of succession is vain unless their descendants conserve safe and uncorrupted the truth of Christ which they have received at their fathers' hands, and abide in it.

3. *The false church, despite its high pretensions, shows that it does not hear God's Word*

The Romanists, therefore, today make no other pretension than what the Jews once apparently claimed when they were reproved for blindness, ungodliness, and idolatry by the Lord's prophets. For like the Romanists, they boasted gloriously of Temple, ceremonies, and priestly functions, and measured the church very convincingly, as it seemed to them, by these. So in place of the church the Romanists display certain outward appearances which are often far removed from the church and without which the church can very well stand. Accordingly, we are to refute them by the very argument with which Jeremiah combatted the stupid confidence of the Jews. That is, "Let them not boast in lying words, saying, 'This is the Temple of the Lord, the Temple of the Lord, the Temple of the Lord.'" For the Lord nowhere recognizes any temple as his save where his Word is heard and scrupulously observed. So, although the glory of God sat between the cherubim in the sanctuary, and he promised his people that this would be his abiding seat; when the priests corrupt his worship with wicked superstitions, he moves elsewhere and strips the place of holiness. If that Temple, which seemed consecrated as God's everlasting abode, could be abandoned by God and become profane, there is no reason why these men should pretend to us that God is so bound to persons and places, and attached to external observances, that he has to remain among those who have only the title and appearance of the church.

4. *The church is founded upon God's Word*

In this same way the Romanists vex us today and frighten the un-educated with the name of the church, even though they are Christ's chief adversaries. Therefore, although they put forward Temple, priest-hood, and the rest of the outward shows, this empty glitter which blinds the eyes of the simple ought not to move us a whit to grant that the church exists where God's Word is not found. For this is the abiding mark with which our Lord has sealed his own: "Everyone who is of the truth hears my voice." Likewise: "I am the Good Shepherd; I know my sheep, and they know me." "My sheep hear my voice, and I know them, and they follow me." But a little before, he had said: "The sheep follow their shepherd, for they know his voice. A stranger they do not follow but flee from him, for they do not know the voice of strangers." Why do we willfully act like madmen in searching out the church when Christ has marked it with an unmistakable sign, which, wherever it is seen, cannot fail to show the church there; while where it is absent, nothing remains that can give the true meaning of the church? Paul reminds us that the church was founded not upon men's judgments, not upon priesthoods, but upon the teaching of apostles and prophets. Nay, Jerusalem is to be distinguished from Babylon, Christ's church from Satan's cabal, by the very difference with which Christ distinguishes between them. He says: "He who is of God hears the words of God. The reason why you do not hear them is that you are not of God."

To sum up, since the church is Christ's Kingdom, and he reigns by his Word alone, will it not be clear to any man that those are lying words by which the Kingdom of Christ is imagined to exist apart from his scepter (that is, his most holy Word)?

5. *Defense against the charge of schism and heresy*

Now they treat us as persons guilty of schism and heresy because we preach a doctrine unlike theirs, do not obey their laws, and hold our separate assemblies for prayers, baptism and the celebration of the Supper, and other holy activities.

This is indeed a very grave accusation but one that needs no long and labored defense. Those who, by making dissension, break the communion of the church are called heretics and schismatics. Now this communion is held together by two bonds, agreement in sound doctrine and brotherly love. Hence, between heretics and schismatics Augustine makes this sort of distinction: heretics corrupt the sincerity of the faith with false dogmas; but schismatics, while sometimes even of the same faith, break the bond of fellowship.

But it must also be noted that this conjunction of love so depends upon unity of faith that it ought to be its beginning, end, and, in fine, its sole rule. Let us therefore remember that whenever church unity is commended to us, this is required: that while our minds agree in Christ, our wills should also be joined with mutual benevolence in Christ. Paul, therefore, while urging us to it, takes it as his foundation that "there is . . . one God, one faith, and one baptism." Indeed, wherever Paul teaches us to feel the same and will the same, he immediately adds, "in Christ" or "according to Christ." He means that apart from the Lord's Word there is not an agreement of believers but a faction of wicked men.

The Counter Reformation

Vincent Cronin

The Reformation sparked a strong reaction in the Catholic Church. Once it became clear that the break was permanent and Protestantism was here to stay, Catholic religious and governmental leaders did their best to entice wayward Protestants back into the fold—and, more obviously, to ensure that those who were still Roman Catholic remained that way. The official Catholic response to Lutheranism was formulated partly at the Council of Trent, a gathering of bishops that met, on and off, between 1547 and 1563 in the German town of Trent. The council dealt mainly with religious issues, devising statements that would let people know what the church stood for and in what areas it differed from the beliefs of those who followed Luther.

However, as Vincent Cronin describes in this excerpt from his book *The Flowering of the Renaissance*, the council also addressed more secular concerns. Here, Cronin argues, the council was less successful, and the methods the church used to carry out its wishes were less than ideal. Rather than moving toward reform, church leaders lashed out at those who dared to question its dogma. Censorship of new ideas and suggestions became the order of the day. This so-called Counter-Reformation, in Cronin's view, was a disaster, though he points out ways in which the Protestants were equally intolerant, rigid, and unwilling to listen to opposition. In the short run, the Reformation led to heightened tensions, and a climate of fear on both sides in which none but the most orthodox dared to speak out.

It was right that the Church should . . . answer views she considered heretical by restating the truth as she saw it. But in the third and last period the Council [of Trent] extended its scope to spheres well beyond religion. It pronounced certain decrees which were to have the very widest bearing on the lives not only of Italians but of all Catholics, not only in the sixteenth century, but for three hundred years to come.

The man who more than any other gave the impulse in this direction was Gianpietro Carafa. Born in 1476 into one of the oldest families of Naples, as a boy he twice tried to join the Dominicans, and although prevented, he was always at heart a 'hound of the Lord'. Tall, with deep-set dark eyes, burning with energy, passionate, an incessant talker, he ate little but drank a dark red Neapolitan wine which he called his 'war-horse'. Appointed Bishop of Chieti in 1503, he took as his motto a text from St Peter: 'The time is ripe for judgment to begin, and to begin with God's own household.' His stern principles appear in his rule for the Theatines [an order of monks], of which he was co-founder: members were vowed to absolute poverty and, though they might receive alms, were forbidden to ask for them. As a Cardinal, Carafa consistently worked against . . . the Emperor, whom he believed—unjustly—really favoured the Protestants in Germany.

It is characteristic of the new mood in Italy that such a man was elected Pope in 1555. The first in a series of reforming pontiffs, he took the name Paul IV. He was already in his eightieth year, but is described by the Florentine ambassador as 'a man of iron, and the very stones over which he walks emit sparks'. He informed the Venetian ambassador that he would skin himself and then proceed to skin others, priests as well as laymen, if by so doing he could effect a single reform. The 'skinning' began with the Jews of Rome. Reversing the liberal policy of previous sixteenth-century Popes, Paul IV shut up the Jews in an overcrowded three-acre ghetto, the doors of which were locked at night; the men had to wear a yellow hat, the women a yellow star of David. They were forbidden to own property outside the ghetto or to speak to Christians except on business.

It is a notorious fact of history that when a society finds its beliefs threatened and at the same time is lacking in the vigour to defend them intellectually, it will seek to stir up another kind of vigour by singling out 'enemies'. It then galvanizes itself to frenzied activity through fear and hatred. So it is not surprising to find that Paul IV's detestable conduct towards the Jews was only one part of a larger whole. As early as 1542, while still a cardinal, he had persuaded Paul III to constitute the Inquisition as the 'Holy Office', and during his own pontificate he vastly extended its range of victims to include sodomites [that is, homosexuals] and even those who failed to observe a fast-day. He also extended the word 'heresy' to include 'simoniacal heresy' [buying church offices or benefits] . . . offenders under these headings could now be sent to the stake. One of his Cardinals, Giovanni Morone, had unwittingly distributed a book of Lutheran tinge entitled *The Benefits of Christ's Death*, whereupon the Pope had Morone flung into prison. Reginald Pole, also suspected of Lutheran sympathies, he dismissed from his post as Legate to England. 'Heresy,' he told the Venetian ambassador, 'must be rigorously crushed like the plague, because in fact it is the plague of the soul. If we burn infected houses and clothes, with the same severity we must extirpate, annihilate and drive out heresy.' As a Greek scholar praised by Erasmus, Paul should have known that heresy was originally a neutral word meaning free choice, and therefore that his metaphor was quite inapplicable. Indeed, there seems to be something deeply irrational in the Pope's fury against heretics. It may have been partly an attempt to compensate for a family scandal: his great-nephew Galeazzo Caraccioli renounced Catholicism and in 1551 deserted his wife and children to settle in Geneva, where he became one of the pillars of Calvin's Church.

Banning Books

Books, thought Paul IV, are one of the chief 'carriers' of heresy. In 1559, the last year of his pontificate, he officially sanctioned the censorship of books and issued the first *Index Purgatorius* [a list of books officially banned]. Paul's memoranda on the subject were forwarded to Trent by his successor, and the Council in its final stages debated them. The Venetian delegate Daniele Barbaro pleaded for the exemption of indiscreet works written in their youth by writers since famous, and for a graduated system of penalties, whereby excommunication would follow from violating an article of faith, but not for lesser errors. Neither plea was heeded, for the Council was now in a rabid mood. In its decree on the subject, promulgated by Pius IV in 1564, the Council kept closely to Paul IV's intentions and in so doing jettisoned two of the main principles of Christian humanism: openmindedness and free enquiry.

The Council laid down that of books published before 1515, the most dangerous should be banned altogether. These included the Koran, all the works of [twelfth-century theologian Peter] Abérlard, [fourteenth-century theologian John] Wycliffe and [fifteenth-century theologian Jan] Huss, and Dante's *De Monarchia*. Only approved Catholic versions of Scripture might be published. As regards pious books and books of religious controversy, these had to be sanctioned by the local Bishop. . . . Obscene books were forbidden, unless by pagan authors and in elegant language: these, however, must not be taught to children. . . . Books with a few reprehensible passages were permitted, provided the offending matter was corrected. Books of superstition and astrology were forbidden (this was the only category for which a precedent exists in Scripture: St Paul, in *Acts*, is said to have publicly burned such works at Ephesus). Finally, rules were laid down regarding publication. Outside Rome every book must be examined by the Bishop and a local Inquisitor before being sent to the printer, and inspectors must visit bookshops and printing houses. Every piece of writing whatsoever, if it were destined for the press, would henceforth come under the Church's scrutiny.

The situation is shot through with tragic irony. It had been the pride of Athens and of republican Rome that a society can exist and be strong without being totalitarian; that it can endure considerable divisions of sentiment within it, and that it can even protect the right of individual conscience without paralysing the communal will. Now the very men who had rediscovered this ideal and made it their own, turned against it, ran their pens through whole paragraphs praising the conciliatory [Dutch Protestant scholar] Erasmus. Just as the Academies [Italian councils] sought to purge the Italian tongue of rough, barbarous words, and artists sought to give a smooth, rounded form to their simpering saints and plump cherubs, so legislators at every level sought to bring society into what they imagined was a polished unified whole, such as Aristotle and Cicero would have approved. With the knife of classical form they gelded the classical ideal.

Most people would probably grant that we cannot have Christianity in this world without some sort of authority, and that, given the variety of human nature, such authority should be flexible, allowing as wide a play as possible to individual development and freedom. Indeed authority has no value or meaning except in a context of freedom. That had been the lesson even of the Roman Empire. Foreign cults were tolerated provided they did not pretend to be substitutes for the official cult. . . . How, then, had the idea of religious intolerance come to birth? The question is important enough to call for a full answer.

Religion and Tolerance

Early Christians had believed in tolerance. [Roman emperor] Tertullian in the third century declared 'According to both human and natural law every man is free to adore the god of his choice; an individual's religion neither harms nor profits anyone else. It is against the nature of religion to force religion . . .' But when Christianity became the only State cult, opinion hardened. Contradicting his own famous phrase, *'Credere non potest homo nisi volens*—No man can believe against his will,' St Augustine was one of the first to urge constraint of heretics, citing the Gospel text, 'Compel them to come in.' But he never demanded the death penalty. It was the canon lawyers of the twelfth century who, confusing the spiritual and temporal, asserted that political unity depends on unity of belief, and it was they who invoked Old Testament texts to bear out the principle that heresy is punishable by death: the laws of *Deuteronomy* and the terrible sentence of *Exodus:* 'He who sacrifices to the gods, let him be wiped out.' The principle was first put into effect on a large scale against the Albigensians [a group of dissident French Christians] at the beginning of the thirteenth century; in Italy a few years later. Between 1224 and 1238 the Emperor Frederick II decreed the death-penalty for obstinate heretics in the territories under his jurisdiction, including Sicily and North Italy. In 1252 Innocent IV made Frederick's decrees applicable to the Catholic world at large by inserting them in his bull *Cum adversus hereticam pravitatem*. Aquinas countenanced [approved] them: 'heretics may rightly be put to death by the secular authorities, even if they do not pervert others, for they blaspheme against God by following a false faith.'

Around 1400, when detailed study of Greece and Rome began, Italians stood amazed before the variety of ancient religious opinions and the tolerance accorded them. Socrates, it is true, had been put to death, but for political not religious motives, and by and large all men were free to follow Epicurus or Plato or the latest philosopher from the East, to profess that the soul survived or did not, to worship Astarte [a Phoenician goddess] or Poseidon. By studying such men Italians learned a new notion of human dignity and the rights of the individual conscience. Although they never abandoned their search for unity of belief, they became large-minded. They believed in tolerance for the time being, until all men should be gathered, at God's discretion, into a single fold. During the fifteenth and first half of the sixteenth centuries Italy became the most tolerant country in Europe. In fact censorship, like the death-penalty for heretics, originated not in Italy but abroad: the first known censorship office was established in Mainz [Germany] as early as 1486.

We have a glimpse of the ordinary educated Italian's attitude in this matter in a short *Life of Christ based on the Four Gospels* written around 1540 by a physician and expert on herbs, one Antonio Brasavola of Ferrara. Brasavola states his view that no punitive action at all should be taken against Protestants who do not actively proselytize [try to spread their faith]. As for proselytizers, they should be warned three times before action is taken against them, and then it should be tempered by consideration of the parable of the tares and the wheat. [Matt. 13:24–30; the moral is that God will separate the good from the bad] Brasavola's tolerance is compounded partly of a compassionate nature and partly of recognition that Catholic failings had prompted the Protestant revolt, but above all of classical humanism.

In 1530 the same Luther who two years before had declared the burning of heretics to be contrary to the will of the Spirit, demanded against the Anabaptists [radical Protestants] those terrible punishments which were promulgated against blasphemy in the Old Testament. In 1536 he said that the parable of the tares applied to preachers but not to the state, which 'is bound to repress blasphemy, false doctrine and heresy, and to inflict corporal punishment on those that support such things'. Not one of the founders of the Reformation tried to undo that rigid principle of the Middle Ages: one religion in one state. In a way they even reinforced it, since they put the power to rule religion into secular hands.

Faced with such rigorous methods on the part of their opponents, and finding precedents for them in their own earlier history, it would have required more moral courage than they were capable of for the Italians not to abandon the classical precept of tolerance. From 1542, the year when the 'Holy Office' was constituted, the Catholic reaction gathered force, and it is so unpleasant a phenomenon that more than one historian, in his love of Italy and the Italians, has claimed that the Catholic reaction was not Italian at all, but a hateful importation from medieval Spain foisted on Italy by the early Jesuits [an order of monks]. This theory fails to fit the facts and contains two profound psychological errors. No civilized people has ever allowed or could allow a dozen or so foreigners to impose against the general will a policy touching almost every aspect of their lives; secondly, because a people has behaved adventurously for several generations, that is no guarantee that it will continue to behave adventurously. . . . No, the Catholic reaction is an expression of the Italians' own character, and their responsibility alone. It is doubly tragic in that it was quite unnecessary. Lutheranism had made almost no inroads in Italy and, even before repressive measures were introduced, was on the wane. As a result the full weight of the new measures was to fall, in default of Lutherans, on Catholics of an inquiring turn of mind.

Chapter
6

Beyond Europe

Although many of the most important events of the sixteenth century exclusively involved Europe, the rest of the world was also active. Large sections of the globe beyond Europe flourished, both culturally and politically. India, for instance, became united under one leader, a Muslim king named Akbar, and began a period of growth that would last well into future centuries. China's Ming dynasty was far from new, but it was still powerful and widely admired for the artworks it produced. And few New World empires throughout history approached the splendor, power, and wealth of the Aztecs and the Inca in the early years of the sixteenth century.

These were not isolated examples. Asiatic Turkey and much of North Africa thrived during most of the century. The Iroquois Confederacy, at once a cultural leader and a dangerous imperial power, formed in North America. Likewise, Japan and Korea underwent major changes that affected life in eastern Asia for years to come.

Many of these non-European nations had a great deal in common with Europe. Europeans would have recognized the political systems, the social structure, and the cultural landscapes of any number of peoples living miles from the European border. Most countries of the world, for instance, were ruled by hereditary kings and queens, just as was most of Europe. Social systems across the globe were usually as rigid as those found in Europe: Women had few rights, class divisions were strict, and peasants had their masters and were answerable to them. And although a painting from Europe would necessarily look different in many particulars from the paintings of China or India, art filled similar functions in cultures across the world: Artistic works were things of beauty, religious symbols, signs that a society valued leisure, and much more.

That being said, there were also many significant differences. The terms *Catholic* and *Protestant* meant little or nothing beyond western Europe. The rest of the world was Muslim, Hindu, Buddhist, and a host of other religions, but Christianity was as yet far from widespread. Individual social customs varied widely from one continent to the next. So did weapons, food, military strategies, and much more.

In fact, these differences helped spark greater connections between Europe and the rest of the globe. Europeans had begun to look out from their continent and to wonder what else there was. Rather than simply dismissing the outside world as a dangerous and evil place, as their ancestors had often done, Europeans of the sixteenth century were increasingly eager to learn about it; they wanted to know more about the peoples, the places, and especially the materials various countries had to offer.

That process was already under way by the time the century began. The great motivator was trade. Spices, slaves, food, cloth, metals, weapons, and indeed almost anything that had any value quickly began to change hands. As the known world expanded, the variety of available goods and materials increased. The result was a mix of cultures that affected people in all corners of the globe—a mix that was unlike anything that had been seen before, and one that would irrevocably change the world.

The Atlantic Slave Trade

Basil Davidson

One of the most tragic events of the sixteenth century was the opening of the African slave trade. By 1510, only eighteen years after Columbus's arrival in America, black slaves were routinely imported to the West Indies. Few Europeans saw anything wrong with the practice. Racism played a major role: Most whites of the time did not see Africans as entirely human. Other Europeans pointed out that many African societies held slaves themselves, and in any case the cheap labor was essential to the growth of sugar plantations in Brazil and the Caribbean. The trade began sporadically but increased throughout the century. By 1600 the institution of slavery was entrenched.

This excerpt from Basil Davidson's *The African Slave Trade,* gives an overview of the trade as it developed throughout the 1500s. Davidson discusses the economic reasons for slavery and explains how it developed into a big business. He also touches on the lives of the slaves themselves and the desperation many of them felt at being taken from their homes and consigned to a life of hard labor and grim punishment.

The slave trade to the Americas began, at least in rudimentary form, with the earliest ships that crossed the Atlantic; but it was not at first a specially African trade. Domestic hands were needed, and these could also be found in Europe.

Yet the demand for labor in the West Indies and the mines of Central America grew with frantic speed. The conquerors began by enslaving the populations they had found, the "Indians," but death robbed them of these. Next they turned back again to Europe and attempted to fill the ranks with "indentured" or near-slave workers from home. When this would not suffice, they applied to Africa; and there at last they saw their problem solved.

By as early as 1501, only nine years after the first voyage of Columbus, the Spanish throne had issued its initial proclamation on laws for the export of slaves to America—mainly, as yet, to Hispaniola (Haiti and the Dominican Republic today). These slaves were white—whether from Spain or North Africa—more often than black; for the black slaves, it was early found, were turbulent and hard to tame. How poorly grounded in fact was the old legend of "African docility" may be seen from the events of 1503. In that year the Spanish governor of Hispaniola, Ovando, complained to the Spanish Court that fugitive Negro slaves among the Indians were teaching disobedience, and that it was impossible to re-capture them. Ovando asked for an end to the export of Negro slaves, and Queen Isabella consented. She seems to have decided to allow the export to the Indies only of white slaves, although her motive was no doubt different from Ovando's: she hoped that Christian slaves would help in the work of converting the heathen, not knowing, of course, that most of the heathen would soon be dead.

Export of Christian slaves continued, though in small numbers, until the end of the seventeenth century; generally they were women, and they were for use but not for sale. Thus in 1526 a license was granted to a certain Bartolomeo Conejo for the opening of a brothel at Puerto Rico, and to Sanchez Sarmento for the establishment of another in Santo Domingo; and white girls were needed for these. A few years later the Spanish governor of Peru secured a license through his brother Fernando Pizarro for the import from Spain of four girls who, the license stipulated, "must be born in Castile and Christians baptized before the age of ten"—not, that is to say, converted Moorish or Negro women. This early white-slave traffic dwindled after the middle of the sixteenth century; yet as late as 1692 there is record of a permit issued for the export of four girls to Veracruz in Mexico.

The African Connection

The trade in Negro captives became important as early as 1510. Before that, there had been sporadic shipments whenever the need for labor was especially acute. Ovando, in Hispaniola, had soon been forced to change his mind about suppression of the Negro trade; already in 1505, thirteen years after Columbus had made his crossing, the Spanish archives mention a caravel [small ship] sailing from Seville with seventeen Negro slaves and some mining equipment. Soon Ovando was asking for many more Negro workers. And in

1510 there came the beginning of the African slave trade in its massive and special form: royal orders were given for the transport first of fifty and then of two hundred slaves for sale in the Indies. Throughout the years that followed it was to be the searing brand of this trade that it would consider its victims, not as servants or domestic slaves who deserved respect in spite of their servile condition, but as chattel slaves, commodities that could and should be sold at whim or will.

From its earliest growth this trade bore the marks of an exceptional cruelty and waste. Yet these were not peculiar to the Negro trade. European slaves and near-slaves were treated little or no better. Irish and other prisoners transported to the West Indies in Cromwellian and later times—all those, in the slang of the period, who were "barbadoe'd"—suffering appalling conditions. A petition to Parliament in 1659 described how seventy-two unfortunates from England had been locked up below deck during the whole passage of five and a half weeks, "amongst horses, that their souls through heat and steam under the tropic, fainted in them."

Transport conditions for slaves from Africa were generally worse: witness a well-known letter of the Spanish king to a certain Sampier, in Hispaniola, in the year 1511, in which the king complains that "I cannot understand why so many Negroes die." Yet the intolerable and special aspect of Negro slavery was its very permanence; even though manumission [freeing] of slaves was always less resisted in the Catholic Indies and South America than in the Protestant states of North America, Negroes were everywhere intended to occupy the lowest ranks of society and to stay there.

This the Negro slaves resisted. They escaped when they could. They rose in bloody rebellion. They fought for their lives. The first notable Negro slave revolt in Hispaniola broke out as early as 1522. Five years later there was another in Puerto Rico. A third at Santa Marta in 1529. A fourth in Panama in 1531. By 1532 the Spanish had established a special police for chasing fugitive slaves.

Becoming an Institution

Yet nothing could stop the trade. There was too much money in it for the courts of Europe. The Spanish king was probably in receipt of cash from slaving taxes even before 1510, the date of the first big "license" for Negro slaves. In 1513 a royal tax was promulgated which made every license cost two ducats, a license being understood as the permit for shipping a single slave; on top of this there was an export tax. These taxes immediately provoked smuggling; and it appears that the earliest African slaves shipped from Portugal to the Indies were sent out clandestinely by tax evaders.

In 1515 there came the first Spanish shipment of slave-grown

West Indian sugar and in 1518, as though by the sheer logic of the thing, the first cargo of African slaves directly from Africa to the West Indies. Royal authority was given for transporting four thousand black slaves. These were to be obtained directly from the Guinea Coast to obviate any danger that North African captivity might have tainted them with Muslim loyalties; but it is quite clear, of course, that so large a number could not possibly have been gotten from anywhere except the Guinea Coast. The "Black Mother" [that is, Africa] had already shown how fertile she could be, and how blind to the consequences.

After 1518 the trade became increasingly an institution, a part of the Spanish economy, an absolutely essential aspect of the whole Spanish-American adventure. The kings of Spain lived off the trade. Even the licenses they authorized and sold became, with time, salable property in themselves—shares in the great process of colonial pilfering and pillage that were exchanged in the money markets of Spain just as government stock is bought and sold today.

As with other economic enterprises, the right to collect and deal in slaves remained a royal property. The kings themselves took no direct part in the business, but farmed it out to wealthy merchants and mariners. This method of farming out the right to buy slaves in Africa and sell them in the Americas was that of the assiento, in essence a royal permit carrying strict conditions of time and price. So far as slaving was concerned, the assiento system applied only to Guinea slaves, since Christianity forbade the sale (though not the use) of Christian slaves, and discouraged the export of North African slaves because they were Muslims and might make anti-Christian propaganda.

High Profit

There were assientos for every branch of business that royalty could lay its hands on, but the slaving assiento topped them all. The system really began to show its value in 1592. Before that, the king had granted licenses for small numbers of captives and on few occasions. But in 1592, trying to meet a demand for slaves that was rendered practically inexhaustible by the holocausts of those who died, the court spewed up a monster of an assiento. No longer was it a question of delivering a few hundred African captives to the Americas; the new license was for the transport of 38,250 slaves. Gomes Reynal, who bought this license, was to deliver his captives over a period of nine years at the rate of 4,250 a year; of these, it was stipulated, at least 3,500 a year must be landed alive. Reynal had to pay nearly a million ducats for this concession and agreed to forfeit ten ducats for every slave short of 3,500 a year. The captives were to be fresh from the Guinea Coast and were to include "no mulattoes, nor mestizos, nor Turks, nor Moors." (They would have included many Negro Muslims, of course, but nobody in Spain would have known this, and perhaps nobody would much have cared.)

The profits of slaving came from many regions. A report of 1520 shows that Portuguese planters were already producing sugar by slave labor in the South Atlantic island of São Tomé, off the coast of Angola. Yet the main profits were always in the Americas. By 1540 the annual rate of direct shipment from Africa to the other side of the Atlantic was already running at several thousand captives, although fewer than fifty years had passed since the discovery of America.

Other maritime nations watched with gathering interest. Though formally debarred from any part in this promising enterprise, English and French interlopers soon took a hand. Nothing more clearly shows how things were moving than the contrast between most of the early English and French voyages to the Guinea Coast, whose object was gold and pepper and ivory, and the slaving ventures of John Hawkins at about the same time. . . .

John Hawkins began his oversea trading with the Canaries [the Canary Islands]. "There," says the record, "by his good and upright dealing being growen in love and favour with the people, be informed himselfe amongst them by diligent inquisition, of the state of the West India [Indies]. . . . And being amongst other particulars assured, that Negroes were very good merchandise in Hispaniola, and that store of Negroes might easily bee bad upon the coast of Guinea, resolved with himselfe to make triall thereof. . . ."

England Joins In

Merchants in London liked the scheme and backed Hawkins with "three good ships," the *Salomon*, the *Swallow*, and the *Jonas*. With crews totaling a hundred, Hawkins "put off and departed from the coast of England in the moneth of October 1562 and . . . passed to the coast of Guinea . . . where he stayed some time and got into his possession, partly by the sword and partly by other meanes, to the number of three hundred Negroes at the least. . . ." This is all that the English documents have to say; but the Portuguese, who suffered from Hawkins's largehanded piracy, add something to the tale. Their records complain that Hawkins seized a Portuguese slaver with 200 Negroes aboard, three other vessels with 70 apiece, and a fifth with 500. But these numbers seem exaggerated, for Hawkins's ships were small.

"With this praye," [prey] whatever its true dimensions, Hawkins "sayled over the ocean sea unto the iland of Hispaniola . . . and there hee had reasonable utterance of his English commodities, as also of some part of his Negroes. . . ." Thence he went on from port to port, "standing alwaies upon his guard," and finally disposed of all his cargoes. For these he received "such quantities of merchandise, that hee did not onely lade his owne three shippes with hides, ginger, sugars, and some quantities of pearles, but he fraighted also two other hulkes with hides and the like commodities, which hee sent into Spain." (Why he should have sent goods to Spain remains obscure; they were seized on arrival, along with the crews of the ships that carried them, and Hawkins estimated his loss at £20,000 in the money of the time.)

Triangular Trade

Thus began the "Great Circuit" trade that was to dominate much of the commerce of the western world for many years thereafter. This circuit consisted in the export of cheap manufactured goods from Europe to Africa; the purchase or seizure of slaves on the Guinea Coast and their transportation across the Atlantic; the exchange of these slaves for minerals and foodstuffs in the West Indies and Americas; and, lastly, the sale of these raw materials and foods in Europe.

By this triangular system three separate profits were taken, all high and all in Europe: the first profit was that of selling consumer goods to the slavers; the second derived from selling slaves to the planters and mine-owners of the Americas; while the third (and biggest) was realized on the sale of American and West Indian cargoes in Europe. It was largely on the steady and often stupendous profits of this circuitous enterprise that France and England would ground their commercial supremacy.

Hawkins sailed again in 1564 and a third time in 1567; on both occasions he went mainly for slaves, and with like success. He fi-

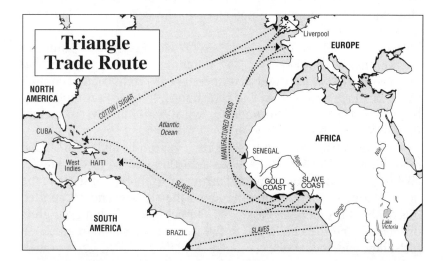

nanced at least one other slaving voyage on which he did not sail himself, that of Lovell in 1566. The king of Spain was furious but as yet unprepared to act—not for another twenty years would the Armada sail for England. Meanwhile, Queen Elizabeth returned soft, misleading answers to the protests of Guzman de Silva, Philip's ambassador at the Court of St. James; and so did Cecil, her principal minister.

"I have spoken to the queen about the six ships that are being fitted out for Hawkins," de Silva wrote to his master on the eve of the third voyage. "She says she has had the merchants"—the London backers of the venture—"into her presence and made them swear that they are not going to any place prohibited by your Majesty. . . . Cecil also says they are not going to your Majesty's dominions but still I am doubtful, because what they seek in Guinea most are slaves to take to the West Indies. I will use all efforts to prevent their going, but the greed of these people is great and they are not only merchants who have shares in these adventures but secretly many of the queen's Council. . . ." Philip might grieve for his slaving taxes. So much the worse for him. The gentlemen of England wanted their share as well.

Ruthless Competition

Yet the slave trade of the sixteenth century, despite these occasional raids from the north, was essentially a Spanish-Portuguese monopoly. The French and English, early on the Guinea Coast in the wake of the Portuguese and Spanish, sometimes worked together against a common enemy, and sometimes fell out and fought. Their interest in any case was not in slaving. Towerson, on his second voyage, that of 1566–1567, both worked with the French and came to blows with them; his dramatic story illustrates the ruthless competition that would accompany the Guinea trade to the very threshold of the twentieth century.

Returning westward, Towerson says, "we had sight of a shippe in the weather of us, which was a Frenchman of ninety tunne who came with us as stoutly and as desperately as might be, and coming neere us, perceived that we had bene upon a long voyage, and judging us to be weake, as indeed we were, came neerer to us and thought to have layed us aboard.

"And there stept up some of his men in armour and commanded us to strike saile; whereupon we sent them some of our stuffe, crosse-barres and chainshot and arrowes, so thick that it made the upper worke of their shippe flie about their eares, and we spoiled him with all his men, and toare his shippe miserably with our great ordinance, and then he began to fall asterne of us, and to packe on his sailes, and get away.

"And we, seeing that, gave him four or five good pieces more for his farewell; and thus we were rid of this Frenchman, who did us no harme at all. We had aboord us a Frenchman, a trumpetter, who, being sicke and lying in his bed, tooke his trumpet notwithstanding, and sounded till he could sound no more, and so died. . . ."

Out of these grim rivalries, in small ships and with small crews, attacked by fevers and the furies of the sea, wrecked and ruined by one another in sudden battles from the coast of Senegal to the Bight of Benin and far beyond, there nonetheless emerged a pattern of commercial exchange and, gradually, a recognized order of behavior.

North African Culture

E.W. Bovill

Before the sixteenth century Europeans and Africans had relatively little contact. Increased European exploration began to change that situation during the 1500s; unfortunately, Europeans of the period typically
dismissed Africans and their culture as backward, an idea that led to the
opening of the slave trade. However, some Africans—notably those
from the northern part of the continent, near the Mediterranean Sea—
were treated differently.

    The following excerpt describes the adventures of Leo Africanus, a young
African widely admired in Europe for his knowledge and achievements.
While focusing on Leo, the article also explains that ideas and knowledge
were sometimes traded on equal footing between Europe and Africa, even
as European sea captains were transporting African slaves to the New World.
Above all, the article provides insight into the life of North Africans during
this time, often in Leo's own words. The excerpt is from E.W. Bovill's *The
Golden Trade of the Moors*, a British book dating from the 1950s. In accordance with the style of this time, Bovill sometimes uses the word "Moor"
where we would be inclined to use "Muslim" today.

In 1518 or 1520 an Arab galley, homeward bound from Constantinople, was captured by Christian corsairs [pirates] off Jerba, the Island of the Lotus Eaters, just as it was approaching the Tunisian shore.
Among those on board was an unusually intelligent Moor who, although still in his twenties, had travelled widely in countries then un-

known to Europe. So, instead of selling the young man into slavery, which was then the common fate of captives, the corsairs carried him to Rome and presented him to Pope Leo X, hoping thereby to turn him to better account than they would be able to do in the great slave markets of [the Italian cities] Pisa and Genoa.

Leo X was a Medici, a son of Lorenzo the Magnificent. He won the praise of his contemporaries for his munificence to men of letters, and the respect of posterity for his patronage of the arts, if for nothing else. All with claims to intellectual distinction were warmly welcomed to his court. Nevertheless, nothing could have seemed less probable than that a young Moor taken from a galley should become an honoured member of the papal court, and his 'discovery' the Pope's chief contribution to letters and science. The young man's name was El-Hassan ibn Wezaz, but he probably preferred to be called El-Fasi, the man of Fez, the great seat of learning to which he owed his education. As he spoke Spanish it was not difficult for the Pope to discover his literary attainments and, much more important, his astonishing knowledge of remote and inaccessible African kingdoms only vaguely known to Europe through the writings of [Arab Authors] El-Bekri and Edrisi. The Pope immediately freed the young man, granted him a pension and secured his conversion to Christianity. At his baptism he gave him his own names, Giovanni Leone, from which he became commonly known as Leo Africanus.

When he was captured, Leo Africanus had with him a rough draft in Arabic of the work which made him famous, *The History and Description of Africa and the Notable Things therein contained.* He completed this work in the Italian language in 1526, three years after his patron's death. In 1550 the manuscript fell into the hands of Ramusio who published it in his collection of *Voyages and Travels.* It was translated into English by John Pory, a scholarly friend of Richard Hakluyt, and was published in London in 1600.

Apart from his African travels and the circumstances of his arrival in Rome, we know little of the life of Leo. Here and there in his published work we find a clue to his early history and his travels outside Africa, but these are not always very helpful. 'For mine own part,' he tells us, 'when I hear the Africans evil spoken of, I will affirm myself to be one of Granada, and when I perceive the nation of Granada to be discommended, then will I profess myself to be an African.' Such candour is certainly engaging, but it is sadly provoking to the student wanting to know where he was born.

It has, however, now been established beyond reasonable doubt that Leo was born in Granada in 1493 or 1494 of well-to-do Moorish parents. . . . The infant and his parents [soon] joined the stream of cultured emigrants who were continually drifting from Granada to [the Moroccan city] Fez and other African centres of Muslim culture. Arrived in Fez, they found themselves part of a large community of recent exiles from Spain who were settling in large numbers in the city and its neighbourhood.

Morocco was in a state of political disintegration. The Portuguese were in occupation of much of the coast and endeavouring to extend their influence inland. The south was in the hands of the Sa'adian Shereefs, under whose dominion Fez was shortly to fall. At the end of the fifteenth century, however, Fez was still enjoying great commercial prosperity and was at the peak of its fame as a seat of learning, its mosques and libraries being the resort of students from many parts of the Muslim world. It was therefore the most natural haven for the exiles from Granada.

Leo's father, a man of wealth and consequence, was accorded in Fez the same honour that he had enjoyed in Granada, together with unusual facilities for educating his son under some of the most distinguished scholars of the Muslim world. Of these opportunities the child took full advantage, soon proving himself to be exceptionally intelligent. He started earning his own living at a very early age as a notary in the Moristane, the Hospital for Aliens in Fez. But it was not long before he began the wanderings which brought him fame. As he travelled from town to town in the Maghreb, his knowledge of the law brought him plenty of work. Sometimes he acted as a *qadi* or judge, but more usually as a clerk or notary to merchants and government officials. Occasionally he traded on his own account. At times he served the sultan on diplomatic missions; at others he lived by hawking verses of his own composition. This varied life brought him adventures and took him far afield. His many coastal voyages and inland journeys in the company of merchants familiarized him with the length and breadth of Barbary and gave him an intimate knowledge of its trade. . . .

Trade

The principal goods exported to the Western Sudan were European trade goods (especially cloth), sugar from Sus in southern Morocco, wearing apparel, brass vessels, horses, and books. The principal commodities for which these goods were exchanged were gold, slaves, and civet [a type of perfume]: Leo mentions a present given by the sultan of Fez which consisted almost entirely of produce of the Sudan:

> Fifty men slaves and fifty women slaves brought out of the land of the Negroes, ten eunuchs, twelve camels, one giraffe, sixteen civet-cats, one pound of civet, a pound of amber (ambergris), and almost six hundred skins of a certain beast called by them elamt (addax gazelle) whereof they make their shields, every skin being worth at Fez eight ducats;[1] twenty of the men slaves cost twenty ducats apiece, and so did fifteen of the women

1. The Tuareg make their shields of addax skins. The horns are said to have been used by the Greeks to make their lyres.

slaves; every eunuch was valued at forty, every camel at fifty, and every civet-cat at two hundred ducats; and a pound of civet and amber is sold at Fez for three score ducats.

Happily for posterity, Leo was to see for himself the countries from which the slaves, the eunuchs, the gold, and the civet all came.

Travel

The most important event in Leo's life in the eyes of his contemporaries, though probably not in his own, was his journey to the Western Sudan, for it enabled him to give to Europe the first detailed account of the interior of Africa, of which men's conception was so blurred that they could not distinguish fact from legend. Many competent Muslim observers had previously visited the country and some had recorded what they had seen, but never in sufficient detail to satisfy the curious. This was because of the traditional contempt of the Muslim for the negro to which both [Moslem travelers] Ibn Haukal and Ibn Battuta had given expression. Leo was a shade less supercilious than either of them, and quicker to overcome his prejudice. . . .

The occasion of this important journey was a mission, of which Leo was a member and his uncle the leader, sent to Songhai by the Shereef of Fez, Mulai Muhammed el-Kaim, the founder of the Sa'adian dynasty. The date appears to have been about 1510, when Leo was still under twenty years of age.

There is much doubt about the routes the mission followed, because Leo, who never forgot that he was writing a description of Africa and not a personal narrative, tells us little of his own experiences. He appears, however, to have had personal knowledge of two of the trans-Saharan caravan routes, the Sijilmasa–Taghaza road to Timbuktu, which the mission naturally followed on its outward journey, and the Agades–Tuat–Tlemcen road, to which he refers so often that it is probably the route by which he himself returned.[2] . . .

Effects on Europe

In the first half of the sixteenth century men's minds were too occupied with stirring events much farther afield to be greatly concerned with Africa. The old century had closed with the discoveries of a new world by Columbus, and of a sea route to India and the Far East by Vasco da Gama. The former suggested possibilities so vast that they could not be assessed; the latter presented the certainty of immense gain. In the space of five years the horizon of civilized man

2. When a recently discovered Italian MS. of Leo's *Description of Africa*, dated about 1526, is published we may find ourselves better informed about him and his travels. The new MS. is said to show that he twice visited the Sudan, in 1509 and 1513, and that he returned from his second journey by way of Bornu and the Nile valley. (R. Mauny, *Hespéris,* XLI, 1954, pp. 379–94.)

had been broadened to an extent which he found impossible to comprehend. But that was not all. The new century had opened with the discovery of Brazil, the first sighting of the Pacific, the founding of a Portuguese empire in India, and the first circumnavigation of the globe.

All this had happened between Leo's birth and his writing about his travels in Africa which, compared with the great geographical events through which he had lived, must have seemed to him and to others of comparatively small account. It is, therefore, not altogether surprising that his story remained almost, if not quite, unknown until its publication by Ramusio in the middle of the century. Before the end of the century Ramusio's *Voyages and Travels* had run through several editions, and Leo had become well known.

Meanwhile, the cartographers had been redrawing the map of Africa in the light of Leo's glowing narrative, their dependence on which remained almost complete until the coming of Mungo Park and the other great African explorers of more than two centuries later. Unfortunately, the work on which the cartographers drew so heavily was marred by a blunder as great as it was inexcusable, a blunder of almost incredible magnitude.

[Roman historian] Herodotus had said that a great river flowing from west to east divided Africa as the Danube divided Europe. This was believed to be the Niger of Pliny and Ptolemy. In the tenth century Ibn Haukal, the first of the Arab geographers to visit the Sudan, confirmed Herodotus's statement that the Niger flowed to the east. Two centuries later, however, the great Edrisi, who never set eyes on the Niger and seems to have confused it with the Senegal, said that it flowed to the west. In the fourteenth century Ibn Battuta was able to declare that he had seen the Niger flowing to the east. But so greatly was Edrisi respected that many preferred what he related at second hand to what lesser men reported from personal experience. Consequently there was much doubt in men's minds about who was right. To Leo was given the opportunity of resolving that doubt, and with it one of the oldest mysteries of the geographical world. Alas, he more than failed. 'The Niger', he wrote, 'flows westward into the ocean . . . we navigated it with the current from Timbuktu to Jenne and Mali.'

There is no satisfactory explanation of how Leo came to give the wrong direction to a river which he himself had navigated for five hundred miles or more. It may be that he had been persuaded that he was wrong when he was right by the 'cosmographers' of Rome, who, he tells us, believed the Niger to be a branch of the Nile, and who, we may presume, were not going to allow their faith in Edrisi to be shaken by a young Moorish captive. Whatever the reason for the extraordinary blunder, the cartographers continued to give the

Niger a westerly course until Leo was proved wrong on that great day at Segu in 1796 when Mungo Park beheld it flowing to the east.

New Information

Leo's *History and Description of Africa* was not a gazetteer, but, as the title says, a description of African countries through most of which the author had travelled. He was writing for readers seeking information about Africa, not for makers of maps. Inevitably, when the latter started work on the text they did not always find its interpretation for their purpose very easy. Sometimes passages were read in different ways by different cartographers. Lack of clarity in the text contributed to the mistakes, but the blame for an important one rests wholly with the map-makers.

Leo said that in the Hausa kingdom of Gobir there was 'abundance of rice. . . . At the inundation of the Niger all the fields of this region are overflowed, and then the inhabitants cast their seed into the water only.' To begin with, the cartographers quite reasonably took this to mean that in Gobir there was a vast marsh, which in 1554 Tramezino, for example, showed on his map as *Nigritis Palus*. They then, it seems, began to suspect that this passage in Leo referred to the great lake which in the previous century Diego Gomez, one of Prince Henry's captains, had reported to be somewhere in the interior of West Africa, his informant probably having in mind the great lakes, Debo and Fagbine, above Timbuktu. Starting with Giacomo di Gastaldi's map of 1564 a big lake, which he called *Lago de Guber*, begins to appear on the maps and there it remained until nearly the end of the eighteenth century.[3]

Nothing could be less fair to Leo than to judge him by what the map-makers made of his text. His *History and Description of Africa* was a mine of new and long-sought information, and for two and a half centuries as indispensable to all who were concerned with Africa as it is today in the narrower field of historical study. If we close a kindly eye to his amazing blunder about the course of the Niger, no comment on his work is more apt than his own condescending reference to Pliny: 'He erred a little in some matters concerning Africa: howbeit a little blemish ought not quite to disgrace all the beauty of a fair and amiable body.'

---

3. The lake was also sometimes called *Sigismes* and sometimes *Guarde*, but why has never been explained in either case. I. Blaeu in 1659 and J. Senex in about 1700 named one half of the lake *Sigismes* and the other *Guarde*. N. de Fer in 1698 and H. Moll in about 1710, having a more critical sense than their predecessors, thought it better to stick more closely to Leo. The one gave *Marais de Guarde*, and the other *Bogs and Morasses de Garde*. D'Anville and Robert in their map of 1770 showed the lake but gave it no name.

Suleyman the Magnificent

Jason Goodwin

The great rulers of the sixteenth century include Henry VIII and Elizabeth I, figures familiar to Americans today. The list also includes monarchs outside Western Europe—less well remembered, perhaps, but no less effective in their day. Among the greatest of these was the Ottoman Empire's Suleyman the Magnificent. Under Suleyman, the Ottomans reached perhaps their greatest influence. This passage describes Suleyman and gives a brief outline of his life, as well as touching on his significance to Turkey and the wider world. It is taken from Jason Goodwin's *Lords of the Horizons*, a recent history of the Ottoman Empire.

On 18 July 1520, [Suleyman's father] Sultan Selim left Constantinople to join his army assembling near Edirne, a hundred miles to the west [and in Europe]. All Selim's campaigns to date had been into Persia, and Arabia, and Egypt; but for the first time in his eight-year reign the horsetails stood at the Edirne Gate; old symbols of Turkish authority, they announced to the world, and the mustering troops, that the pride of Ottoman arms was moving west, towards Europe. Only halfway to Edirne, on 21 September, Selim died, a chronicler wrote, 'of an infected boil, and thereby Hungary was spared'.

The traditions which governed Ottoman succession moved smoothly into operation. Selim's Grand Vizier kept the news of his master's death secret in the camp, while the fastest messenger service in the world carried word to Selim's only son, Suleyman, currently acting as military governor of Manisa across the Dardanelles. Because

Suleyman had no brothers, on this occasion the empire would escape the conflict which usually marred Ottoman succession by the implementation of the law of fratricide.

Suleyman, then twenty-six years old, reached Constantinople on Sunday 30 September, within eight days of his father's death. There he was escorted to the mosque and tomb at Eyup, on the upper reaches of the Golden Horn, outside the city walls. To Ottoman believers, this was the third holiest site in the world, after Mecca and Jerusalem, the spot where Eyup Ensari, the Prophet's friend and standard bearer, had been buried during the first Arab siege of Constantinople, which took place between AD 674 and 678. The siege had failed, the burial site was lost, and Constantinople remained in Christian hands for another eight centuries; but during the successful Ottoman siege of the city in 1453 Eyup's tomb was miraculously rediscovered, and Mehmet the Conqueror had a *kulliye*, or mosque complex, erected there. After his own death, it became the custom for all succeeding sultans to be girded with the sword of their illustrious ancestor, Osman Gazi, at Eyup's tomb, and then to visit the tomb of the Conqueror himself, in the great kulliye he had built in the middle of Constantinople, over the old Byzantine Church of the Holy Apostles.

At dawn the following day—Monday 1 October 1520—he received the homage of the high officials at the gate of the third court, in the Topkapi Palace. In the afternoon he met his father's funeral procession at the Edirne Gate, and escorted the body to its burial place: his first official decree was to order the erection of a kulliye in Selim's honour. Two days later he distributed the now customary donative, or bakshish [tip], to the Janissary Corps [elite Turkish fighters]: a larger sum, it was noted, than his father had thought necessary to give them eight years before. He also gave money to the other household troops, and various palace functionaries. To demonstrate his own regard for mercy and justice he decreed that some Cairene [from Cairo in Egypt] intellectuals Selim had brought to Constantinople by force should be allowed home; a boycott of Iranian goods was lifted, with compensation; and a few persistent evildoers were executed.

'He is tall, but wiry, and of a delicate complexion. His neck is a little too long, his face thin, and his nose aquiline . . . a pleasant mien, though his skin tends to pallor. He is said to be a wise lord, fond of study, and all men hope for good from his rule.' So [Italian writer] Bernardo Contarini summed up the new Sultan at his accession. Selim's conquests had given Europe a breathing space of some twenty years. 'A gentle lamb had succeeded a fierce lion,' Jovius wrote, while Pope Leo X had prayers sung all over Rome.

While the earliest Ottoman sultans had been dubbed 'Gran Turco' by the Italian city-states, later, as their prestige and power grew, they were referred to as 'Gran Signor'. For Suleyman the West reserved its highest commendation. Suleyman the Magnificent signed himself ruler of thirty-seven kingdoms, lord of

> the realms of the Romans, and the Persians and the Arabs, hero of all that is, pride of the arena of earth and time! Of the Mediterranean and the Black Sea;
>
> Of the glorified Kaaba [building in Mecca of religious importance to Moslems] and the illumined Medina [city of Islamic religious significance], the noble Jerusalem and the throne of Egypt, that rarity of the age;
>
> Of the province of Yemen, and Aden and Sana, and of Baghdad the abode of rectitude, and Basra and al-Hasa and the Cities of Nushirivan;
>
> Of the lands of Algiers and Azerbaijan, the steppes of the Kipchak and the land of Tartars;
>
> Of Kurdistan and Luristan, and of the countries of Rumelia and Anatolia and Karaman and Wallachia and Moldavia and Hungary all together, and of many more worthy kingdoms and countries:
>
> Sultan and Padishah [sovereign].

Suleyman was sometimes known as Suleyman II, in coy deference to his biblical namesake. He was to be styled 'the Perfecter of the Perfect Number', for his whole existence was hedged about with the number of good fortune, ten—the number of the Commandments, the number of Muhammad's disciples, of the parts and variants of the Koran, of the toes, the fingers, and the astronomical heavens of Islam. Sultan Suleyman was the tenth ruler of his house, born at the beginning of the tenth century, the year 900 of the Hegira [the flight of the prophet Muhammad from Mecca in the seventh century A.D.], AD 1493.

Successive Venetian ambassadors at his court found themselves dealing with a sovereign who could put 100,000 men into the field at no visible cost, whose borders ran for 8,000 miles, who was so exalted that he only gave audience in profile, and then did not deign to speak. In their reports they were puzzled as how best to describe his powers, whether geographically, classically, politically, numerically or financially—so that one pictured his empire in near fantastical terms, saying its borders ran with Spain, Persia and the empire of Prester John [a mythical Christian kink thought to rule parts of Asia or Africa].

"He Roars Like a Lion"

Under no other sultan would the Ottoman Empire be so universally admired or feared. Suleyman's corsairs [pirates] plundered the ports of Spain. Indian rajahs begged his aid. So did the King of France, who once had letters smuggled to the Sultan from an Italian prison cell, hidden in the heel of his envoy's shoe. The Iranians burnt their country on his account. The Hungarians lost their nobility at a stroke. 'He roars like a lion along our frontier,' wrote one foreign ambassador, and even

the Habsburgs [emperors of Spain and Central Europe] gave him tribute. His reputation was so splendid and magnanimous that twenty
years after his death the English begged his successors for a fleet to
help them tackle the Spanish Armada. Thirty years later a Neapolitan
traveller went to admire his sepulchre in Constantinople, 'for surely
though he was a Turk, the least I could do was to look at his coffin
with feeling, for the valorous deeds he accomplished when alive'.
When he went to war—thirteen times on major campaigns, endlessly
on stiletto raids—foreign descriptions of the cavalcade ran to chapters.
The flight of the Knights of Rhodes to Malta in 1526 made the eastern Mediterranean Ottoman; and the coast of North Africa right up to
Algiers was ruled by the Barbary corsairs in the Sultan's name. When
Suleyman went to sleep, four pages watched the candles for him.
When he rode through the city or into battle or out hunting, they went
with him, as one of the overwhelmed Venetian ambassadors reported,
'one to carry his arms, another his rain clothes, the third a pitcher full
of an iced drink, and the fourth something else'.

Better known in Turkish history as Suleyman Kanuni, 'the Law-
giver', Suleyman oversaw the most detailed codification of sultanic
and Koranic law that had ever been known in an Islamic state, surpassed only by the work of [Byzantine emperor] Justinian, in the same
city of Constantinople, almost a thousand years before. The law fixed
the duties and rights of all the Sultan's subjects, in accordance with Islamic precepts, established the relationship between non-Muslims and
Muslims, and laid out the codes by which society was to understand
and comport itself, down to the clothes which different people were to
wear.

He ruled so long that he became something of an Ottoman Queen
Victoria, the very embodiment of his state. Fantastically impassive,
for example, was his reaction to news of a great naval victory over the
Holy Roman Emperor, King of Bohemia and the Low Countries and
Emperor Elect of all the Germanies, Charles V, whom Suleyman referred to as 'the King of Spain'. When the Ottoman admiral sailed his
fleet up the Horn, a little pinnace [small ship] ran ahead trailing the
high standard of Spain in the water from her stern. The admiral's flagship was laden with high-born Christians, including a Spanish
commander-in-chief. A long line of captured vessels, dismasted and
rudderless, bobbed along behind like ducks, while, forty-seven other
ships of the Christian fleet—ships of Naples, Florence, Genoa, Sicily
and Malta (all fitted up by the Pope himself)—were now sunk in the
shallows off the Tunisian coast. The Spanish were chastened by their
attempt on North Africa. Their greatest admiral, Andrea Doria, was
lucky to escape to Italy with his life. Suleyman went down to a kiosk
on the water's edge to give his Kapudan Pasha [admiral] the honour
of his attendance; but not for a second did his expression change, 'the

same severity and gravity as if the victory had nothing concerned him, so capable was the heart of that old sire of any fortune, were it never so great'. . . .

Suleyman's high aspirations warred with his suspicious, gloomy, passionate nature. His long reign is flawed by tragedy more subtle than the hubris which had overcome his ancestor Bayezit the Thunderbolt [who had picked a fight with the Central Asian Warrior Tamerlane, and had lost miserably]; more consequential than the gilded misery reserved for later sultans. The higher men rose in the empire, the closer they got to the bowstring; and the reign of Suleyman seems in retrospect coiled round with a silken garotte.

On 31 August 1526—that buoyant year for Ottoman arms, when the Sultan carried the day at Mohacs [in Hungary], annihilating Hungarian opposition—he penned this most depressing diary entry: 'Rain falls in torrents. 2,000 prisoners executed.' In his lifetime he pushed the borders of the empire further than ever before, but he may have realised, before he died, that he had found their limits, too. He was a poet and a fighter, a patron of the faith, and of the arts and sciences, a monarch who understood his duty, but he was more ruthless within his own borders than in enemy territory. He had his best friend murdered. On the death of one of his children he threw his turban on the ground, ripped off his jewels, stripped all the decorations from the walls of the palace and turned the carpets upside down, before he followed the coffin to its grave in a chariot drawn by weeping horses. Yet his son Mustafa was strangled by mutes whiles Suleyman watched from behind a screen: he had been given to believe that Mustafa was plotting a coup. Another son, Bayezit, saw the writing on the wall; he mounted the coup, was defeated, and fled to Persia from where, after negotiation, the Shah delivered him to Suleyman's executioner. Suleyman left the empire to Selim, a drunkard, but [his wife] Roxelana's child. In his last years, his instinctive morbidity crowded out the high hopes and generosity of his youth—he dressed plainly, dined off earthenware platters, and fostered the triumph of orthodox Islam, making the wisest mullah, the Grand Mufti of Constantinople, into a sort of Muslim Patriarch, in command of a new Islamic hierarchy. But when the Austrian ambassador took leave of Suleyman in his old age, it was scarcely a living being he described, but a sort of metaphor of empire, rotting and majestic, fat, made up, and suffering from an ulcerous leg.

Japan and the West

John Whitney Hall

Until the sixteenth century, Japan and Europe had never come in contact with each other. They had developed societies similar in some ways and strikingly different in others. Then relationship between Japan and the West has often been stormy, even violent, since the first contact between Japanese and Portuguese traders in 1543. At other points it has been marked by mutual admiration and a desire to learn from each other. This excerpt, from John Whitney Hall's *Japan: From Prehistory to Modern Times*, details the first century of Japanese-European relations—connections paralleled in future centuries.

The period of Japanese history from the 1540s to the 1640s has been called the Christian century. The designation is something of a Western conceit. To be sure, Christianity was introduced into Japan at this time and may by the second decade of the seventeenth century have touched close to two percent of the country's population. But the capacity of Westerners to interfere in the national affairs of Japan was slight, and their cultural impact was even less pronounced. The century of contact with Europeans was a significant chapter in Japanese history, but chiefly in terms of the internal dynamics of Japan's own gigantic struggles which led to the reunification of the country and to the reshaping of its basic social and economic institutions.

Yet in terms of world history, the sixteenth and seventeenth centuries in East Asia hold a special interest, for they witnessed the first extensive contact between Europeans and the Chinese and Japanese, and resulted in an initial rebuff of the Westerners by the two prime powers of East Asia. It is well to remember that the first phase of East-West contact involved a very different "West" from that of the nine-

Excerpted from pp. 135–41 of *Japan: From Prehistory to Modern Times*, by John Whitney Hall, Michigan Classics in Japanese Studies, no. 7 (Ann Arbor: Center for Japanese Studies, University of Michigan, 1991). Used with permission.

teenth century. The Portuguese and Spanish who ventured to the Orient in the sixteenth century were stretching their capacities to the limit when they established their colonies in Malaya and the Philippines. Their manpower was limited and their staying power rested as much on the weakness of the peoples they conquered as on their special military superiority. The Dutch and the English who entered Asian waters in the seventeenth century were not yet prepared to exert a major effort to penetrate the China and Japan trade. And so, after a century and a half both China and Japan were able to "control" the Westerners. The Portuguese were expelled from Japan and restricted to the small colony of Macao in China. The Dutch accepted a small, controlled trade with Japan at the one port of Nagasaki. Both China and Japan were able to return to their traditional policies of isolation.

What was it that differentiated this first encounter between Europe and East Asia from the one which came in the nineteenth century? From the Western side, it is generally explained in terms of the rise and decline of European trading activities and the rivalries between the Old World colonial powers and the Dutch and the English who followed. But conditions within China and Japan had a significant influence as well. It is well to remember that in the sixteenth century the Eastern countries were not so inferior to those of Europe in terms of their technologies of government and military defense. The early infiltration of the Portuguese into the China Seas had been facilitated in large measure by the internal weakness of both China and Japan. China was in the last stages of dynastic decline, while Japan was politically disunited and preoccupied by internal rivalries. Once both countries returned to full strength, China under the Ch'ing dynasty and Japan under the Tokugawa house, they regained the ability to control their own frontiers.

The Portuguese reached India in 1498. By 1510 [Portuguese noble Affonso de] Albuquerque had established a military outpost and trading center at Goa [in India], which was to become the hub of Portuguese operations in the East. One year later the Portuguese captured Malacca [in Malaysia] from the Arabs and gained access to the spice trade and the China Seas. They are said to have reached China by 1514, and though they failed to obtain the commercial concessions they sought from the court at Peking, they were able to establish in 1557 a post at Macao from which they had access to trade with Canton. Shortly before this, in 1543, Portuguese traders landed on the small island of Tanegashima south of Kyūshū and made their first contact with the Japanese. The Spanish arrived in 1592, the Dutch in 1600.

These were years of confusion and high adventure in the China Seas. The official Japanese trade with China had broken down and the seas swarmed with Japanese and Chinese freebooters. The Japanese before long established bases in Annam [in Vietnam], Siam, and Luzon [in the Philippines] and had entered the spice trade. The islands

off the coast of China became the haunts of pirates, while Japanese
ships so frequently carried out raids on the China coast that the weak-
ening Ming government in desperation forcibly rolled back the coastal
population of central China several miles inland. China remained an
important element in the Japan trade, since the chief profit for Japanese traders came from importing Chinese silk and gold to Japan in
exchange for Japanese silver and copper. It was into this regional trade
that the Portuguese intruded themselves.

Portuguese trade with Japan began in 1545, and soon the daimyo [lo-
cal rulers] of Kyūshū were vying with each other to lure the Europeans
to their ports. Within a decade the Portuguese had practically run the
Chinese traders out of Japanese ports by their more aggressive tactics
and because of the greater maneuverability and greater size of their
ships. The novelty of the European commodities which the Portuguese
brought to Japan was also a major attraction. European firearms, fab-
rics such as velvet and wool cloth, glassware, clocks, tobacco, and spec-
tacles appealed to the Japanese and their eclectic tastes. Ports of entry
shifted frequently and often depended on the whims of local daimyo.
Kagoshima seems not to have caught on. Hirado was active in the
1550's, and Fukuda gained favor in the 1560's. With the opening of Nagasaki as a major port in 1571, it became the main Portuguese center
in Japan.

The effect of this trade upon Japan was considerable. For one thing,
it accentuated the commercial factor in the national economy, making
it possible for great wealth to be accumulated by trade rather than exclusively by control of land. The growth of trade was not a sudden phenomenon, of course, and it was not just the arrival of the Portuguese
that brought into being the flourishing activity in the ports of Kyūshū.
But the Europeans enlivened the trade and helped to augment its dis-
ruptive aspects. The manner in which certain of the lesser daimyo of
Kyūshū were able to increase their local prestige out of all proportion
to their territorial size eventually became a major concern for the land-
based daimyo of central and eastern Japan who led in the process of
military unification after the middle of the sixteenth century.

There were other measurable influences, of which two need particular attention: one was the introduction of new firearms and military technology, the other was the introduction of Christianity. The Japanese were
not ignorant of gunpowder, which they had faced in the Mongol invasions. The freebooting Japanese Wakō [pirates] were also frequently sub-
jected to explosive missiles from Chinese and Korean coastal defenses.
But the Portuguese arquebus was the first accurately firing weapon the
Japanese had witnessed. Its introduction into Japan had an immediate
impact on the nature of Japanese warfare. Within ten years after the
Japanese first caught sight of the arquebus at Tanegashima, the daimyo
of western Japan were avidly importing Western arms, and Japanese ar-

tisans were turning out replicas in large numbers. The "Tanegashima" became the new weapon of the rising daimyo. The Ōtomo of north Kyūshū apparently were the first, in 1558, to put cannon into the field. By the 1570's musket corps were entering the battle lines of troops along with pikemen and archers, and in 1575 Oda Nobunaga won a major battle against the Takeda forces by employing three thousand musketmen in recurring waves. This was something of a turning point in the warfare which preceded Japan's military unification. Thereafter superior firepower was to determine the contest of strength, and the small mountain castles which had held out against the bow and the cavalry-fighter were brought within reach of musket and cannon. Daimyo were obliged to build massive castles with far-flung battlements and moats to protect their forces. Only the daimyo with the greatest of resources were able to survive. The importation of the musket probably hastened by several decades the ultimate unification of the country.

Christian Missionary Work

The impact of Christianity upon the Japanese of the sixteenth century was largely a product of the Jesuit missionary effort. The tremendous vitality of the European missionary activity is seen when we realize that only ten years after the founding of the Society of Jesus in 1539, Francis Xavier, one of its founders, was preaching in Japan. Xavier (1506–1552) arrived in Goa in 1542. Disappointed in the Indian response to his message, he eventually made his way to Japan guided by a Japanese castaway named Yajirō. He arrived at Kagoshima in 1549. Here he was welcomed by the daimyo who hoped trade would follow when he granted Xavier permission to preach. Within a year Xavier had been expelled from Satsuma and was obliged to move to Hirado. From there he travelled through Hakata and Yamaguchi to Kyōto where he attempted to obtain a license to preach from the Ashikaga Shogun. Failing this he returned to Kyūshū through Sakai, established the first church in Yamaguchi and obtained the support of the Ōuchi and Ōtomo houses. He left Japan in 1551 with the hope of carrying his message to China, but died near Canton in 1552.

The brief two years during which Xavier travelled in Japan laid the basis of the greatest missionary success the Jesuits had in all of Asia. Yet he and his successors faced insuperable odds in conveying the Christian messages to the Japanese. Handicapped by the difficulty of making Christian principles comprehensible to the Japanese, it is probable that for many years they could achieve no meaningful appeal other than through personal conduct and example. The Japanese called the Portuguese and Italians "Southern Barbarians" (Namban), noting their arrival from the south seas, and at first considered Christianity just another version of Buddhism. Yet for some reason the Japanese were attracted to the men from afar. Their frankness and resoluteness, their absolute faith and strength of character were attractive features in an age of warfare when the Buddhist priesthood showed signs of materialism and corruption.

The missionaries were also men of learning who brought with them knowledge of a new civilization. Xavier, who had begun his mission with the attempt to reach the common man by streetcorner preaching, learned quickly to make his appeal to the ruling class and to coat his religious message with the attractions of European material civilization. Missionaries therefore brought trade in their wake and entered their audiences with the daimyo bearing curious gifts. Several daimyo of Kyūshū, in large measure influenced by thoughts of trade, adopted the new religion and some even ordered all their subjects to follow suit. The arrival of Father Gaspar Vilela (1525–1572) in Kyōto in 1559 established the capital as a second major center of Christian activity, and for a time the Jesuit missionaries had the active support of Oda Nobunaga, one of the prime military leaders of Japan.

Three daimyo of Kyūshū provided the most conspicuous support of Christianity. It was Ōmura Sumitada who in 1570 created the port of Nagasaki, permitted the Jesuits to establish a church there, and in 1580 turned over the administration of the town to the missionaries. Having become Christian in 1563 he later ordered his entire domain to do likewise. Arima Harunobu and Ōtomo Yoshishige (better known by his Buddhist name of Sōrin) made up the rest of the so-called "Three Christian Daimyo." These men in 1582 sent a group of four Japanese Christian envoys to the Papal court in Rome by Portuguese carrack. Itō Mancio, Chijiiwa Miguel, Nakaura Julião, and Hara Martinho took the long route via Macao, Portuguese India, and the Cape of Good Hope to Lisbon, returning to Japan in 1590. In 1613 Date Masamune sent a similar mission by Spanish galleon across the Pacific to Acapulco and then on across the Atlantic to Spain and Italy. By 1582 when the Jesuit Visitor Valignano (1539–1606) reported on his findings in Japan he estimated that there was a total of two hundred churches and 150,000 converts, all the work of seventy-five Jesuit missionaries.

But already the willingness of the Japanese leaders to tolerate the foreign religion had begun to change. For as the tide of unification and consolidation swept over the country, the open conditions which had greeted the Western traders and missionaries began to disappear. Christianity was not to be interdicted until 1587, and the first martyrdoms were not to come until 1597. But after 1612 the Tokugawa authorities set to work to exterminate the religion with ruthless determination and great loss of life. Foreign trade was still encouraged for several decades more, but it too was placed under heavy restriction as the newly established central authority jealously prohibited the Kyūshū daimyo from enriching themselves through foreign contact. By 1640 Japan had adopted a rigid policy of national seclusion and suppression of Christianity.

The Mughal Empire of India

Stanley Wolpert

Among the many non-European empires that flourished during the 1500s was the Muslim Mughal Empire of India. The Mughals had been a powerful force in Indian politics for many years. In 1556, they beat back several rivals and claimed the entire country for themselves, under the reign of the teenage king Akbar.

This excerpt by India specialist Stanley Wolpert details the founding of the Mughal dynasty and describes the social and governmental structure that prevailed under Akbar. One of the main problems faced by the Mughal Empire was to win the support of the large Hindu population. Akbar did this rather effectively, as Wolpert points out, but tensions between Muslims and Hindi in India, Pakistan, and surrounding countries persist today.

Jalal-ud-din Muhammad Akbar was born on October 15, 1542, at Amarkot in the Sind desert, while his father was fleeing toward Persian [present-day Iran] exile. The infant Akbar was left with his Persian mother, Hamīda Bānū Begum, and his head nurse, Māham Anaga, at the Afghan fortress of Kandahar, under guard of his father's trusted lieutenant, Bayram Khan, who remained at his side after he ascended the throne. Reared in rugged Afghan exile rather than [the capital city] Delhi's palatial ease, Akbar spent his youth learning to hunt, run, and fight and never found time to read or write. He was the only great Mughal who was illiterate, but he later noted that the prophets were illiterate and advised believers to keep at least one son in that unlet-

Excerpted from *A New History of India*, fifth edition, by Stanley Wolpert. Copyright © 1997 by Oxford University Press, Inc. Reprinted with permission from Oxford University Press, Inc.

tered condition. Perhaps illiteracy predisposed him toward mysticism, as did his love of animals and nature and the early hardships he endured.

Akbar was thirteen when Humayun [his father] died, and Bayram Khan, knowing there would be rival claimants to Delhi's throne, quickly crowned the boy at Kalānaur in the Punjab, where Akbar had been serving as his father's governor. Several heirs to the Afghan Sur dynasty did, in fact, claim to inherit control over North India, but none of them proved formidable obstacles to Akbar's force, led by his chief minister and general, Bayram Khan. A Hindu named Hemū however, who had served as *vazir* of the Sur dynasty, marched against Agra and Delhi at the time of Humayun's death, seeking to restore Hindu power. He seized both cities and proclaimed himself *Rājā Vikramāditya* ("King Whose Effulgence is Equal to the Sun's"), winning enough Afghan support to muster 100,000 horses in his army. Hemu also kept his elephant corps well fed, even though each of his 1,500 war elephants ate an average of 600 pounds of grain a day while the populace of Delhi starved through one of India's worst famine years. But despite Hemu's military strength, the Mughal army won the prize of North India once again on the battlefield of Panipat on November 5,1556.

For the first five years of his reign, Akbar remained subservient to Bayram Khan, until the regent was deposed at the instigation of Akbar's nurse, who hoped to run the empire herself. The faithful old regent, hustled off on a pilgrimage to Mecca, was stabbed to death by a band of Pathans in Gujarat in 1561. For a few years, the ambitious nurse, Māham Anaga, enjoyed the prerogatives of court patronage and petty power, but in 1562, the seventh year of his reign, Akbar liberated himself from harem rule and took firm personal command of his court and its policy. Akbar's unique achievement was based on his recognition of the pluralistic character of Indian society and his acceptance of the imperative of winning Hindu cooperation if he hoped to rule this elephantine empire for any length of time. First of all, he decided to woo the Rajputs, marrying the daughter of Raja Bhārmal of Amber in 1562, thus luring that Hindu chief with his son and grandson as well to his capital at Agra, the start of four generations of loyal service by that Rajput house in the Mughal army. That same year, Akbar showed his capacity for wise as well as generous rule by abolishing the practice of enslaving prisoners of war and their families, no longer even forcibly converting them to Islam. The following year (1563), he abolished the tax that from time immemorial had been exacted by kings from Hindu pilgrims traveling to worship at sacred spots throughout India. Akbar had been tiger hunting around Mathura when he chanced to learn of the pilgrim tax and, insisting it was contrary to God's will, ordered it abolished immediately. In 1564 he remitted [forgave] the hated *jizya* (non-Muslim poll tax), which was not reimposed for more than a century, and with that single stroke of royal generosity won more support from the majority of India's population than all other Mughal emperors combined managed to muster by their conquests.

War

Not that Akbar was adverse to using force as well as conciliation in unifying India. When the *rana* of Mewar refused to follow Amber's example of joining the Mughal army and Akbar realized that repeated attempts at diplomacy simply inflated the pride of the Rajput heirs to Rana Sanga, he personally led the seige of Chitor in October 1567 and ordered the massacre of some thirty thousand of its defendants when it fell in February 1568. No prisoners were taken; only the massive regalia, Mewar's kettledrums and candelabra, were dragged back to Agra as symbols of the Mughal victory, which broke the back of remaining Rajput resistance. Ranthambhor surrendered in March 1569, and Kalinjar that August. By November 1570, virtually all the chiefs of Rājasthan—except for the *rana* of Mewar, who had fled to the hills—had sworn allegiance to Akbar.

The picture of Akbar preserved by a number of contemporary historians, the best of whom was Abu-1 Fazl (1551–1602), and by foreign visitors, including several Jesuits at court, is of a most energetic and powerful, yet singularly sensitive, often melancholy man, whose fits of depression were as prolonged and profound as his flights of manic celebration were frequent. He seems to have been epileptic, and until the age of twenty-seven, he remained childless. (Twin sons born to his wife in 1564 died after only a month.) Anxiety that he might leave no heir to his empire weighed so heavily upon his consciousness that Akbar went to seek help from a Sufi saint, Shaikh Salim of the Chishti order, who lived at a spot called Sīkri, some twenty-three miles from Agra. Repeated sessions with the shaikh seemed to soothe the emperor's troubled spirit, and a year later, in 1569, his first son and heir, Salim, was born to the daughter of Raja Bharmal. The next year a second son was born, and two years later, a third. Akbar's gratitude to his sufi guide went far beyond the mere naming of his heir after the shaikh, for in 1571 at the village sight of Sikri he erected a magnificent red sandstone palace-fort, moving his entire household and court to that "sacred" spot, thereafter called Fatehpur ("Fortress of Victory") Sikri. To accommodate the sudden influx of people, an artificial lake had to be dug, but by 1585 that supply of water proved so inadequate or polluted that the splendid new capital city had to be abandoned. It stands to this day as a ghostly reminder of Akbar's reign, at once a tribute to the impulsive grandeur of his spirit and a symbol of the evanescence of power.

Expansion

Akbar invaded wealthy Gujarat in November 1572, personally marching at the head of his army into Ahmadabad, then capturing Surat in February 1573. With great Mughal power thus securely anchored in the Arabian Sea, Akbar could turn his attention east to Bengal, where he marched in 1574, finally integrating that hitherto independent region into his imperial scheme in 1576. The northwestern limits of Akbar's power were firmly fixed by August of 1581, when he marched triumphantly into Kabul with no fewer than 50,000 cavalry and 500 elephants at his command. By pacifying Afghanistan for the remaining quarter century of his rule, Akbar managed to achieve more than British arms [in later centuries] would ever be able to command. In 1592 he added Orissa, and in 1595 Baluchistan, to his imperial domain. His effective control over northern and central India was, in fact, greater than that of either the [ancient] Mauryas or the British, and after conquering those regions he established stable administrations within them, creating a pattern followed by his Mughal descendants as well as by early British administrators.

The *mansabdari* (*mansab* is Persian for "office" and *mansabdars* were "officeholders") system of administration developed by Akbar divided the higher echelons of Mughal officialdom into thirty-three ranks. Each "rank" was classified on the basis of the number of cavalry an official of that *mansab* was expected to raise and lead in the emperor's service at a time of martial emergency. The princes of royal blood were given the highest *mansabs*, ranging from five to ten thousand, while lesser nobility would be assigned *mansabs* of from five hundred to five thousand. The lowest *mansabdar* was a "commander of ten," whose appointment would come from the emperor through nomination by some court *amir* (noble). All of the higher ranks were hand-picked officials drawn mostly (70 percent) from Muslim soldiers born outside of India, but they also included many major ethnic, regional, and religious groups within India, about fifteen percent Hindus, most of whom were Rajputs. Akbar's administration thus relied, as would the British Raj, primarily upon foreign administrators, but it also contained some of the most talented as well as vigorously ambitious young Indians, many of whom might have raised armies against Mughal power had they not been invited to share in it. Twenty-one Hindus held *mansabs* of five thousand and above during Akbar's reign, and Raja Todar Mal, who was Hindu by birth, held the second most powerful post in the bureaucracy—*diwan*, or minister of revenue—and was for a brief interlude elevated to the premiership, as *vakil*, the emperor's bureaucratic right hand.

Akbar's empire was divided into twelve provinces (*subas*), and subdivided into districts (*sarkars*), which were in turn usually broken down into *parganas* (subdistricts). Each province was ruled by its *sub-*

adar ("governor"), whose lavish court was a miniature reflection of the great Mughal's. Municipalities were separately administered by a *kotwal* ("city governor"), who supervised the various bureaucratic boards. Cities supported their own police force, while the countryside was secured by district military commanders (*faujdars*), who assisted the district revenue collectors (*amalguzars*) in gathering the emperor's "share" at each harvest. Though the decennial revenue "settlement" reached with each peasant (*ryot*) or landed overlord (*zamindar*) in Akbar's time varied from region to region, depending upon the fertility of the soil, actual crops grown, availability of irrigation water, and other factors, the average overall assessment was about one-third of the total annual harvest, or one-third of its cash value, somewhat lower than it had been before or was to be later. To help peasants survive seasons of drought or crop failure, moreover, Akbar's revenue collectors were ordered to remit taxes in afflicted districts, and thanks to the sympathetic administration of that ministry by Hindus, there was far less coercion or brutality used in the general collection of revenue during Akbar's reign than at any other era of Muslim rule. Islamic law, codified in the orthodox *Shari'at* ("Highways") and interpreted by learned scholars (*ulama*), was enforced by judges (*qazis*), whose decisions could always be appealed to the emperor. After 1579, Akbar asserted that as God's earthly representative he would always judge correctly. Few prisons were maintained in Mughal India. Whipping, public humiliation and display, banishment, and death were the usual forms of punishment. At the local level, wherever a legal dispute involved two Hindus, Hindu law (*Dharma-shastra*) was applied, and Brahmanic opinion, or the decision of the village *panchayat* would generally be accepted as final, unless appealed to the emperor.

Economics Under Akbar

A total population of about a hundred million, less than one-seventh the density of modern South Asia, and a total revenue demand of little more than one-third the yield of the land, meant that the average inhabitant of Akbar's India was economically better off than his peasant heirs have subsequently been. As for the elite courtiers, indeed all *mansabdars*, their descendants would never again attain such affluence, enjoy so much power, or live in such luxurious splendor. A mere *mansabdar* of one thousand received the rupee equivalent in salary of a British lieutenant governor, and his pay permitted him to live in thoroughly regal luxury. Mughal grandees knew that their wealth and property would revert to the emperor when they died, so their level of conspicuous consumption was even greater than their exorbitant salaries alone dictated. There was very little opportunity for capital investment, hence lavish spending on high living became the order of daily Mughal society. Grandees kept their stables full of Arabian horses, their harems replete with Indian and African dancing girls, their servants' quarters crammed with slaves, and their jewel boxes overflowing. India's premier industry in Akbar's day was the production of textiles for export, as well as for domestic sale. Gujarati cotton goods clothed most of Africa and Asia at this time, and Indian peasant weavers did not yet face competition from Lancashire [English] mills for the home market. Impoverished Bengali peasants wore sackcloth woven of jute; the wealthy covered themselves in homespun silk; and Northerners who could afford to wore wool during the brief but often bitter winters. In addition, Kashmiri shawls and carpets were prized both at home and abroad for their soft warmth and the brilliance of their artistic design. Indigo and opium were other important Mughal exports, but they ranked far below cotton cloth and spices in total value.

Not only did Akbar's efficient administrative system help stimulate and expand India's economic development and trade, foreign as well as domestic, but it also resurrected Ashoka's imperial idea of bringing the entire subcontinent under a single "white umbrella." Like the ancient Guptan and Mauryan emperors, Akbar endowed his high office with trappings of divinity, which he may have based more on contemporary Persian models than on early Indian ones, but which were clearly popular with most of his subjects. For it was not as an orthodox Muslim monarch that Akbar ruled, but rather as a divine Indian emperor, the spiritual as well as the secular father of all his people. Perhaps, like the predisposition to a social system based on a hierarchy of "castes" where birth alone confers high or low status for life, something in the "soil" or "climate" of India made its populace more amenable to royal rule (*raj*) of a "divinely" imperial variety than to other forms of government. Akbar, at least, seems to have perceived such a predilection. He made the most of his imperial position not merely by issuing his "infallibility decree," which raised the decisions of "a most God-fearing king . . . for the benefit of the nation" above those of sectarian Islamic law, but also by founding a "Divine Faith" (*Din-i-Ilahi*) at his court in 1581. The motto of that court religion, used as a salutation by its devotees, was *Allahu Akbar*, which could mean either "God is great" or "Akbar is God." It was doubtless interpreted both ways, depending on whether the person using it was more of a devout Muslim or an imperial Mughal. Akbar himself had by then abandoned orthodox Islam for its mystic Sufi form, and much of the ritual associated with his court religion was derived from the practice of Sufi orders. Some of his ideas came from Hinduism and Jainism, however, and others were borrowed from Parsis, Sikhs, and Christians, who were regularly invited to Fatehpur Sikri to discuss their beliefs with the ever-curious emperor. One of the most interesting buildings at Akbar's capital was his octagonal "Hall of Private Audience"

(*Diwan-i-Khas*), a small chamber whose central support is a stout pillar from which catwalk spokes emerge about eight feet above floor level. Akbar would stand on the catwalk and, looking down at the gathering of learned leaders of every religion attending below, throw out provocative questions to one and then another wise man, vigorously engaging them in debate and inciting arguments among them while he listened and paced overhead.

Cultural Issues

Orthodox Muslim leaders like the *mulla* of Jaunpur came to fear that the emperor had abandoned Islam entirely, and called upon their congregations of the faithful to rise in revolt. In 1581 rebellion flared in Bengal and Kabul, but Akbar managed easily to suppress such opposition to his popular "national" policy. Akbar went so far as to forbid cow slaughter by imperial decree, making that offense against Hinduism and his Divine Faith punishable by death. During the final decade of his reign, orthodox Muslim opposition mounted in the north, while much of his time and fortune was lavished on expeditions to overwhelm Shi'ite Muslim sultanates of the Deccan. The sultanates of Ahmadnagar, Khandesh, and Berar, heirs to the northern half of the Bahmani sultanate, were all defeated by Akbar's forces and incorporated (nominally, at least) within the Mughal Empire. Lacking a modern railroad or telegraph system, however, the Mughals were to find it much more difficult to retain effective control south of the Vindhya-Satpura divide than to win martial victories there. Though Akbar and his successors repeatedly tried to consolidate their tenuous grip over the south, their invasions served more to stimulate local opposition than to unite the subcontinent permanently. Indeed, it proved easier for Akbar to expand his hold over Afghanistan than over the Deccan, weaning Kandahar from Persia and adding it to Mughal domain in 1595.

The importance of Persian cultural influence on the Mughal Empire and court can hardly be exaggerated; it was found not only in Akbar's Sufism, but in the reintroduction of Persian as the official language of Mughal administration and law. . . . The elegant decadence of Mughal dress, decor, manners, and morals all reflected Persian court life and custom. Mughal culture was, however, more than an import; by Akbar's era, it had acquired something of a "national" patina, the cultural equivalent of the Mughal-Rajput alliance. That new syncretism, which has come to be called "Mughlai," is exemplified by Akbar's encouragement of Hindi literature and its development. While the Persian and Urdu languages and literatures received the most royal patronage and noble as well as martial attention, the emperor also appointed a poet laureate for Hindi. Raja Birbal (1528–83) was the first poet to hold that honored title, thanks to which many other young men of the sixteenth century were induced to study the northern vernacular that has now become India's national tongue, helping to popularize it through their poetry and translations of Persian classics. Most popular and famous of the Hindi works in this era was the translation of the epic *Ramayana* by Tulsi Das (1532–1623).

In architecture as well as painting, Akbar's era reflects a blend of Perso-Islamic and Rajput-Hindu styles and motifs. The buildings at Fatehpur Sikri are a unique synthesis of Indian craftsmanship and design employed in the service of one of Islam's most liberal monarchs. . . . In painting, even more vividly than in architecture, the central theme of Akbar's policy of fashioning a Mughal-Rajput alliance reached its peak of artistic expression. More than a hundred painters were employed at court, honored with *mansabdar* rank, and constantly encouraged by the emperor himself to improve their magnificent pictures, which would be exhibited each week before him. Their portraiture, book illumination, and naturalistic animal and bird paintings remain among the most beautiful treasures of Indian civilization. The Persian calligrapher par excellence of Akbar's court was Khwaja Abdul Samad, but most of the great artists were Hindus: Daswanath, Basawan, Lala Kesu, Haribans, and others whose names were recorded by Abu-l Fazl, though much of their work has perished or been lost. We do, however, have a number of portraits and miniatures dating from this era, the finest fruit of the union of Hinduism and Islam. When challenged by orthodox Sunnis, who reminded him that Islam prohibited depiction of the human form, Akbar replied that he could not believe God, the "Giver of Life," would be repelled by the human beauty portrayed in works of true art.

The last four years of Akbar's life were plagued by his eldest son's rebellion, the curse of an inherited pattern of Central Asian succession struggles that haunted the Mughals and proved so debilitating a drain on Indian resources. Prince Salim proclaimed himself *padishah* in Allahabad in 1601, while his father was preoccupied with Deccan warfare. Akbar deputed his most trusted lieutenant, Abu-l Fazl to "take care" of his wayward son, but the loyal Fazl was murdered on his way back to Agra by an assassin hired by Salim. Akbar reasserted his paternal power briefly, but the following year, on October 17, 1605, the great Mughal emperor died of what seems to have been a dose of poison administered by his son. Salim now assumed his Persian title name Jahāngīr ("World Seizer"), starting his twenty-two year reign at the age of thirty-six. The empire he inherited was probably the most powerful in the world at the time, and certainly the strongest in Indian history to date.

Expanding the Menu

Reay Tannahill

The cultures of the Old and New Worlds influenced each other in many ways during the era of exploration. Europeans brought gold, jewels, and other valuables back from voyages to the Americas, but perhaps the most significant new discoveries they made had to do with food. Explorers traveling to distant places brought back many unfamiliar foods which soon became an important part of the European and African diet. Among these foods were maize, chocolate, turkey, potatoes, peppers, and tomatoes. In this excerpt from her book *Food in History*, British food historian Reay Tannahill describes some of these new foods and examines their effects on Old World culture.

W hen Columbus first sighted America, its inhabitants had already developed more than 200 types of maize—one of the most remarkable plant breeding achievements in history. On his early visits to Cuba Columbus noted that it was 'most tasty boiled, roasted or ground into flour'. When he arrived back in Spain, his most popular exhibits from the New World were a few specimen 'Indians' and some handfuls of gold dust, but he seems also to have carried maize seeds in his baggage. Soon afterwards the Spaniards began distributing maize around the Mediterranean, although it was the Venetians who took it to the Near East, from which it travelled up to the Balkans and also back to France, Britain and Holland. For a time Britain, Germany, Holland and Russia called it 'Turkish wheat'. In parts of France it was

Rhodes, Spanish or Barbary corn; in Italy, Sicilian or Turkish corn. And in Turkey? '*Roums* corn'—foreign corn.

When, in 1519, Magellan set out on a new Spanish attempt to reach the Spice Islands by a westward route, he took maize with him. It was known in the Philippines soon after, and by 1555 was sufficiently important in some parts of China to rate a mention in a regional history of the province of Henan (Honan). In the seventeenth century it was to transform agricultural life in Yunnan and Sichuan (Szechuan) and become a life-saving crop for migrants forced out into the hills from the overpopulated Yangtze delta.

To Portugal, however, belongs the dubious credit for having introduced maize farming to Africa to provide ships' stores for the slave trade. Among history's many ironies is the fact that a cheap food designed to feed African slaves on their way to America should have resulted, in Africa itself, in a population increase substantial enough to ensure that the slavers would never sail empty of human cargo.

Maize was accepted quickly in Africa because, in comparison with other grains, it grew rapidly and its cultivation was undemanding (which is not, however, true of the modern, heavy-cropping varieties). A woman working alone could plant her seeds, leave them to grow and harvest the crop as and when she needed it; when one patch of soil became exhausted, she moved on to another. It was poor agriculture, but it sustained life and made few demands.

In time the health of the Old World peoples who adopted maize as their staple began to deteriorate. Africa today is still only too familiar with the 'disease of the mealies', otherwise known as pellagra, which results from eating too much maize and not enough foods containing the vitamin C and nicotinic acid that maize lacks. In much of the African interior, except in banana-growing regions, useful fruits and vegetables were in short supply until the American introductions (including manioc, the sweet potato, groundnuts and French beans) became widely established, while in Europe foods with a high nicotinic acid content were not, with the exception of cheese, easy for the poor to come by, especially when they were unaware of the need for them. As a result, maize soon lost much of its initial popularity in Europe (if not in Africa, where the options were fewer) and did not regain it until a wider-ranging diet became common.

Beans and Tomatoes

In Central and South America pellagra was rare because the deficiencies in maize were amply remedied by other items in the diet—tomatoes, avocados, beans, capsicums [peppers] and fish.

Beans, which provided useful protein when eaten in conjunction with maize, were usually boiled, though if they were young and small they may have been eaten raw. The *refrito* beans that are a speciality of Mexico today—boiled, mashed, fried and served with a topping of grated cheese—evolved only after the Spaniards introduced the cow and other domesticated animals to Central America. Before that, there seems to have been no reliable supply of fat or oil; what little fat there was came from dry-fleshed game animals or birds, and although oil was sometimes extracted from groundnuts, maize or sunflower seeds, there is some academic doubt as to whether technology was far enough advanced for this kind of extraction to be practised on any scale.

Tomatoes had made their first appearance as weeds in prehistoric times, but careful cultivation had enormously increased both yield and varieties by the time Cortés and his 400 Spaniards reached Mexico in 1519. Like maize, tomatoes were utilized at every stage of growth; thin shavings of the green and unripe fruit were incorporated in many dishes, while the ripe fruits were mixed with chillis to make a strong-tasting sauce to go with cooked beans.

The tomato introduced into Europe in the sixteenth century may have been an orange-yellow variety, which would account for one of the early names, 'golden apple', although apples can seldom have been as heavily ribbed and misshapen as tomatoes were until the beginning of the twentieth century. Another name was 'love apple', which derived either from the fruit's reputation as an aphrodisiac or from the French *pomme d'amour*, itself a corruption either of *pomi di Mori* ('apple of the Moors'), or of *pomodoro* ('golden apple'). The Spaniards, better informed, called it *tomate* (from the Aztec tomatl) and adopted it as readily into their diet as they did all other introductions from their American empire.

Italy also acquired a taste for it some time later, when two Jesuit priests brought a red variety back from America. 'Apples of Love', reported the Quaker merchant Peter Collinson in 1742, 'are very much used in Italy to putt when ripe into their Brooths & Soops giving it a pretty Tart Tast. A Lady just come from Leghorn says she thinks it gives an Agreeable tartness & Relish to them & she likes it Much.' Tomato sauce as an accompaniment to pasta put in an appearance a few decades later.

Not until the twentieth century did Britain acquire a taste for tomatoes—and, with it, a passion for tinned tomato soup—and America was almost equally slow, possibly influenced by the same arguments that discouraged the peoples of northern and western Europe. Tomatoes were described as being . . . a cause of gout and lacking in both nourishment and substance.

Peppers

The Central American capsicum 'pepper', which like the tomato has a high vitamin C content, bore no family relationship to the *piper nigrum* [that is, black pepper used as a spice] of India, but the Spaniards were swift to apply the old name *pimienta* to the hot-tasting capsicums they found in Mexico—an excusable piece of wishful thinking, on the whole, since it was the search for pepper that had taken them to the New World in the first place.

The inevitable confusion over names and classifications of peppers has not diminished with the centuries but, loosely, chilli peppers—which come in various sizes and shapes, the small ones being most familiar—are used for seasoning; the gamut of flavour runs from inflammatory to blistering (and the seeds can in fact, burn). Some are dried to make chilli powder or the more refined cayenne paper, some pickled in vinegar for Tabasco sauce, and others can be used in sauces and chutneys, or as direct flavourings in meat dishes. The large, sweet, fleshy bell pepper is the one that is used, green, yellow or red according to ripeness, as a vegetable or in salads. Special varieties of it are dried to make the mild spice known as paprika, which has none of the searing pungency of the chilli.

The people of tropical America used, and still use, capsicums with everything. In early post-Columbian times capsicums went into soups, stews, sauces and vegetable preparations, sometimes four or five different kinds in the same dish; they were dried and pickled, too, as a portable relish for travellers. In the early seventeenth century it was estimated that there were at least forty varieties of capsicum; in Mexico today there are said to be ninety-two.

Food in Mexico

In Aztec times most Mexicans breakfasted long after they had begun the day, stopping only at about 10 A.M. for a bowl of maize porridge flavoured with honey or capsicums, which sustained them until the main meal taken in the early afternoon, when it was too hot to do anything else. This commonly consisted of tortillas, a dish of beans and a sauce made from tomatoes or peppers.

When the conquistadors reached the Aztec capital, Tenochtitlan, and saw the market there, one of them, Bernal Diaz del Castillo, reported how astonished they were 'at the number of people and the quantity of merchandise that it contained, and at the good order and control that was maintained. . . . Each kind of merchandise was kept by itself and had its fixed place marked out.' Some stallholders sold 'beans and sage and other vegetables and herbs', some 'rabbits, hare, deer, young ducks, little dogs [bred for the table] and other such creatures', some fruit, some salt, some honey and some 'cooked food, dough and tripe'.

The 'cooked food' would consist of stews, spiced maize porridge and stuffed tortillas; the 'dough' would be tortilla paste. Tortillas were Mexico's daily bread. Kernels of dried maize, boiled in water with a little charcoal or lime to loosen the skins, were crushed to a paste with a stone roller. The paste was then kneaded and slapped into thin round cakes, and cooked on a special hotplate, the *comalli*, that rested over a small fire.

Tortillas could be rolled and stuffed, when they were known as tacos (or enchiladas), or the mixture could be made into tamales, in which the uncooked dough was plastered onto corn husks, spread with a mixture of beans, capsicums, green tomato shavings and shreds of meat or fish, folded like an envelope and then steamed. The result, after the husk was stripped off, was a portable individual pie, Mexico's answer to Scotland's Forfar bridie and China's spring roll. . . .

There were some foods that gave the conquistadors pause, especially those drawn from the lakes on which the capital was built. As well as conventional pond life such as frogs and freshwater shrimps, there were tadpoles, water flies, larvae, white worms and a curious froth from the surface of the water that could be compressed into a substance not unlike cheese. At the court of Montezuma, a variety of newt peculiar to Mexico (the *axolotl*) was something of a delicacy and so, too, were winged ants and the large tree lizard, the iguana, which even Columbus's sailors had thought 'white, soft and tasty'. That other luxury, the agave worm or maguey slug, was often served with guacamole, the sauce that even in Aztec times was made with tomatoes, capsicums and avocados—rich in protein, fat and A, B, C and E vitamins.

Mexico's only domesticated livestock were the turkey and the dog, which was regarded as a useful but inferior meat. 'The turkey meat was put on top and the dog underneath, to make it seem more.' After the Spanish conquest and the introduction of European cattle, the dog began to lose its usefulness as a food animal, but the turkey entered on a wider stage.

The Turkey

It is possible—just—to make sense of how the turkey got its name. The bird itself seems to have reached England soon after its first arrival in Europe (in about 1523–4) through the agency of the Levant or Turkey merchants, who usually touched in at Seville on their way to and from the eastern Mediterranean. Not familiar with its Mexican name, *uexolotl*, or understandably reluctant to pronounce it, the English called it the 'turkie cock'.

Unfortunately, in about 1530 the Portuguese brought the guinea-fowl back to Europe from one of its homelands in West Africa, and the Levant merchants seem to have picked it up, too, and transported it onward to an England that had forgotten it since Roman times.

Confusion ensued. The guinea-fowl was not unlike a miniaturized version of the turkey in looks and in its reluctance to fly, and it seems to have been assumed that they belonged to the same family. But although some sources claim that in sixteenth-century England any reference to 'turkey' really meant guinea-fowl, this is not the case. When Archbishop Cranmer framed his sumptuary [regulatory] laws of 1541 he classed turkey-cocks with birds of the size of crane and swan, not—as he would have done with guinea-fowl—with capons and pheasants. At much the same time a certain Sir William Petre was keeping his table birds alive until wanted in a large cage in his Essex orchard, 'partridges, pheasants, guinea-hens, turkey hens and such like'. And the heraldic arms granted in 1550 to William Strickland of Boynton-on-the-Wold—the crest 'a turkey-cock in his pride proper'—show a bird that is, without doubt, a turkey proper. . . .

Elsewhere in Europe there was confusion of a different kind. In France the name most generally favoured was *coq d'Inde* ('cock of India'; not, it should be noted, 'of the Indies'), which was later corrupted to *dinde* or *dindon*. In Italy it was *galle d'India*; in Germany, *indian-ische Henn*. The sex of the names might vary, but the principle was the same, and it was, on the whole, reasonable enough that the bird should have been attributed to India—even (or perhaps especially) by the Turks, who called it *hindi*. The New World stubbornly remained 'the new Indies' long after the error had been discovered.

But it was a pity that the Germans, Dutch and Scandinavians should have chosen to embroider further on the Indian theme, producing the *calecutische Hahn*, the *Kalkoen* and the *Kalkon* that suggest an origin in Calicut, the place where da Gama first landed on the south-west coast of India. The Persians also had a contribution to make, calling the turkey the *filmurgh* or 'elephant bird'—without specifying whether it was an Indian or an African elephant they had in mind. No doubt they simply meant 'large'.

As if all this were not enough, in India itself the bird became known as *peru*, which was geographically a good deal closer to the mark than most, even if still a few hundred miles out. The bird, as it happened, was no more Peruvian than it was Turkish (or Indian). It seems to have reached India, as something new and exotic, in the second decade of the seventeenth century, probably by way of the Philippines, a Spanish possession ruled direct from Mexico.

At least one thing all these names do make clear: the turkey established itself quickly and firmly on most of the tables of the Old World.

The Age of Exploration

PREFACE

By the end of the fifteenth century Christopher Columbus had visited America and ships from Portugal and the Netherlands had sailed down the coast of Africa and as far as India. The age of exploration was well underway. Events of the sixteenth century built on the foundation begun by Columbus and others. By the end of the 1500s the portion of the world known to Europeans was far larger than it had been at the start of the century.

The list of new places visited by Europeans is both long and impressive. Portuguese expeditions under a variety of captains sailed south and then east, snaking closer and closer to the Pacific Ocean. In 1511 they reached Malaysia. The following year they pushed as far as the islands of Indonesia. A scant few years later, a Portuguese ship sailed into the harbor at Canton, China. Not to be outdone, the Spanish made voyages of discovery of their own. Spanish captains and commanders explored the coast of Florida, the isthmus of Panama, and the Gulf of Mexico; later, hiring the Portuguese navigator Ferdinand Magellan, the Spanish commissioned a voyage that would ultimately circumnavigate the entire globe.

The age of exploration helped fill in empty places on the map. Mapmakers found out about the landscapes of the African interior and the nooks and crannies of the Atlantic shoreline off Newfoundland. They began to be able to sketch a reasonable picture of the various islands and rivers of the world. These voyages helped to answer pressing questions that had dogged geographers for centuries. Did the sea really begin to boil as you sailed farther south? How thick did the ice become in the North Atlantic? Were there ways of reaching the Pacific without having to go around the Cape of Good Hope in extreme southern Africa? As explorers and navigators brought in readings and observations, the mapmakers turned the information into drawings—drawings that increasingly matched the actual shape of the globe and its landmasses.

One effect of the age of discovery involved control. Europe's edge in technology, weaponry, and navigation helped give it dominion over much of the rest of the world. To European merchants, explorers, and royalty, the rest of the world was akin to a tasty plum, ripe and ready to be plucked and eaten. Europeans tended not to consider those outside Christendom to have any rights to speak of, and they viewed the natives of Africa and the Americas with particular disdain. The result, too often, was harsh and unreasonable treatment of native inhabitants—treatment that involved enslavement, robbery, and outright murder.

However, not all voyages of exploration resulted in the immediate destruction of an empire. Nor did they all damage cultures by bringing in diseases, firearms, or new and alien ways of thinking. Many of the native peoples "discovered" by the Europeans gave as good as they got. Magellan, for instance, was killed by inhabitants of the Philippine Islands, and similar fates befell several other explorers. And the reaction to a clash of cultures, on both sides, was surprisingly often not one of fear and hatred but rather one of genuine curiosity and mutual respect. In many ways, the age of exploration made the world a very different place from what it had been before.

Portuguese Arrival in Brazil

Pedro Vâs de Caminha

The Portuguese were among Europe's first great navigators. Under the guidance of Prince Henry the Navigator, Portugal sent ships to places unknown to the rest of Europe during the fifteenth century. When the sixteenth century dawned, the Portuguese continued their seafaring tradition. This excerpt describes the arrival of the Portuguese explorer Pedro Alvares Cabral in what is now Brazil early in the year 1500. Written to the king of Portugal by Cabral's personal scribe, the letter provides an excellent insight into the European view of the people they encountered as their explorations continued.

Sire, the admiral of this fleet, besides the other captains, will write to Your Majesty telling you the news of the finding of this new territory of Your Majesty's which has just been discovered on this voyage. But I, too, cannot but give my account of this matter to Your Majesty, as well as I can, though I know that my powers of telling and relating it are less than any man's.[1] May it please Your Majesty, however, to let my good faith serve as an excuse for my ignorance, and to rest assured that I shall not set down anything beyond what I have seen and reflected on, either to add beauty or ugliness to the narrative. I shall not give any account of the crew or the ship's course, since that is the pilot's concern, and I should not know how to do so. Therefore, Sire, I begin what I have to tell thus:

1. One should not forget that this is modesty and that Caminha was a highly trained professional scribe.

Excerpted from "The Discovery of Brazil," by Pedro Vâs de Caminha, translated by Charles David Ley in *Portuguese Voyages, 1498–1663* (London: J.M. Dent & Sons, 1947).

And I say that our departure from Belém [in Portugal] was, as Your Majesty knows, on Monday, 9th March. On Saturday, the 14th of the same month, between eight and nine o'clock we sailed between the Canary Islands,[2] going in nearest to the Grand Canary. We were becalmed in sight of them the whole day, for some three or four leagues. On Sunday the 22nd of the same month, at about ten o'clock, we came in sight of the Cape Verde Islands,[3] or, to be precise, St. Nicholas's Island, as the pilot, Pero Escobar,[4] declared.

On the following night, the Monday, we discovered at dawn that Vasca de Ataide and his ship had been lost, though there was no strong or contrary wind to account for this.[5] The admiral sought him diligently in all directions, but he did not appear again. So we continued on our way across the ocean until on the Tuesday of Easter week, which was 21st April, we came across some signs of being near land, at some 660 or 670 leagues from the aforesaid island, by the pilot's computation. These signs were a great quantity of those long seaweeds sailors call *botelho*. . . . On the following morning, Wednesday, we came across the birds they call 'belly-rippers.'

This same day, at the hour of vespers we sighted land, that is to say, first a very high rounded mountain, then other lower ranges of hills to the south of it, and a plain covered with large trees. The admiral named the mountain Easter Mount and the country the Land of the True Cross.

He ordered them to drop the plumb-line, and they measured twenty-five fathoms. At sunset, about six leagues from the shore, we dropped anchor in nineteen fathoms, and it was a good clean anchorage. There we lay all that night. On Thursday morning we set sail and made straight for land, with the smaller ships leading, the water being seventeen, sixteen, fifteen, fourteen, thirteen, twelve, ten and nine fathoms deep, until we were half a league from the shore. Here we all cast anchor opposite a river mouth. It must have been more or less ten o'clock when we reached this anchorage.

Human Inhabitants

From there we caught sight of men walking on the beaches. The small ships which arrived first said that they had seen some seven or eight of them. We let down the longboats and the skiffs. The captains of the other ships came straight to this flagship, where they had speech with the admiral. He sent [sailor] Nicolau Coelho on shore to examine the river. As soon as the latter began to approach it, men came out on to the beach in groups of twos and threes, so that, when the longboat reached the river mouth, there were eighteen or twenty waiting.

---

2. recently colonized by the Spanish 3. recently colonized by the Portuguese 4. pilot of the *Berrio* on da Gama's expedition 5. He later rejoined them.

They were dark brown and naked, and had no covering for their private parts, and they carried bows and arrows in their hands. They all came determinedly towards the boat. Nicolau Coelho made a sign to them to put down their bows, and they put them down. But he could not speak to them or make himself understood in any other way because of the waves which were breaking on the shore. He merely threw them a red cap, and a linen bonnet he had on his head, and a black hat. And one of them threw him a hat of large feathers with a small crown of red and grey feathers, like a parrot's. Another gave him a large bough covered with little white beads which looked like seed-pearls. I believe that the admiral is sending these articles to Your Majesty. After this, as it was late, the expedition returned to the ships, without succeeding in having further communication with them, because of the sea.

That night there was such a strong south-easterly wind and squalls that it dragged the ships out of their position, more especially the flag-ship. On Friday morning at about eight o'clock, by the pilot's advice, the captain ordered the anchors to be weighed and the sails hoisted. We went up the coast to the northwards with the longboats and skiffs tied to our sterns, to see if we could find a sheltered spot to anchor in where we could stay to take in water and wood. Not that these were lacking to us, but so as to be provided with everything now, in good time. At the hour when we set sail about sixty or seventy men had gradually come up and were seated near the river. We sailed on, and the admiral told the small ships to run under the shore and to slacken sails if they found a sufficiently protected spot for the ships.

Thus we sailed along the coast, and, ten leagues from the spot where we had weighed anchor, the aforesaid small ships found a ridge of rock which contained a very good, safe port with a very large entrance. So they went in and struck sails. The bigger ships came up behind them, and, a little while after sundown, they struck sails also, perhaps at a league from the rocks, and anchored in eleven fathoms.

Our pilot, Afonso Lopes, was in one of the small ships, and he received orders from the admiral to go in the skiff to take the soundings inside the port, for he was a lively and capable man for the work. He took up two of the men of the country from a canoe. They were young and well formed and one of them had a bow and six or seven arrows. There were many others on the shore with bows and arrows, but they did not use them. Later, in the evening, he took the two men to the flag-ship where they were received with great rejoicings and festivities.

The Brazilians

They are of a dark brown, rather reddish colour. They have good well-made faces and noses. They go naked, with no sort of covering. They attach no more importance to covering up their private parts or leaving them uncovered than they do to showing their faces. They are very in-genuous in that matter. They both had holes in their lower lips and a bone in them as broad as the knuckles of a hand and as thick as a cotton spin-dle and sharp at one end like a bodkin [hairpin]. They put these bones in from inside the lip and the part which is placed between the lip and the teeth is made like a rook in chess. They fit them in in such a way that they do not hurt them nor hinder them talking or eating or drinking.

Their hair is straight. They shear their hair, but leave it a certain length, not cutting it to the roots, though they shave it above the ears. One of them had on a kind of wig covered with yellow feathers which ran round from behind the cavity of the skull, from temple to temple, and so to the back of the head; it must have been about a hand's breadth wide, was very close-set and thick, and covered his occiput [back of the head] and his ears. It was fastened, feather by feather, to his hair with a white paste like wax (but it was not wax), so that the wig was very round and full and regular, and did not need to be spe-cially cleaned when the head was washed, only lifted up.

When they came, the admiral was seated on a chair, with a carpet at his feet instead of a dais. He was finely dressed, with a very big golden collar round his neck. Sancho de Toar, Simão de Miranda, Nicolau Coelho, Aires Correia, and the rest of us who were in the ship with him were seated on this carpet. Torches were lit. They entered. However, they made no gesture of courtesy or sign of a wish to speak to the admiral or any one else.

For all that, one of them gazed at the admiral's collar and began to point towards the land and then at the collar as if he wished to tell us that there was gold in the country. And he also looked at a silver can-dlestick and pointed at the land in the same way, and at the candle-stick, as if there was silver there, too. We showed them a grey parrot the admiral had brought with him. They took it in their hands at once and pointed to the land, as if there were others there. We showed them a ram, but they took no notice of it. We showed them a hen, and they were almost afraid of it and did not want to take it in their hands; fi-nally they did, but as if alarmed by it. We gave them things to eat: bread, boiled fish, comfits, sweetmeats, cakes, honey, dried figs. They would hardly eat anything of all this, and, if they tasted it, they spat it out at once. We brought them wine in a cup; they merely sipped it, did not like it at all, and did not want any more of it. We brought them wa-ter in a pitcher, and they each took a mouthful, but did not drink it; they just put it in their mouths and spat it out.

One of them saw the white beads of a rosary. He made a sign to be given them and was very pleased with them, and put them round his neck. Then he took them off and put them round his arm, pointing to the land, and again at the beads and at the captain's collar, as if he meant they would give gold for them.

We took it in this sense, because we preferred to. If, however, he was trying to tell us that he would take the beads and the collar as well, we did not choose to understand him, because we were not going to give it to him. Then he returned the beads to the man who had given them to him. Finally they lay on their backs on the carpet to sleep. They did not try to cover up their private parts in any way; these were uncircumcised and had their hairs well shaved and arranged.

The admiral ordered one of his cushions to be put under either of their heads, and the one in the wig took care that this should not be spoiled. They had a cloak spread over them. They consented to this, pulled it over themselves, and slept.

Magellan in the Pacific

Charles McKew Parr

Ferdinand Magellan was one of the great early navigators. In 1518, after a career in the Portuguese navy, Magellan was hired by the Spanish to discover a new route to the East Indies. Magellan chose to sail across the Atlantic and into the Pacific via the tip of South America, a route which was difficult and dangerous but which ultimately proved successful. Though Magellan himself died in the Philippines later in the voyage, some of his crew continued on to Europe, thus circumnavigating the world and proving that the world's oceans are interconnected. This excerpt, from Charles McKew Parr's *So Noble a Captain: The Life and Times of Ferdinand Magellan*, describes one portion of Magellan's journey.

Editor's Note: The narrative begins with the passage of Magellan's fleet through the straits at the southern tip of South America and into the Pacific Ocean, a passage still known today as the Straits of Magellan. Heady with the success of having made it through the straits, Magellan was anxious to strike out for the Philippines and other East Asian ports. Unfortunately, lack of geographic knowledge led him to believe that Asia was closer than it actually was, leading to disaster.

Magellan's fleet was called the Armada de Maluco. By this time in the voyage it consisted of three ships: the Victoria, *the* Concepción, *and the flagship, the* Trinidad. *Another ship, the* San Antonio, *had just deserted and returned to Europe. The expedition was outfitted by Spain, but Magellan's crews came from many nations, among them Italy, Germany, Portugal, and various South American countries. There were several differ-*

ent ranks aboard ship. Among them were maestres, or ship masters, second in authority to the captain; contra-maestres, or boatswains, who commanded the crew; pilots, or navigators; the alguacil, or master-at-arms, who was in charge of discipline; his assistants, the merinos; the bombarderos, or artillerymen; the marineros, or experienced sailors; and the ordinary seamen known as the grumetes.

Even though it was summer [in the Southern Hemisphere], the air was chilly, for the frigid zone was near. The crews felt the cold keenly, so Magellan gave orders to turn sharply and steer as nearly due north as possible; as the wind was from the northwest, he kept well away from the lee coast. On December 2nd [1520], they encountered winds from the southwest and were picked up by a favorable northward-flowing current that aided the steady gale to carry the ships along at a good speed. For over two weeks they followed the northerly route with the wind abeam in a smooth sea. The weather was clear and the temperature gradually became mild, like that of Andalusia [a Spanish region] in springtime. The sea was alive with strange fish, and the men trailed baited lines in the wake of the ships. Having little work to do, they spent lazy hours betting on the sea swallows, as they called the flying fish, and whether or not they would be snapped up by the large bonitos who followed their shadows, as they soared desperately above the waves before they landed back in the brine.

At about 42° S. latitude, Magellan discerned the promontory of Cape Tres Montes [in Chile]; thereafter they kept the brown, mountainous coastal range in sight. Therefore modern Chile ranks him as its discoverer. The somewhat conjectural charts which he had brought showed the unknown West Coast of South America meeting the eastward-jutting shores of Asia at a latitude of about 35° S.; he continued on his northward course, seeking the supposed point of juncture, until they reached 32° S. latitude. On December 18th, seeing no sign of the nearness of the coast of Asia, he steered away from the continent on his starboard and struck a course northwest in the hope of reaching Asia on this line. Had he chanced to adopt this northwest route a few days earlier, he would have reached the large island of Juan Fernandez, where he could have taken on water, wood, and some food. As it was, he barely missed the two little islets which lie to the east of it. If he had taken a northwest course even earlier, he would have sighted Easter Island, and from there on would have encountered a series of archipelagos that would have provided a continuous supply of victuals and water. However, the stumpy masts of his little ships were so near sea level that the lookouts in the crows' nests were not high enough to pick up the islands that lay just over the horizon. Even if they had had some form of telescope, which they did not, it could not have helped them in this case.

Magellan now had a steady, strong wind astern, and, with the sails once set, there was little for the crew to do except search the horizon and imagine that every low-lying cloud was land. The smoked fish and seafowl from the straits supplied ample rations, and the water from the River of Sardines [in South America] was still palatable. But now that the weather was pleasant and the hardships had disappeared, tempers became testy and there were frequent quarrels. With light duties and no discomfort, friendliness was succeeded by fretfulness, and there was boasting and sneering [among the ethnic groups that made up the crew]. The Gallegos and Basques resented the assumption of superiority by the Castilians, and the French and Flemings, being northerners, banded together against the southerners, the Iberians and Italians.

However, the jarring factions were in accord on one subject, that the Isles of Spice were just over the horizon. They agreed that soon they would be at Ternate [a south-eastern Asian island], loading the ships with the mace, cinnamon, cloves, and nutmegs that Francisco Serrano [Magellan's cousin] had accumulated for them. Then it would be up with the sails and across the Atlantic to Spain, with everyone's fortune made. . . .

Magellan had Master Andrew of Bristol, the English constable of the *bombarderos*, give gun drills daily. He also had *Alguacil* [Gonzalo Gomez de] Espinosa practice the crew in repelling boarders and in defending the forecastle from mock attack from the waist deck. But the men went about the drills half-heartedly, and even the rope's end hardly quickened them. They fumbled at the routine, and the lackluster eyes and shambling movements showed that this was due to malnutrition.

In the cooking arrangements of the *Trinidad* there were three distinct messes. All were rationed, and there was no favoritism as to size in the small portions doled out. No one any longer had wine, the staple of the Mediterranean sailor's diet which was more missed than anything else. However, the nature of the food differed. The officers' larder still had garlic, figs, and raisins left. The marines' steward also had garlic on hand, but the pantry of the forecastle had only ship biscuit, salted fish, and smoked sea birds. Consequently, without calculation, the officers and the men-at-arms had the benefit of antiscorbutics [vitamins that warded off the sailor's disease called scurvy] which maintained their health somewhat better than did the common sailor's diet. Had the effect of diet on scurvy been known, an equitable distribution of the garlic would have been made; as it was, the *marineros* were weakened, while the guards retained somewhat more vigor. However, everyone was debilitated by the meager diet, and before long the small rations were cut in half. Unless someone managed to catch a fish or hook a shark, a man did not receive enough to still the normal complaint of an empty stomach.

Now the blistering sun of the equator blazed down upon the fleet every day. The improperly smoked penguin meat, of which there were many barrels, spoiled in the tropical heat and bred long, fat, white worms, disgusting to look at, which crawled everywhere about the ship. The worms ate woolen clothing and leather, and their pincer jaws gnawed into the hull of the ship itself. The water in the casks turned yellow, became alive, and stank, so that to drink it one had to hold one's nostrils. Everyone tried to keep to windward of the hold, for the odor of the bilge became overpowering, and the air beneath the deck was suffocating. The listless men no longer could be forced to drill, but lay moodily about the deck.

The first victim of scurvy was a Brazilian stowaway, referred to in the official records only as "the Indian from the Land of Verzin"; he was quickly followed by the giant Patagonian called Juan Gigante. . . .

Although the Europeans resisted malnutrition better than the two Indians, their health began to deteriorate rapidly, and soon the strain became pronounced. According to all Magellan's charts, the armada should by now have crossed the Great South Sea. What if the old legends were true and it was really an endless sea? Now they had passed the point where they could turn back, for the supply of food would not suffice for the return voyage. In any case, they could not double back against the vigorous west wind. Each day was like the last. The monotony of the days and of the unending gale astern told on the nerves of all aboard. The same clear horizon, the same unclouded, blazing sky, the same blue and white waves, and astern the two other little *naos* [ships], met their gaze each day; and the same hunger ached in every man's stomach. Never, in all the African or Asian experience of any of the veteran navigators aboard, had any voyage lasted as much as a month without landfall. The compasses began acting queerly, and the older common seamen worried when they learned of it; the Captain General ordered the pilots to reinforce the needles' magnetism with their loadstones. The men also were superstitiously fearful of the two hitherto unknown galaxies of stars which are now known as the Magellanic clouds; these had first appeared high in the firmament after the armada had entered the Pacific. The astrologer, Andres de San Martin, was besieged by nervous inquiries about their import, and he had to admit his ignorance of their celestial influence, whether malign or benign. . . .

At last Magellan threw the charts aside. It was clear they were worse than useless, and that the renowned geographers who had drawn them up were scholarly humbugs. Day after day, week after week, he peered ahead for land. Again and again a cloud formation or a mirage deceived him.

After two months of sailing, on St. Paul's Day, January 24, 1521, Magellan described a brilliant green patch diffused over the surface of some low-hanging white clouds. From his experience in eastern seas, he was sure the phenomenon was the reflection of sunlight on the waters of a shallow lagoon on an island at some distance. Soon the call "Land ho!" rang out. An island could now be seen far ahead, just under the green reflection. Everyone was galvanized into new life; eyes shone, lips smiled, and there was a sudden outburst of horseplay and practical joking. As they drew near, Magellan could see no signs of habitation; there were only sea birds and a growth of verdant bushes, but no trees. The leadsmen taking soundings from the bows kept reporting no bottom, and hence, although the ships had the anchors ready, they could not let them go. With the fresh wind and a strong set of current, the squadron could not maneuver into a position where Magellan dared launch a boat to go ashore; unanchored, the ships might be swept past the island and be unable to recover the boat. For a few moments it looked as if they were going to be as much tantalized as if the island were a pure mirage. just as they gave up hope of landing, the *Trinidad*'s leadsman shouted that he had found shallows; the Captain General had anchors dropped and sails furled at once, and the consorts followed suit. The *Trinidad*'s longboat dashed into the breakers and got through safely; the men clambered out, capering and scampering like children on the sandy beach.

The island, named St. Paul's Island because it was the saint's feast day, was a rounded atoll made up of the circular walls of the crater of a submerged volcano. On the inner side, the emerald color of the lagoon was so vivid that its reflection made the breasts of white sea birds hovering over its surface seem green. Don Antonio was captivated by the contrast between the cobalt blue of the encircling ocean, the white of the tumbling surf, and the green of the interior lagoon. The windward shore of the island was a mass of tumbled coral rocks shattered by the constant impact of the surf. The landing party found these rocks alive with crabs and the waters offshore swarming with brilliantly colored fish. In the breakers, grayish sharks darted like dim shadows within the flanks of the waves. The hungry men expertly hooked sharks and other large fish off the reef and netted a number of small fish in the shallow lagoon.

There was no firewood to be had, for the only growth was a stunted bush with glossy leaves like a magnolia shrub and yielded no worthwhile fuel. Magellan had wood brought ashore and drying racks erected. The sharks' flesh was cut into strips, thoroughly smoked, and salted away in casks, and similar treatment was given the carcasses of numerous large gray gulls, or goonies.

The island was densely populated by sea birds. Evidently none of them had ever seen men before, and they made no attempt to escape when the sailors walked up to them. Nests were everywhere, and the eggs provided a variety of dishes for the famished men. There was much experimentation with roasting, broiling, and stewing the various water fowl, including black terns, white love birds, wingless rails, sea eagles, goonies, and pirate birds. . . .

During the four days they were on St. Paul, the navigators tried to ascertain its longitude, or east-west position on the globe. Magellan knew, from his own experience, the distance from Malacca westward to the Cape of Good Hope, and he could make a fair guess as to the distance across the Atlantic from the Cape of Good Hope to the Straits of Magellan. He therefore knew the approximate distance from Malacca westward around the world via the Cape of Good Hope to St. Paul's Island in the Pacific, where they now were. The difference between this known distance and the world's circumference would represent the distance they still had to sail to reach Malacca. The difficulty, of course, was that nobody had yet traveled clear around the world, so the best estimate could only be a guess. Magellan, like most of the astronomers of his day, much underestimated the size of the globe, and he therefore miscalculated the distance the armada yet had to sail from St. Paul's Island to reach the East Indies. He probably calculated St. Paul's latitude, or north-south position, correctly; apparently it was about 15° south of the equator, but since its longitude was not ascertained we cannot identify it today.

The discovery of St. Paul had banished the secret terror of an unending waste of waters which had possessed Magellan for a fortnight. He felt confident that from now on they would encounter other similar islands which would supply seafood and bird flesh, and that certainly fruits and greenstuffs would be found to cure the scurvy. There was less than a month's supply of food on hand, but with frequent landfalls that would do.

It was probably at this council at St. Paul's that Magellan divulged his determination to sail to the Philippines first, there to establish a safe Spanish base of operations, before entering the area about Maluco [an Indonesian island off south-east Asia] patroled by Portuguese ships. There is no doubt that the archipelago he had discovered on his secret eastern voyage from Malacca [in Malaysia], about 1512, was the Philippines. The course he steered after leaving St. Paul and his subsequent statements and movements bear out the conviction that he meant to plant the flag of Spain on the Philippines and then operate from there. . . .

By the fourth day at St. Paul, they had barreled much smoked shark meat, fish, and the carcasses of many birds. Magellan judged it time to weigh anchor, and the armada continued on its westward route. The crews had relished the abundance of diet afforded by the island and had benefited by the recreation, but since they secured no vegetables nor fruits, the change did not improve their health as much as Magellan had hoped. During the first two weeks after leaving St. Paul, a spirit of optimism prevailed in the three ships, no doubt due to fresh water and good food. In this fortnight they sailed two hundred leagues north-northwest with a sustained following wind. The pilots' observations showed them to be at 10°15' S. latitude when they perceived at dawn, just ahead of them, another island similar to St. Paul.

As the ships drew near, the excited crews saw it to be an uninhab-ited atoll, with much herbage, and swarming with birds. The most com-forting sight to Magellan was that of heavy clusters of coconuts, which he could see upon the tops of the nodding palms. This would mean the banishment of scurvy. As they neared the windward reef, the leadsmen taking soundings kept chanting that they found no bottom; the ships divided and passed to each side of the island, casting the lead anxiously and hurriedly. When the vessels united at leeward, having circled the atoll, and still the leadsmen could reach no bottom, fear gripped every heart. Magellan had the *Trinidad* hastily drop sail, followed by its con-sorts, and all three continued feverishly to sound the depths,while the crews stood tensely ready to drop anchor at the signal.

When there still were no soundings, consternation spread through the armada. Could it be possible they could not land? The ships had now drifted well beyond where there was any reasonable hope of find-ing bottom, but the leadsmen continued stubbornly to sound. Magel-lan hastily conferred across the waters with the captains on the other two ships as to the advisability of launching all batels [ship's boats] to try to tow the *capitana* back. But time and distance had now slipped past. It would be a desperate move to send the longboats back alone, for even though the sails of the ships were furled, their high super-structure, both fore and aft, caught the wind almost like sails. The men on the batels would never be able to land, load with coconuts, and overtake the fleet. The armada was unable to sail back to the island against the wind and current. This could be attempted only by sailing a triangular course, and it was decided not to lose days of time in mak-ing the effort.

Magellan was confident that the westward crossing of the Great South Sea must by now be almost completed, and he expected to reach other islands in a short time. He gave the unattained island a name on his chart, Sharks' Island. Its longitude is unknown and we cannot identify it, but perhaps it was the islet we now know as Caro-line Island.

On February 13th, after leaving Sharks' Island in the wake, the *cap-itana* changed the course to northwest; we calculate that Magellan crossed the Equator at about the longitude of 160° W. of Greenwich. He thereby missed finding Christmas Island and Jarvis Island, where he could have procured ample supplies. He must have passed very near the Marshall, Gilbert, and Mulgraves archipelagoes without sighting a single island. We do not know if the little flotilla sailed in close formation or in single file, but one wonders why the three *naos* did not spread fanwise across the sea, keeping barely in touch with one another. However, the fear that a storm might separate them under those circumstances probably led the three frightened commanders to keep close together.

The voyage became more and more terrible. Under the heat of the Equator, almost all the crew and many of the men-at-arms were down with scurvy. Stricken men lay groaning wherever there was a bit of shade, and those still on their feet tottered and staggered. The sick had such swollen joints that they shrieked when they had to move a hand or foot. Ulcers broke out all over their bodies. Their gums were puffed out and their teeth were covered by the pulpy growth; when they tried to eat, their teeth loosened in the sockets and fell out. Their palates became so enlarged and sore that men died of starvation rather than swallow what food was available. The fetid breath of the sufferers was almost unbearable, and this, together with the putrifying odors from the bilge, made the ship's atmosphere nauseating even to those hitherto inured to it. . . .

When there was no longer any fish nor meat [to make] broth, Magellan collected the stony fragments of biscuits that were the leavings of the bread casks, stained yellow with the urine of rats, and had these crumbs pounded into powder, being careful to include all the maggots, as these might contain some nourishment. Some casks in the hold had once held raisins, honey, and preserved quinces; he had the enriched, sweet slivers of wood cut from the inside of these barrels. He also scraped the inside of empty pork barrels with a knife and added the greasy sawdust to the pitiful mess, moistening it with hot water and pretending bravely to the patients that they were being fed a gruel.

Next he had the rawhide wrapping which encased the mainyard, to protect it from chafing against the shrouds, cut from the spar. It had been exposed to the sun and wind for two years and was as hard as wood, but after it was trailed overboard for three days it became softened. It was then boiled in water, cut into bits, and grilled upon embers. Only those without scurvy could chew upon it, but the Captain General [Magellan] doled out this tough ration to such few able bodied men as were able to gain sustenance from it. . . .

At last, on March 5, 1521, there was absolutely nothing left to eat. Twenty-five men in the fleet were so weakened by scurvy and hunger that they could not stand, but lay helpless on the decks. Nineteen members of the company bad been buried at sea, dead of scurvy. Those who had escaped the acute attacks of the disease were so weakened by starvation that they had to cling to the rail or rigging as they lurched about, and some crawled on their hands and knees to save themselves from falling. The hallucinations of seeing land increased, and the cry of "Land ho!" sounded feebly at intervals all during the day. Nobody any longer paid it any attention.

At dusk, the Captain General sent a *grumete* named Navarro to the crow's nest to look ahead for reefs, for by now the armada no longer hove to [took down the sails] at night, in spite of the danger of driving ahead in the darkness in an unknown ocean. The crews lacked the strength and the will to haul upon the heavy sails twice daily, and Magellan had fatalistically decided to run whatever risk there might be. Moreover, he knew that in their desperate situation they could not afford to lose the fifty or sixty miles of westing progress which the nightly run represented.

When young Navarro had laboriously climbed to the crow's nest at the masthead, he peered across the sea and thought he saw a dim, low-lying cloud on the horizon. In the twilight it looked convincingly like an island, but he could not be sure; the darkness closed in and he lost it to view. When he came down upon the deck, he mentioned his vivid impression. His statement was listened to with skepticism, and one of the men told Navarro feelingly that he gladly would give him the gold ring he wore if they saw land in the morning. Several others made similar pledges. The canny sailor extended the conversation and secured additional promises of jewelry from others of the circle about him.

At the first break of day, Navarro climbed the ratlines to the main top. Sure enough, far ahead on the starboard was a mountain peak. He could hardly doubt it, but he held his peace and waited impatiently as the false dawn disappeared and darkness again reigned. Shortly the sky again lightened, and he saw clearly a land mass with a high mountain. Twice he wet his lips and swallowed, twice he tried to cry out, and only a squawk came. Then he mastered himself and, with tears running down his cheeks and in a queer, cracking voice that was not his own, he screamed, "Praise God! Praise God! Land! Land! Land! Land!" Then he burst out in a fit of weeping.

Below him on the deck there were raucous shouts, shrill laughter, and yells. Dying men tottered to the rail, men previously too weak to walk clambered up the shrouds like monkeys. Someone touched off the lombard that was kept loaded on the poop as an emergency signal. Minutes later there were answering flashes and loud booms from the *Victoria* and the *Concepción,* and the standard of Castile was hoisted on each ship. Everyone was drunk with joy, laughing, leaping, hugging his neighbor, thumping him on the back. Men who had not spoken to each other for weeks exchanged friendly grins. Magellan, standing aloft on the poop deck, smiled through his tears like an indulgent father. Father Valderrama raised the Cross, and the ship's company wept unashamedly as they intoned the *Laudate Domine.* The men crowded about Navarro, the sailor who had first seen land, and insisted on carrying out their half jocular promises of reward to him. So many pieces of jewelry were pressed upon the simple sailor that Gines de Mafra, the pilot, records that their total value must have amounted to a hundred ducats, about fifteen hundred dollars today, and a snug fortune at that time.

The Northeast Passage: The Search of the Impossible Grail

Isabel Barclay

Few sixteenth-century nations sponsored exploratory expeditions for the joy of discovery; the primary motivation was economic. Gold was one possible outcome of voyages of discovery, jewels another. And profitable trade was a third, and perhaps the most important of all.Whichever nation could find a new, more direct way to East Asia would have an advantage in obtaining and carrying spices, silk, and other products to the West; moreover, a quicker route would provide a ready-made market for the goods that country produced. Some nations sent explorers to sail southeast around the southern tip of Africa. Others struck out for the West, hoping that easy sea passages to Asia would lie through or around the Americas. And a few explorers tried a new, and ultimately impossible way, to the northeast.

A quick look at a globe shows us that this attempt was doomed to disaster, but to merchants, sailors, and officials of the sixteenth century the problem would have been a good deal less obvious. This excerpt from *Worlds Without End* by Isabel Barclay describes the efforts of Dutch explorer William Barents to find a path into and through the Arctic.

Excerpted from *Worlds Without End,* by Isabel Barclay. Copyright © 1956 by Isabel Barclay. Reprinted with permission from Doubleday, a division of Random House, Inc.

William Barents was a well-educated and well-to-do citizen of Amsterdam. He was a practical seaman, an able navigator, and a determined and resourceful man. He had spent most of his life at sea and was known to have more than his share of courage. He was loved and respected by the men who served under him and greatly admired by his fellow countrymen. The Dutch merchants could hardly have found a more ideal leader for their enterprise. Barents's first expedition set sail from Holland in June 1594 but failed to break through the ice pack and returned, like so many before it, with its mission unaccomplished. However, neither Barents nor the merchants were discouraged, and the next spring a new expedition set out.

This time there was a fleet of seven ships, a double complement of men and supplies for eighteen months. Barents rounded the North Cape and then, bearing east, made his way through the ice pack into the turbulent waters of the White Sea.

Here there was less ice and the climate grew milder. The Dutch decided that the ancient theory that Arctic seas were unnavigable was nonsense. Perhaps once the ice cap was passed the seas grew warmer. Possibly the Pole itself was hot. How could it be? Well, for that matter, why must it be cold? Just because it was farther from the sun than the equator did not necessarily mean that it was colder. After all, the men pointed out to one another, it is colder on the top of a mountain than in a valley and yet the mountain top is nearer the sun. Might this not also be true of the earth? . . . William Barents and his men knew no facts about the North Pole and very few about the Arctic and even the world as a whole. What they were on was a *fact-finding* expedition.

After rounding the cape, Barents sailed into what is now called Train-Oil Bay. Here some of the men went ashore and found "divers[e] footsteps of men and deer." Finally they came across a boatload of hunters who had come over the ice from northern Russia in search of game. Luckily Barents's interpreters could understand their language, and so they questioned them about the nature of the northern seas.

"In winter," the hunters said, "the seas freeze so hard that it is possible to go over the sea into Tartaria [Russia]."

These hunters were wild-looking men "dressed in harte's skins from head to feet." They were described as having "broad, flat faces, small eyes, short legs" and the habit of "being very quick to go and leap."

These goers and leapers were of course Laplanders, and the "harte's skins" in which they were dressed were reindeer hides. The Laplanders are a people akin to the Eskimo of northern Canada.

Another Attempt

After learning about the frozen seas, Barents continued on his way. The ships ran into fog and storm. Finally the other captains, who were worried by the ice and lateness of the season, prevailed on Barents to return to Holland. The merchants who had financed the expedition were relieved to see the ships return safely to port. They wanted to find a northeast passage but not at the risk of losing their ships. William Barents was willing to find it at the risk of everything, including his life.

Perhaps it was for this reason that he was not placed in command of the expedition which put to sea the following year. He was still chief pilot and navigator, but a stout sea captain, Jacob van Heemskerk, was in command. Barents accepted this change in fortune cheerfully. Van Heemskerk treated him as co-commander and looked upon him, as did the men, as the real leader of the expedition. Most of the crew were unmarried "that they might not be dissuaded by means of their wives and children to leave off the voyage."

The ships, two in number, left Holland in May. They had good winds and by June were in the Arctic. Van Heemskerk's instructions were to find a northeast passage and to come to "an agreement for fair, faithful, upright, and uninterrupted trade, traffic, and navigation with the people of China." He was also "to keep a good and accurate account of everything that shall occur during the voyage." This good and accurate account was kept by Groot de Veer, the fleet's surgeon-barber. To think of a surgeon-barber seems curious to us, but the very first surgeons *were* barbers, just as the first dentists were blacksmiths. In the sixteenth century and for some time afterwards the blacksmith and the barber looked after the sick of the community. Medicine as we know it simply did not exist. And so Groot de Veer with his scissors and razors and leeches and boxes of pills went along to cut either hair or limbs as the need arose. He probably was a very good barber, and it is from the record which he so faithfully kept that we have learned the details of Barents's final and remarkable voyage.

The ships left Holland in May, and by June they were off the North Cape. Barents wanted to sail east again but Van Ryp, the captain of the second ship, and Van Heemskerk decided to go north in the direction of Greenland. The ice grew thicker with each hour. The seas were stormy and there was almost continual fog. It was dangerous and difficult navigating but Barents managed to maneuver the ships through the ice floes, and in September they came to a hitherto unknown island. Some of the men landed to go in search of food and fuel when suddenly two of them were attacked by a polar bear, "a great, lean, white bear," which came suddenly stealing out and grabbed one of the men by the neck. His companions yelled in terror and the rest of the landing party rushed to the rescue. But it was too late. The bear had bitten off the man's head and seemed not to be in the least scared by his companions. The Dutch attacked the beast with pikes and muskets, but instead of running away she ran at them, grabbed another man, and proceeded to tear him in pieces. "Wherewith," De Veer says, "all the rest ran away." Small wonder! Eventually Barents led a well-armed rescue party and killed the bear by shooting it between the eyes. The Dutchmen buried their dead companions, and for obvious reasons named the island Bear Island. . . . It lies in the east of Barents Sea about midway between the northern tip of Norway and Spitzbergen.

From Bear Island the ships sailed on until suddenly through the ice and fog and mists, Barents caught sight of lofty mountains. He christened this new land Spitzbergen, "the land of the jagged peaks," and decided it was part of Greenland. As you know, he was wrong.

More Discovery

On the crags of Spitzbergen the Dutch saw geese nesting, and this interested them greatly. Until then no man had known where the wild geese bred. Their nests had never been found and even scientists believed that they grew on trees! In a botany book of the time it is written that in the islands of the North there was a special tree that grew near the water. In the spring these trees produced eggs instead of blossoms and, says the writer, "out of these come living creatures which falling into the water do become fowls." In the summer of 1596 Barents's men learned that this was a lot of nonsense. Geese did not grow on trees, not even on special trees; they simply built their nests and hatched their young in the Far North where Europeans were not in the habit of traveling. Mysteries often have very simple explanations.

After exploring some of the Spitzbergen coast they put about and returned to Bear Island. From here, following Barents's original plan, Van Heemskerk and Barents sailed northeast. Van Ryp returned to Holland. On July 17, after a day's voyage, Barents sighted what is now Novaya Zemlya. The seas round the island were thick with ice and as the Dutch continued to make their way east and north, it grew bitterly cold. Besides the drift ice there were now enormous icebergs, and the little ship was in constant danger of being smashed to pieces. De Veer tells us that they had "to winde about, because of the great quantities of ice. . . . The wind blew so uncertain that we could hold no course but were forced continually to winde and turn about by reason of the ice and the inconstantness of the wind. . . ." To add to their difficulties the weather changed. It had been cold and clear. Now the skies became overcast and it began to snow. Early in September they sought refuge in a harbor on the northeast coast of Novaya Zemlya. They called it Ice Harbor and well they might, for it was here that the ice finally got them. Almost overnight the pack ice closed in and Barents's stout little ship was frozen fast.

The men worked like beavers to try and pry her loose, but to no avail. The ice shifted with wind and weather, and the timbers of the ship cracked and groaned. She did not fall apart but she was in a bad way. Orders were given to shift the stores to land. Here the men pitched tents and waited for a break in the weather. None came. A week passed and it grew still colder. The ship, almost on its side, lay battered and forlorn in the ice. Barents and Van Heemskerk realized they were marooned and that there was nothing for it but to build some sort of shelter and prepare to spend the winter in the Arctic.

And so "we determined to build a house upon the land," De Veer wrote, "to keep and defend ourselves from both the cold and the wild beasts." The question was how to build the house. The ship's carpenter led an expedition inland and by "God's mercie" they found driftwood. This they used for the walls and floor. A sail from the ship was stretched across the top for a roof and packed with sand. The days grew shorter and shorter. Some of the men fell ill and the carpenter died. It was a terrible blow, but the work proceeded according to his plan and by mid-October the house was done. The last of the supplies were brought from the ship, the sick men made as comfortable as possible, and everybody stoically settled down for whatever the winter might bring.

"It is God's will," Van Heemskerk said, and this gave these good, stolid Dutchmen great comfort.

Wintering Over

They went about making the inside of their house as comfortable as possible. They built bunks round the sides and set up a stove from the ship in the center. They even made a bathtub out of a barrel, and De Veer insisted that every man take at least one hot bath a week. This was a most unusual procedure for those times, but De Veer and Barents felt that cleanliness was an important part of their health routine, and they knew that if they were to survive the Arctic winter they must keep fit. With this in view, they organized games and took what exercise they could in the open air.

But the open air became less and less hospitable. De Veer, still faithfully writing his report, at the end of October noted that "the wind blew northeast and it snowed so fast that we could not work without the door. . . . The same day we set up our dial and made the clock strike.". . .

By November the winter had set in in earnest. The winds raged round the little house and the snows "beat sore upon them." The sun disappeared over the horizon and did not reappear. It was the land of eternal night at last, and the thermometer plunged to 60° below zero. The kegs of beer, so carefully brought from the ship, froze and became unfit to drink. There were bears and foxes to eat, but little bread and of course no vegetables. They still had a good supply of wine, but their main drink was water which, De Veer tells us, "we melt out of snow which we gathered without the house."

On New Year's Eve, despite their cold and hunger and fear of the polar bears that prowled hungrily about, they summoned up courage to have a concert. De Veer organized it and it was a great success. Some of the men played and sang, and they had charades. In January the weather improved, and on the twenty-fourth De Veer and Van Heemskerk caught sight of the rim of the sun on the horizon. The men were filled with joy and "gave God hearty thanks for this grace showed unto us that that glorious light appeared unto us again."

But their days of rejoicing were short. Despite the reappearance of the sun the weather was "still foul and bitter cold." Their supply of wood ran out and the men, weakened by cold and hunger, were often too exhausted to go and fetch more. There was nothing to eat but fox stew. Even the polar bears were hibernating! By April many of the men were down with scurvy, but the ice pack began to break up so they had some hope of getting out alive, provided the ship wasn't crushed to pieces in the shoving ice. Of course it was, and nothing Barents or the men did could save it. They salvaged what bits and pieces of timber they could and held council.

"There is nought for it," Barents said, "but to build ships' boats and make our way then as best we can."

Open Boat

And so with what tools and materials they had they fashioned open boats with sails. It took time to make the boats and stow the gear, for the men were very weak. Barents himself was seriously ill, but before abandoning the house he insisted on writing a letter. This letter "he put into a musket charge and hanged it up in the chimney showing how we came out of Holland to saile to the kingdom of China and what had happened to us being there on land . . . that if any man chanced to come thither they might know what had happened unto us and how we had been forced in our extremity to make that house and had dwelt ten months therein."

When all was in readiness Barents was put on a sled and dragged to the water's edge and so "with a west wind and an indifferent open sea" they set sail.

On the west side of Ice Harbor a headland juts into the sea. Barents had christened it Icy Point when the Dutchmen sailed into the bay the year before. Now as the open boats neared the point, Barents called out to De Veer.

"Groot, are we about the Ice Point? If we be, then I pray you lift me up for I must view it once again."

And so they lifted him up.

"How do you?" Jacob van Heemskerk asked, and Barents, cheerful as always, replied, "Well, God be thanked." He was the bravest of men.

The little boats sailed on. The weather instead of improving grew fouler and fouler. It began to snow, and De Veer tells us the ice in the seas battered and buffeted the little boats until they were sure any moment they would be ground to pieces. But somehow or other they survived. They would land from time to time, build fires, catch and cook sea fowls, and then continue on their cold and dangerous way. For a time in June the ice closed in and they "could find no opening in the seas."

"This will be our last abode," one of the men said as they drifted helplessly in the ice. "We shall never get from hence." But De Veer, the surgeon-barber-writer replied, "God has helped us in worse perils. He will still help us at His good will and pleasure."

Remembering the dreadful months through which they had passed the men agreed.

Just at this moment the chief boatswain called to De Veer that one of the men in his boat was dying, whereupon Barents said:

"Methinks I shall not live long after him," and asked De Veer to let him once more read his record of the voyage to make sure all was in order. When he had finished he said in a voice so weak it could hardly be beard:

"Groot, give me some drink." Before De Veer could get him water Barents was "taken with a sodun qualon" and died.

It was the morning of June 28, 1597. For the next three months, with their chief pilot and navigator dead and many of their company sick and dying, this brave little band of Dutchmen made their way across the top of Europe. It was a truly frightful journey. There were ice and fog and gales. The sails were torn to shreds and the boats began to leak. They ran out of food and were attacked by polar bears, but "in the end," De Veer writes in triumph, "God delivered us out of our many dangers of death." In September they reached Holland, after being picked up by Van Ryp, who had been sent to look for them, near the present port of Murmansk [Russia].

Immediately on his return Van Heemskerk made his report.

William Barents was dead, and so were more than half of the men who had sailed with him. They had failed to find a northeast passage but they had survived a winter in the Arctic, the first Europeans ever to do so, and for many generations the last. The centuries passed but though other men sailed to the Arctic none went so far afield as William Barents. It wasn't until 1871 that a Norwegian walrus hunter by the name of Carlsen sailed round Icy Point and into the waters of Ice Harbor. There, to his amazement, he found Barents's house just as Barents and his men had left it nearly three hundred years before. The bathtub was in the corner, the bunks lined the walls, and the frozen sails were still stretched across the roof!

Maps and Atlases

Lloyd A. Brown

The age of exploration sparked an enormous increase in geographic knowledge. To help make this knowledge accurate and available, navigators came up with techniques and mapmakers worked to draw maps that were as realistic as possible. Where earlier maps had been filled with fanciful drawings of sea monsters and other imagined dangers in far-off lands, sixteenth-century maps increasingly reflected the world as it was. In this excerpt from the book *Mapmaking: The Art that Became a Science,* cartographer and author Lloyd A. Brown explains the process by which mapmakers worked, the role of the printing press in cartographic knowledge, and the big business that mapmaking became during the sixteenth century.

The art of printing spread like wildfire across Europe. Every year, it seemed, there were more and more stories to be printed and published. Every year there was a little more to tell others. Knowledge could be traded back and forth in printed books. And after the New World was discovered and explorers brought back wonderful tales about the strange lands and strange people across the ocean, hundreds of books were printed to describe them. Many of these books were illustrated with pictures and maps.

In order to make these illustrations and maps, publishers depended on artists and goldsmiths who made a living by decorating all kinds of silver and gold objects with engraving.

They did this by cutting very fine lines in the polished surface of the metal with delicate tools that had very sharp edges. The designs they cut were beautiful, and many artists and engravers wanted to keep a record of the work they had done. And this is the reason they finally taught themselves how to "print" pictures and maps to illustrate books.

Engraving on wood and metal was not a new idea, but Italian crafts-men showed the world how beautiful it could be. This is the way they did it. After cutting their design in the gold or silver they were deco-rating, they rubbed a gummy black ink into the cuts. Then they wiped the surface clean. After that they pressed a sheet of damp paper against the metal, and the ink that was stuck in the engraved lines came off on the paper in the form of a "print." This simple process made a nice clean copy of the design, and if the artist wanted to make more than one copy, all he had to do was rub more ink into the metal surface and print again.

After years of practice, artists began to engrave their designs and pictures on a sheet or plate of copper; first, because it was a cheaper metal than gold or silver, and second, because it could be hardened or tempered, and the engraved lines on the plate would not get fuzzy af-ter a few prints had been made from it. This was very important after printers began to make as many as a thousand copies of a book. After the discovery of America there were more and more books and maps printed in editions of a thousand copies or more. Every year new books were written that told about the latest discoveries in the New World, and people were anxious to read them and look at the latest maps of America. Some of these new maps could be bought in sepa-rate sheets, but most of them were bound up in books and were used to illustrate the story the book had to tell.

In 1507, one of these maps, drawn and published by a man named Martin Waldseemüller came out with a new name on it. The name was "America," and on his map the name was spread across the new lands that had been discovered by Columbus and explored by others after him. Waldseemüller called the New World "the fourth continent," and he explained to his readers that this land should be named after Amerigo Vespucci, because Vespucci had discovered it. Not many peo-ple agreed with him about the discovery, but his map was so popular and so many copies of it were printed that people got into the habit of calling the New World "America," and the name was accepted by everyone—even those who knew that Columbus had discovered it.

Maps and Books

The business of printing and publishing books and maps was a great success. People everywhere wanted more and more books to read and look at. And because the Netherlands had trained some of the best en-gravers and printers in Europe, that was the place to go to find the best books and maps. By 1550 Antwerp had become the great commercial center of Western Europe. Her craftsmen were turning out thousands of prints of religious scenes, illustrating the lives of the saints, and sto-ries from the Bible, all to be sold in the market place or exported to the Jesuit missions in South America.

The book-making industry in the Netherlands was well organized into guilds. Today we would call them unions. Some men made nothing but title pages and decorative borders for books. Others made nothing but ornaments for artists and architects. Still others made nothing but maps and charts. Their standards of workmanship were high. In their guilds or unions were "wardens" who supervised the work and saw to it that their men did not get careless. They were proud workmen.

About this time two of the most important men in the history of map making were living and working in the Netherlands. One of them was Gerard Mercator, the man who made the first sensible chart for navigators. The other was Abraham Ortelius. Mercator had his shop in Duisburg, after moving from Louvain, and Ortelius worked in Antwerp, sixty miles away. They were competitors in the map business, but they were also friends, and each of them worked hard to improve the maps and charts that were being published all over Europe. They did it in different ways, because Mercator was a map *maker*, who went out with his men and remeasured the land that he wanted to map. Ortelius was a map *seller*, who began his career as a member of the guild that specialized in coloring maps and charts, the Guild of Saint Luke.

When Ortelius was a young man his father died, and the money he earned was not enough to support his mother and two sisters. In order to earn some more money he began to buy maps that were made in Antwerp and other places. His sisters mounted them on linen and Abraham colored them and sold them at the fairs in Frankfurt and other cities. Soon he began to travel abroad to find new markets for his Netherlands maps and to bring back maps that had been published in other countries. He visited France and Italy, where he sold his own beautifully colored maps and brought home copies of the best maps of foreign cities and countries he could find. In a few years he began to plan the first general atlas of the world, and this is how he happened to do it.

The First Atlas

Ortelius had a good customer in Antwerp. His name was Hooftman, and he loved to collect and study maps. He was a merchant, and he wanted to know as much about foreign countries and foreign markets as he could learn. But Hooftman grumbled about his maps. Some of them were big and bulky to handle. Some were so small that the print was hard to read. His eyes bothered him. What he wanted was a collection of maps, each one on a single sheet of paper, that he could read and study without getting a headache. He wanted good maps of the Netherlands, Germany, France and any other countries that could be bought. And he wanted them all the same size so that they could be bound up in a book and stored away on a shelf instead of being spread all over his office.

Abraham Ortelius was called in, and after he heard about Hooftman's problem he went home and began to gather up copies of all the maps he could find in his shop. He picked only the ones that were about the same size, and ended up with about thirty. He took them to a bookbinder and had them bound up in a handsome binding and then delivered the volume to his customer. Hooftman was so pleased with the job that Ortelius decided to make up a few more volumes of the same kind, and he was surprised to find that some of his other customers liked the idea, and the collection of maps as well.

Ortelius was happy about the maps he was selling, but he thought he could do even better if he searched a little harder for the very best maps of every country, and then published them himself in a book that was handsomely printed. He talked it over with Mercator, and his friend encouraged him to go ahead with the idea. He also talked with the best engravers he knew, and they told him they could make some of the large maps smaller so that they would fit the size Ortelius had picked for his book of maps.

The Theater of the World

It took Ortelius ten years to gather together the maps he wanted and have them engraved. When it came time to print the text for his atlas, Ortelius went to his good friend Christopher Plantin, one of the best printers in Europe, whose shop was in Antwerp. The two men decided to call the atlas *The Theater of the World*, and Plantin agreed to print it. There were thirty-five leaves of text and fifty-three maps in the book, and in May of 1570 it was published. The atlas sold so well that in three months a second edition was printed. So many foreigners wanted to buy it that Ortelius had the text translated, and when he died in 1598, at least twenty-eight editions of the big book had been published in Latin, Dutch, German, French, and Spanish.

During all the years Ortelius was selling his atlas, Mercator was working on the same kind of collection of maps, one that could be bound up in a single volume. But he had planned so many maps for his atlas that he did not live long enough to see it completed. However, the finished work was very popular, and copies of it sold for more than fifty years after it was first published. In order to make the atlas even more popular, and cheap enough for a poor man to buy, a pocket-size edition was published. The maps, of course, had to be re-engraved and reprinted, and many of them were very tiny and hard to read, but they were better than nothing to the people who wanted to know something about the world beyond their doorstep.

Geographical atlases became very popular books, and several publishers in Europe copied the ideas of Ortelius and Mercator. One of these was an Italian named Lafreri. Lafreri is interesting to know about because of the title page of his atlas. Mercator had used the word *Atlas* in the title of his map collection instead of some other, such as *Theater of the World*, or *Looking Glass of the World*. Lafreri used the word *Atlas*, too, but he went a step further, and on the title page of his atlas he engraved the figure of the mighty Atlas of Greek mythology, supporting the world on his shoulders. He was the same hero that Homer had written about, and when he appeared on the title page of a book of maps, both his name and his picture, the public liked it, because he represented what the book was trying to tell its readers about—the world. Map publishers tried many other names for their geographic volumes, but the word *atlas* pleased their readers best, and today it is used by geographers all over the world. Everyone knows what it means, and what they can expect to find in the book—a collection of maps.

Chapter

8

The Fall of the Aztecs and Incas

PREFACE

Until the sixteenth century, the great nations of Europe were rivaled by two great cultures of South and Central America: the Aztec of Mexico and the Inca of Peru. Both the Aztec and the Inca civilizations had developed strong, sophisticated systems of communication and transportation. Both societies were military powers that dominated their immediate regions and influenced the course of events many miles from their capitals. Both societies were partly urbanized; both had worked out the logistics of feeding, clothing, and housing large populations. And although neither the Aztec nor the Inca culture had developed phonetic alphabets such as were known in Europe at the time, both had a long and rich tradition of culture: Stories, music, art, and religion were all of great importance in each society.

Through the course of history, great societies have come and gone. The Aztec and Inca had only been dominant for a century or two. At some point in the future they would surely have begun losing their authority, much as had happened to the ancient Greeks, the early Egyptians, or—an earlier example from the New World—the Maya of Mexico's Yucatan Peninsula. However, that slow loss of power never occurred.

The reason was European exploration. In search of gold and other valuables rumored to exist somewhere in the American continent, Spanish voyagers came quickly to the empires ruled by the New World's greatest civilizations. In Mexico, the Spaniards were led by Hernán Cortés; in Peru, the commanding officer was Francisco Pizarro. Each man determined to claim that part of the world for his country. If destroying the power of the present rulers was necessary to accomplish that goal, as it seemed to be, then destruction was called for.

Both Pizarro and Cortés were ruthless in their pursuit of the gold that they believed lay somewhere within the boundaries of the Aztec and Inca lands. Each commander took enormous risks, but each also showed tremendous courage and a thorough understanding of both psychology and tactics. However, the native people had nearly all the advantages. They had a huge edge in manpower and a knowledge of the territory; they had military discipline and allies whose influence stretched well beyond their own borders. But the Aztecs and the Inca had significant weaknesses, too. Their weaponry did not approach the arms the Spanish brought with them. Nor did they take the Spanish invaders as seriously as they might have. The ability of the Spanish to recognize and exploit these weaknesses ultimately led to a political defeat of the empires. Aztec and Inca culture lives on—many people in Central and South America today continue the crafts, religions, and other customs of their ancestors. Politically, however, the loss of the empires cost Mexico and Peru their independence and made them Spanish possessions. No native American dynasty would hold such power again.

Massacre and Siege

Diego Duran

Priest and historian Diego Duran was a native of Spain who came to Mexico around 1542, when he was still a small child. In 1581 he completed a long volume on the history of Mexico; the book began with the Aztec creation stories and ended with the events that led to the downfall of the Aztec empire. Duran's book is one of many such chronicles written during the period. Like the others, he relied on stories told to him by people who had lived through the period, and on pre-Spanish documents, often written in pictures.

The capture of Moctezuma (Motecuhzoma) was by no means the end of the Aztec empire; Cortés and his men had several very narrow escapes over the following months. This excerpt describes a massacre committed by the Spanish and the resulting siege against them led by Moctezuma's replacement, Cuauhtemoc.

The Indians were about to celebrate the solemn feast of Toxcatl, during which the idol of Huitzilopochtli was transferred from one place to another. This was a very important festival and rites were held before and after, like our octaves after a religious ceremony. I have dealt with this in the *Book of Rites*. Every day the natives came out to dance in preparation for their feast, and Cortés asked Motecuhzoma to explain to him the meaning of those dances and ceremonies. [He was afraid of a rebellion and] he warned the Aztec king not to stir up trouble since neither he nor his men wished to harm him. Motecuhzoma reassured Cortés, saying that a rebellion was not their intention. He added that he was a prisoner and that he and his people had no hostile plans. He begged Cortés to be calm as the dances and songs he heard meant only that the feast of the god was approaching and that certain ceremonies must be performed before and after the great day. Cortés then asked him as a favor to order that all the rulers and lords of the city and province gather to dance in the courtyard of the temple, together with the most courageous men, for he wished to take pleasure in observing the grandeur and nobility of Tenochtitlan. But all this was a cunning plan to massacre all those people, which is what happened.

This plan had been communicated to Cortés by Pedro de Alvarado, who had been instigated in turn by the Tlaxcalans, who hated the Aztecs, and who said that the object of this feast and the dances was to stir up a rebellion against the Spaniards and murder them. It is also possible that Alvarado in his cruel nature was desirous of making himself ruler of the land, even though it be at the cost of the lives of many. I have read much about him and his cruelties, and how he boasted about these. Motecuhzoma, who was naive and sincere and did not suspect malice, nor did he realize that such treachery was being planned, called together his dignitaries and told them that the Spaniards wished to enjoy the spectacle of the grandeur of Tenochtitlan and its nobility.

When the day for the Toxcatl feast arrived, when Tezcatlipoca and Huitzilopochtli were honored, the Aztec lords and warriors, unsuspecting, came out to worship their god and to show the splendor of Mexico-Tenochtitlan. Wearing all their finery, their splendid clothing and adornments, they wished to please Cortés in performing their dances and ceremonies before him and the others—although their performance was not appreciated and they received a treacherous attack in compensation, as we shall soon see. Motecuhzoma's order had been heard all through the city, so the principal men and captains prepared themselves with their most magnificent attire in order to participate in the Toxcatl feast.

The day for the festivities having arrived, some eight or ten thousand men of the highest order and purest lineage appeared, wearing all their finery as we have said, and formed a great circle in the temple courtyard. While they were dancing, all with contentment and pleasure, Cortés, instigated by Alvarado, ordered ten soldiers to be placed at each of the four gates of the courtyard so that no one could escape. He sent ten others to stand next to those who were beating drums where the most important lords had gathered. The soldiers were told to kill the drummers and after them all those who surrounded them. In this way the "preachers of the Gospel of Jesus Christ," or rather, disciples of iniquity, without hesitation attacked the unfortunate Indians, who were naked except for a cotton mantle, carrying nothing in their hands but flowers and feathers with which they had been dancing. All of these were killed; and when the other Aztecs saw this and fled to the gates, they were slain by the soldiers who were on guard there. Others tried to take refuge in the rooms of the temple, fleeing from those ministers

This illustration depicts the first meeting between the Spaniard Cortés and the Aztec emperor Moctezuma.

of the devil. As they were unable to do so, all were slain and the court-yard was drenched with the blood of those wretched men. Everywhere were intestines, severed heads, hands and feet. Some men walked around with their entrails hanging out due to knife and lance thrusts. Verily it was a terrible thing to behold, the saddest thing one could imagine, especially when those dreadful screams and lamentations pierced the air! And no one there to aid them!

The entire city became frenzied, and the frightful wails of the women and children resounded in the mountains and were enough to make the stones burst from pain and pity. Eight or ten thousand men, the entire nobility of Mexico-Tenochtitlan, torn to pieces in the court-yard of the temple! They had done nothing to deserve this fate, unless they were being punished for having given of their possessions in abundance to feed and quench the thirst of the Spaniards.

"The Most Atrocious Act"

When the priests saw the cruelty with which their own people were being treated and when they realized that the Spaniards were trying to ascend the steps of the pyramid, they knew that they too were soon to be massacred and that the image of the god was to be cast down the steps. They prepared to defend themselves and, on seeing the ascent of three or four Spaniards whose names I shall not record here, these Aztec priests brought out a large heavy beam and sent it rolling down the steps. But it is said that it stuck on the topmost stairs and its flight was arrested. This was held to be a miraculous thing, and so it was, for divine mercy did not wish those who had committed that wicked and cruel massacre to go straight to Hell but was desirous of giving them an opportunity to do penance—that is, if afterward they really did it. However, they were so lacking in sensitivity that they did not recognize the mercy of God in liberating them from this great peril and continued up the steps, killed all the priests, and cast down the idol of Huitzilopochtli. Many other barbaric acts were committed by them, always in the belief that they were serving God.

At this point [in the *Historia*] it says that some of the captains, hearing the clamor of the women and children and the moaning of the entire city, began to sing the ballad:

> From the Tarpeian Rock
> Nero watched Rome on fire.
> Not even the tears of the women
> His pity did inspire . . .

All of the above I discovered in certain writings, which tell that this was the most atrocious act ever committed in this land. It was the end of the flower and nobility of Tenochtitlan, where so many illustrious and courageous men died.

Motecuhzoma, seeing the treachery and deceit of the Spaniards, wept bitterly and asked the men who guarded him to kill him, for he knew that the Aztecs were wicked, vindictive people who might believe that he had advised the Spaniards to commit that evil act and who might slay him, his children and his wives. He and all the others who were prisoners begged to be slain, and their wishes were to be granted later.

After this the Aztecs and the Tlatelolcas confederated and raised Cuauhtemoc, lord of Tlatelolco, to the kingship. He was a youth about eighteen years old and a nephew of King Motecuhzoma. Everyone conspired against the dethroned Motecuhzoma and killed his wives and children. However, certain people had pity on his family; it is said that they managed to take them out of the city in secret. They were taken to towns in the country, where they remained concealed until the land was at peace again.

Cuauhtemoc

The new king, Cuauhtemoc, had grieved sorely over the death of his kinsmen in the massacre, so he gave orders that all the remaining men take up arms and prepare to attack the houses where the Spaniards were lodged. These houses were then surrounded by a great number of Indians with spears, stones, and arrows, and the attack was so fierce that the Spaniards did not dare appear in the doorways or on the roofs. The courtyards were filled with round stones that had been shot by the slings and that destroyed some of the walls. These courtyards were also filled with spears and arrows and the bonfires and torches lit by the Indians at night were so brilliant that it seemed like day. In this way they did not let the Spaniards rest or sleep and they could no longer obtain food supplies. Their plight was so desperate that they and Cortés repented having followed such bad advice [given by Alvarado].

During all this time Cuauhtemoctzin placed garrisons around the entire city, as he was determined that the Spaniards must die. He ordered all the neighboring towns, especially those that had not yet seen Cortés and his men, to be ready to be called to arms. Some of these towns were Tenayuca, Cuauhtitlan, Tula, Talantzinco, the province of Xilotepec with all of Cuauhtlalpan and the Otomi towns, as well as those of the Matlatzinca region and people from the many towns in the Tezcoco province. He ordered them all to be prepared for war when they might be called. So great was the number of men who answered this call that, if God in His Mercy had not seen the tears of those who invoked Him, none of the Spaniards would have escaped with their lives. Their need for food was so great and their hopes of obtaining any help so slim that they were like men staring into the eyes of death. Among them there were different opinions. Should they go out and die fighting? Escape from the city was impossible! The metropolis was made up of canals with narrow bridges from house to house. These ditches were so deep that horses could not traverse them. Risking their lives, the foot soldiers tried several times to leave, but the rain of stones, darts, and spears was so furious that they were forced to return rapidly. Any barbed dart that entered the body could not be extracted save by pushing it through the flesh. All those who were wounded were in great danger.

Wizards, Visions, and Dreams

During these days when the Spaniards were in deep affliction and dared not leave, the new ruler of Mexico, Cuauhtemoctzin, realized that the Aztecs were unable to force them to leave their quarters, nor could they enter those places because of the artillery that had been placed at the doors. Therefore, he called all the old men of the province and the enchanters and sorcerers and asked them to frighten the Spaniards by showing them nocturnal visions. In this way the Spaniards were to die of fright.

The wizards came and every night they conjured visions and frightful things. Sometimes the Spaniards would see human heads jumping about in the courtyard. At other times they would see a foot still attached to the leg, walking around. Or they beheld corpses rolling on the ground. At other times they heard screams and moans. At length the tension became unbearable. . . .

So it was that the Spaniards became weary of so much sorrow and affliction, but no one knew what to do since Cortés came to no decisions. He said that he was waiting for the right moment. He encouraged his companions, promising them that they would soon find relief, and prayed to Our Lady of Remedies to alleviate the situation. Having great faith in this Virgin, Cortés decided to make Motecuhzoma appear in public and with his own lips command his people to be calm and cease their attacks. One day while the Aztecs were attacking fiercely, almost demolishing with stones the house where the Spaniards had taken refuge, Cortés and one of his soldiers (one carrying a leather shield and the other with a steel one) took Motecuhzoma to the flat roof of a housetop, next to the place where the Indians were fighting most fiercely. Protecting him with the shields, they led the Aztec lord to the edge of the roof, where Motecuhzoma made signs with his hands that the people should stop yelling since he wished to speak to them. There was silence and the assault upon the house ceased. The two shields that covered him were removed and in a loud voice he implored the people to stop attacking the Spaniards.

The Aztec captains who were in the front line, therefore the closest to him, began to insult him with ugly words, telling him that he was a mistress of the Spaniards and, as such, that he had helped them plan the massacre of the great warriors and brave lords. The Aztecs, then, no longer recognized Motecuhzoma as king; he and his children and wives, his whole lineage, were to be killed, erased from the face of the earth! With them would die the wicked Spaniards who had perpetrated such evil among them! Having said these things and before Motecuhzoma could be protected by the shields, one of the Aztecs threw a stone that struck Motecuhzoma high on the forehead. Although he was wounded, it was only a glancing blow that did little harm. Others say that at the same time he was injured by an arrow in one foot. This is mentioned by different authors though our chronicle says nothing about it. It is said to have been an account by a certain Indian. Motecuhzoma, wounded, was then carried down into the palace. His appearance before the crowd had no good effect because the people were possessed by a raging fury against the Spaniards.

The valorous young Cuauhtemoctzin appeared every day to encourage his people and to fight with them. Whenever a Tlaxcalan was captured by them, his life was not spared. The soldiers of Tlaxcala were in the same difficulties as the Spaniards and later were to suffer greatly. Few of them returned to Tlaxcala.

End of Empire

Irwin R. Blacker

In the spring of 1521, Cortés decided to wage total war against the Aztecs. With his Indian allies he surrounded the Aztec capital of Tenochtitlan and cut it off from outside communication and supply. The strategy was successful. By August the Aztecs had been soundly defeated, as this excerpt from Irwin R. Blacker's *Cortés and the Aztec Conquest* explains. Similar stories would be repeated across North and South America throughout the next four centuries whenever Old World explorers encountered indigenous peoples.

More than fifty-five days had passed since the siege had begun, and still the enemy remained unbeaten. Most of the Spanish ammunition and arrows had been used. Some new supplies were received when a ship put in at Villa Rica de Vera Cruz with the remnants of [Spanish explorer] Ponce de León's expedition that had been routed [that is, badly defeated] on the Florida coast.

Finally, Cortes and his men had recovered sufficiently to begin attacking once more. This time he was determined that he would never again be trapped as he had been on the causeway [across the lake leading to Tenochtitlán]. He would leave no roofs for the Aztecs to fight from, no houses for them to hide within, no gaps in the causeways and streets to trap his men. Everything would be razed as the Spaniards moved forward. If need be, the entire city would be leveled, building by building. No stone would remain on another. This was a battle to the end, and Cortes was determined to win it regardless of the cost. Messengers were sent to his allies telling them he was ready to fight again, and many of them rejoined him.

Each day the invaders marched down the causeways, entered the town, and continued their destruction. As the Indian allies tore the buildings apart, Spanish soldiers hid nearby and Spanish horsemen lurked behind the column of soldiers. Invariably the Aztecs took the bait and attacked the invading Indians. Invariably, too, the Spaniards trapped the Aztecs between the hidden soldiers and the cavalry. "With these ambushes," Cortes wrote, "we killed some of them every afternoon."

The Spaniards began to notice signs that the Aztecs were feeling the effects of the siege. At the beginning of the long battle, they had buried their dead with all their accustomed funeral rites. Soon they no longer had time to bury the corpses and merely hid them inside the houses. As the campaign dragged on week after week, they no longer even bothered with their dead. Cut off from the countryside that fed them, the Aztecs were slowly starving. Gnawed roots and the chewed bark of trees were seen in the streets. But still they fought on. The youthful emperor had no intention of surrendering.

Time after time Cortes sent messengers to Cuauhtémoc asking him to abandon the fight, but he always received the same answer, "If there were only one man left, he would die fighting."

Approaching the End

The siege went on and on: a clash in one part of the city, a skirmish in another, ambush and retreat; and forever, the death of Spaniards, allies, and Aztecs. Finally, the representatives of the Aztec emperor agreed that Cuauhtémoc would meet with Cortes. The appointed hour came. Cortés was there, but the emperor never appeared—he had apparently realized that the struggle could end in nothing less than his total victory or total defeat. But Cortes took no pride in the slaughter that then ensued; he called the last phase of the siege a "mockery." The Aztecs no longer had the weapons nor the strength to wield them. They were dying of starvation and thirst.

At last Cortes made what he thought was his last assault. The way through the city was open. No one came out to oppose the invaders. And the Indian allies of the Spaniards avenged themselves. "That day they slaughtered and took prisoner more than forty thousand men. The shrieks and the weeping of the women and children was heartbreaking." The Spaniards were too few to control their allies, and they had to countenance sickening cruelty and barbarism.

That night nearly all of the ruined city was in Cortes' hands. The stench of the dead, left lying in the summer heat for days, permeated the island. Men who had fought most of their adult lives were revolted by it and withdrew.

It was already August 12; although there were lulls, the fighting continued, and it appeared that the brutality of constant battle would last through the rest of the summer. On this day Cortes expected to meet with the emperor to receive a petition for surrender; but once more the Aztecs failed to appear as they had promised. The fighting began again and lasted through most of the day. Hoping to avoid another battle, Cortes went to the top of one of the few remaining buildings and pleaded with the caciques [chiefs] to end the slaughter.

The caciques met together and agreed to parley. For more than five hours the enemies talked. There was so little ground left to the Aztecs that they had to walk on the bodies of their dead. Some of them had withdrawn to the lake where they swam to the far shore or drowned. Cortes noted, "their plight was such it was impossible to conceive how they could endure it."

The Final Assault

As the hours passed, Cortes realized that he would have to order a final assault. He fired a shot, the signal to advance, and watched the death agonies of Tenochtitlán.

> More than fifty thousand of them perished from salt water they drank, or from starvation and pestilence. . . . As the people of the city came toward us, I ordered Spaniards to be stationed in all the streets to prevent our allies from killing those unhappy people. I also ordered the captains of the allies to restrain their men in every way possible. But our allies were so many we could not prevent a massacre, and that day more than fifteen thousand were killed.

In the late afternoon, the captain of one of the ships stopped an escaping canoe. The men aboard the Spanish craft leveled their guns and prepared to fire when those in the canoe cried out that the emperor was among them.

As soon as Cortes heard that the young Aztec had been taken prisoner, he sent for him. The captain general had his men carpet a terrace with crimson cloth and matting, and he waited for his prisoner to appear. Doña Marina was at his side. As Cuauhtémoc mounted the terrace where Cortes sat, the Spanish leader rose to his feet and stepped forward. For a time both men were silent. Then Cuauhtémoc told Cortes that he had done all that he could to defend himself and his people. Now reduced to his present wretched state, he asked Cortes to deal with him as the conquering Spaniard wished.

Cortes, filled with admiration for the bravery and determination of the young Aztec, told him that he respected valor even in an enemy. He called for Cuauhtémoc's wife to join her husband, and in peace at long last, they sat down together.

After seventy-five days, Tenochtitlán had finally been subdued by the persistent Spaniards and abandoned by its people. The war with the Mexicans had come to an end. The Aztec empire had crumbled with the destruction of its great and beautiful city. The breaking of the siege of Tenochtitlán marked the beginning of Spanish rule on the mainland of the New World. Yet the shift from conquerors to colonial administrators did not come easily for most of the officers who had sailed with Cortes. They were not by nature bureaucrats. They had started out as adventurers hoping to find riches and converts for their religion and way of life. But once the adventure was over and the conquest complete, they wanted their share of the spoils of victory.

The Spaniards had fought long and hard; they had almost all been wounded one or more times; they had seen their companions killed on the battlefield or on the altars of the enemy. Now they wanted to be paid, and to the surprise of everyone, including Cortes, there was very little treasure to be found.

Aftermath

No one really knows just what happened to the great treasure amassed before the *noche triste* [a battle] and abandoned during that fateful night. When Cortes and his men set out to recover it upon their return to the city, only a small part of it could be found. Some of the conquistadors claimed that the Aztecs had taken it out of the city before the siege began. Some claimed that Cortes and his captains actually found it and confiscated it for their own use. Still others believed the story told by some of the Aztec leaders that the treasure had been thrown into the lake to thwart the conquerors. Whatever the answer, only a few golden reminders of the original treasure remained.

The Aztecs nominally continued to rule for a time, with the conquistadors and caciques ruling together under the direction of the Spanish court and the Church. But soon the temptation to use the Indians as slaves became too great to be resisted. Christianity was forgotten as the Indians were herded together, branded, and forced to toil in the gold and silver mines and on the great plantations that were parceled out to the conquerors of New Spain.

While Mexico City was being rebuilt and the country explored and exploited, Cortes waited for word from Spain concerning the legality of his own position. He had notified King Charles of his victory and of the establishment of the new empire, but both [Cuban governor Diego de la] Velásquez and the Bishop of Burgos were determined to destroy Cortes.

Finally, the wrangling for power reached such proportions that both the king and the pope entered into the argument. Special committees were established to study the various claims, and the results completely vindicated Cortes. An order went out on October 15, 1522, naming Cortes governor, captain general, and chief justice of

New Spain. At last, after hazarding his life and fortune, he was recognized by his king. With a strong hand, but with love for his adopted land, Cortes ruled until 1534 when Charles made Antonio de Mendoza the viceroy of New Spain, with authority to act with royal power. Cortes retained his titles and rank, but never again was he to wield the power he held at the moment the conquest ended.

He arranged a marriage for Doña Marina to Juan Jaramillo, one of his captains, and then returned for what he thought would be a brief visit to Spain. But when his visit was completed in 1547 and he was on his way to embark for Mexico at the Spanish port of Seville, his great strength began to fail. Within a few days he died—not on a charging horse or in combat on the causeway, but peacefully in bed. His family, knowing that that would have been his wish, moved his body to Mexico.

Today there are no statues of Cortes in the land he conquered; he and his fellow conquistadors have been rejected by more recent generations. But the great civilization that he overcame with steel and courage is remembered everywhere in modern Mexico. Pride in the Aztec past and delight in rediscovery of Aztec culture are strong. The Aztecs who conquered and then were conquered are winning, through history, the final victory.

The Fall of the Inca

Henry F. Dobyns and Paul L. Doughty

Few New World civilizations were as advanced as the Inca of the sixteenth century. From a base in present-day Peru, the Incas had built a network of roads throughout the Andes mountains. They used the roads to extend their political and economic superiority over the region. By the sixteenth century, their king, Atahualpa, ruled an area that could fairly be called an empire. And rule he did: Atahualpa, like all his ancestors, was a supreme ruler and a descendant of the gods. He was the so-called *Sapa Inca* or "sole Lord" of the society. Unfortunately for Atahualpa, in 1532 he would preside over the destruction of his empire at the hands of Spanish conquerors led by Francisco Pizarro.

In this excerpt, historians Henry F. Dobyns and Paul L. Doughty describe some of the factors that allowed the Spanish to defeat the Inca. They examine the effects of armor, weapons, and other technical superiority of the Spanish, but they also discuss the role of diseases introduced by the conquerors; the problems associated with civil strife in Inca territory; and the similarity of Spanish and Inca cultures and institutions.

Editor's Note: In 1524, the Inca emperor Huayna Capac died, leaving an uncertain succession behind him. Power was ultimately seized by his son Atahualpa, who reigned over what was increasingly a troubled empire, its population diminished by disease and its political allegiances split between claimants to the throne. In 1532, a small Spanish force led by Francisco Pizarro began to make its way into Inca territory. Atahualpa had known for some time that they were on the way but had done nothing to stop them. That November, however, Atahualpa went to meet the Spanish at the city of Cajamarca. Riding in a litter and surrounded by several thousand of his finest warriors and lords, he spoke to Pizarro's chaplain, who asked him to accept Christianity. Insulted, Atahualpa refused, whereupon Pizarro's men attacked without warning. The result was a massacre. Estimates of the dead range between three and four thousand, all Inca. Atahualpa was taken prisoner. Though there would be several further attempts by the Inca to reclaim power, none were successful. The Inca Empire was at an end.

*S*antiago! The Spanish war cry echoed off the walls of the royal buildings around the square of the Inca city of Cajamarca on the evening of November 16, 1532. In less than two bloody hours, Francisco Pizarro and 167 companions seized effective control of the *Tawantinsuyu* [that is, the Inca Empire], slaughtering several thousand Inca nobles and troops, with cannon and war horse, sword, and lance. The Spaniards captured Atahuallpa, the son of Huayna Capac [the previous emperor, who died in 1524] who had just won the War of Inca Succession. Astonishingly, within a few years after Cajamarca, an amazingly small number of Spaniards replaced the *Tawantinsuyu* with colonial political, social, and economic institutions that would endure essentially unchanged for centuries.

The very rapidity with which Spaniards successfully imposed a "conquest culture" on the *Tawantinsuyu* highlights how alike in some respects Spanish colonial and Inca colonial cultures were in 1532. The easy substitution of a Spanish elite for a Native American elite meant that the Spaniards had themselves developed a "conquest culture" well adapted to the task of ruling by seizing power from a wealthy, autocratic Native American imperial lineage dominating masses of peasant horticulturists. Pizarro's conquest of the Inca empire benefited not only from the forty-year experience Spaniards had in subjugating other New World states, but also from the evolution during the long Spanish reconquest of the Iberian Peninsula [present-day Spain and Portugal] from the Moors of a distinctive "conquest society" within Spain.

By the fifteenth century, Spanish Christians had come to regard themselves as a "chosen people" engaged in a religious crusade in the Mediterranean basin. This fanatic psychology led to the expulsion from the Iberian Peninsula of Moors who would not accept baptism as Christians. In the critical year 1492, moreover, the Spaniards also expelled from their homeland its large Jewish population. Spaniards naturally transferred to their new American conquests many of the Peninsular institutions and customs that had developed during their earlier religious crusades at home.

Basic differences between the Peninsular reconquest and the subjugation of Native American peoples quickly forced Spain to modify Peninsular conquest culture in the New World. New conditions that demanded institutional changes included the sheer population size of Native American states and the geographic distance of the New World from Spain. By the time Pizarro's men set foot on Peruvian soil, Spaniards had already carried out many innovations in their overseas institutions in the course of conquering the Caribbean islands, Mexico, and the Isthmus of Panamá.

The moment Spanish conquerors decided to rule and exploit the native populations in the Caribbean, they realized that Peninsular conquest culture could not totally cope with the conditions of New World dominion. Not only did the native peoples of the Americas greatly outnumber the population of Spain, but the New World also bulked vastly larger. Thus the new colonial enterprise demanded that the Spaniards live among Native Americans to maintain Spanish sovereignty and to rule the teeming population through a new "conquest culture." This followed Iberian models closely, however, so no historian should seek to defend the thesis that the Indian frontier in Hispanic America generated a more democratic society than the homeland on the Peninsula, as has been asserted with regard to North America.

The distant overseas location of the New World demanded further Spanish cultural change. Spain was not a great maritime power in 1492. That technological deficiency forced the Spaniards to compensate in terms of institutional flexibility in the Indies. The Spaniards improved Peninsular colonial institutions to create a class of social, economic, and political mechanisms with no precise equivalents in Iberia.

In addition, by the time Francisco Pizarro led his private army into the *Tawantinsuyu*, the biological Columbian exchange [that is, the introduction of diseases] between the Old and New Worlds was already well advanced, to the advantage of the Old World. The great smallpox pandemic that reached Mexico in 1519 decimated the population of *Tawantinsuyu* in 1524. It probably more than halved the peak imperial population and left in its wake an Inca War of Succession that opened an easy path to the Spanish conquerors. It also set in motion a crippling depopulation trend among Andean region Indians that would endure, apparently, for two-and-a-half centuries.

Because of the relationship between disease mortality and the absolute number of persons in a given population susceptible to infectious epidemics, the first introduction of each Old World disease—smallpox, measles, whooping cough, bubonic plague, typhoid, influenza, malaria, and yellow fever—tended to exact its largest human toll. Consequently the loss in absolute numbers evidently was greatest during early colonial times. The imperial Inca population that had been pressing hard against natural resources ranged perhaps around 32,000,000 persons about 1520. It dropped to less than 16,000,000 after 1524, and continued to decline with succeeding disease introductions to probably 5,000,000 individuals by 1548.

Thus, when after several years of exploring and probing the Pacific coast of South America, Francisco Pizarro landed in the *Tawantinsuyu* near Tumbes early in 1532, several key factors had already combined to allow Pizarro and his Spanish coconquerors to seize Inca power rapidly. One key to the situation was the horrible death of the Sapa Inca Huayna Capac during the smallpox plague of 1524, at the apogee of his military and civil power. His crown prince died in the same epidemic, leaving the empire not only demoralized but disoriented as well. Atahuallpa, offspring of Huayna Capac and a Quito wife, fought Huascar, son of Huayna Capac and a Cuzco wife, for the emperor's scarlet fringe. Their contest so splintered authority that Pizarro never faced more than a fraction of the prepandemic might of the *Tawantinsuyu*. The Inca army never unified to engage the Spaniards and large field forces remained uncommitted to imperial defense.

In contrast, the motley force of conquerors assembled in Spain and Panamá by Francisco Pizarro and Diego de Almagro evinced total commitment to its purpose. Members of the expedition represented a cross-section of Spanish overseas conquest society, acting with decision under the stern hand of Pizarro. Of the 168 conquerors present at Cajamarca, 21 percent came from Extremadura, 20 percent from Andalucia, and 19 percent from Old and New Castille. Most had emigrated, in other words, from poverty-stricken Peninsular provinces. The largest single contingent, some 8 percent, came from Pizarro's home town, the city of Trujillo, and reflected the prevailing preference for one's genetic kinsmen and coresidents. A quarter of the men at Cajamarca claimed noble blood, and as many as 30 percent may have been literate, so they were not representative of the Peninsular population. Some 3 percent, including the expedition's chaplain, Valverde, may have been recent Jewish converts to Christianity. The members of the expedition included 7 percent former white-collar workers, 8 percent merchants, and 13 percent artisans, demonstrating how gold-fever cut across social status groups.

Significantly, Francisco Pizarro also obtained royal permission, three years before he undertook Peru's official conquest, to add fifty Negro slaves to his 1529 expedition. Evidently he was well aware of the attrition in Native Americans already well underway. Consequently, a Black man became the first "Spaniard" ashore at Tumbes when Pizarro landed his force on the soil of the *Tawantinsuyu*.

The invaders from the Old World appeared strange and exotic to the natives of the *Tawantinsuyu*, lending them a certain psychological advantage. The Spaniards also enjoyed a tremendous technological superiority over Native American armament which greatly added to their psychological advantage, with particular effect in face-to-face combat. When the two forces met at Cajamarca, 37 percent of the Spaniards were mounted on imposing war horses hung with noisemakers and armor.

The Spaniards could bring to bear nonhuman energy on a scale that no Indian could possibly match. At Cajamarca they possessed, in addition to war horses, the further advantage of firearms, including cannon. Thus, the disparity in numbers between the conquerors and their Inca opponents was not nearly as large as it seemed.

Even when the Indians overcame their fear of horses and guns, the Spaniards still held a distinct edge in hand-to-hand combat. They wielded very high-quality steel swords—often the justly famous Toledo blades. Inca clubs, maces, or halberds simply could not match the steel sword or saber. Native American projectiles, whether arrows or spears or sling-thrown stones, could not penetrate metal or mail, so armored Spaniards ran little risk in battle.

The psychology of the Inca approach to the unparalleled circumstance of invasion by bearded men with skins both lighter and darker than any Incas had ever seen played another key role in this conquest, as it had in the earlier Aztec reception of Spaniards. The Inca rulers traced their ancestry to a deified predecessor who was reputedly also bearded and light-skinned. The Inca elite's image of its own ancestry clearly influenced Atahuallpa at first in dealing with the strange new beings. Nevertheless, one surely cannot conceive of the contender Atahuallpa ordering his litter-bearers to carry him right up to Pizarro and his men in the provincial city of Cajamarca had he not thoroughly expected to receive obedience and respect as heir and member of the sacred royal lineage. Atahuallpa regarded the Spaniards as either supernatural, or at least honorable and honest men.

In fact, Pizarro and his Spaniards were only too mortal. Greedy for riches such as the precious metal litter that bore the Quitan contender for the imperial throne, they also felt contempt for any non-Christian, regardless of exalted rank. Thus the psychological orientation of the Spaniards and the Inca leadership upon initial contact helped to set the stage for the decisive hours in the later afternoon of November 16, 1532. The Spaniards immediately seized the initiative. From that moment on they never looked back, as Pizarro and his followers went about substituting themselves for the Inca ruling nobility.

The hostage Atahuallpa perceived by the end of 1532 how greedy the Spaniards at Cajamarca were for silver and gold. He sagaciously attempted to buy his freedom with royal treasure, but failed to discern the duplicity of the Spaniards. Atahuallpa lacked, after all, any previous experience with Europeans to serve him in his hour of need. The quantity of precious metal collected for Atahuallpa's ransom staggered the 168 Spaniards at Cajamarca. Gold alone filled a room 22 feet long by 18 feet wide to a height of 9 feet. Silver filled a smaller room twice. When they melted most of the artistic creations, the Spaniards divided up 13,420 pounds of 22 1/2-carat gold and 26,000 pounds of silver. This treasure bulked three times greater than Cortez's spectacular garnerings from the Aztec capital in 1521. At fluctuating current prices for precious metal bullion, the Cajamarca ransom was worth on the order of $30-50 million in gold and $1.5-2 million in silver. The present value of the unmelted artistic works is incalculable.

To the Cajamarca ransom, the now enlarged conquistador task force soon added an even greater treasure looted from the public buildings of the Inca capital of Cuzco, further supplemented with precious metals from administrative cities throughout the *Tawan-tinsuyu*. In mid–1533 Pizarro allowed twenty men to hurry home to the Peninsula with their sudden riches. Some conducted royal bullion to the Spanish court. Others acted as Pizarro family stewards. All recruited reinforcements by stirring Peninsular gold-fever.

While gold was a prime motivation in bringing people to Peru, the key to Spanish colonial rule in the Andean region lay in rapid substitution of Spaniards for members of the Inca royal *ayllus* [ruling clans]. This process met with astonishingly little resistance. A nearly total transfer of power occurred between a few hundred men within less than half a decade.

The Inca nobility of the eleven royal *ayllus* that exercised absolute power over the teeming imperial populace appears to have numbered no more than about 500 individuals at the time of the conquest, although it could well have been more numerous prior to the devastating smallpox pandemic. The great mass of Indian peasants who could have acted as a major force were not motivated to defend in battle the interests of the numerically small group of Inca overlords.

When Manco Inca, the leader of the Neo-Inca state [an Inca group attempting to regain power], besieged Cuzco and the Rímac Valley in 1536, a few hundred Spaniards and Indian allies were able to defend themselves successfully. By that time, the Neo-Inca forces even used horses, captured Spanish swords, and hardened, copper-tipped lances. The crucial difference appears to have been that the Indian masses took little part in the struggle. Commoners served either Spaniards or noble Incas as personal servants, burden-bearers, grooms, and so on, but a very small elite group apparently did the decisive fighting. This parallel between the overseas Spanish conquest state and the Inca conquest state tremendously facilitated transition of sovereignty from one small elite to the other.

CHRONOLOGY

1500
The Portuguese arrive in Brazil.

1501
Michelangelo begins sculpting *David*.

1502
Columbus begins his last voyage.

1503
Leonardo da Vinci paints the *Mona Lisa*.

1507
Martin Luther is ordained a Roman Catholic priest.

1508
Maximilian I becomes Holy Roman Emperor.

1508
Michelangelo begins to paint the ceiling of the Sistine Chapel.

1509
Henry VIII ascends to the throne of England.

1510
The approximate beginning of the slave trade; the drama *Everyman* appears.

1512
War between France and Spain.

1513
Balboa crosses Panama to the Pacific.

1514
Portuguese ships sail to China.

1517
Luther posts his ninety-five theses.

1519
Magellan sets out to circumnavigate the globe.

1520
Suleyman the Magnificent becomes the leader of Turkey; chocolate arrives in Spain from the New World; Luther is excommunicated.

1521
Cortés destroys the Aztec empire; the Diet of Worms takes place.

1526
Babur founds the Mughal dynasty in India.

1527
Troops of the Holy Roman Empire sack Rome.

1528
Paracelsus writes a manual of surgery.

1529
Jean de Bourdigne writes the *Chronicle of Anjou.*

1532
John Calvin leads Reformation activities in France.

1533
Francisco Pizarro executes the Sapa Inca of Peru.

1535
Thomas More is tried for treason and is executed.

1541
Hernando de Soto finds the Mississippi River.

1543
The Portuguese land in Japan; Spanish Inquisition begins; Copernicus dies.

1545
Truce of Adrianople is signed between Turkey and Austria.

1552
Ivan IV of Russia begins to attack neighboring countries.

1555
The Peace of Augsburg is signed in Germany.

1556
Akbar the Great becomes ruler of India.

1559
Elizabeth I is crowned queen of England.

1562
The first religious war in France between Huguenots and Catholics begins.

1563
Council of Trent ends.

1564
Spanish occupy the Philippine Islands; Shakespeare is born.

1565
The sweet potato is introduced to England.

1567
Spain extends rule over the Netherlands; Japan's government is centralized.

1568
Gerardus Mercator devises the map projection that bears his name.

1570
Japan opens to international trade.

1571
Don Juan of Austria defeats Turks in the Battle of Lepanto.

1573
Wan-Li becomes thirteenth emperor of China's Ming dynasty.

1577
William Harrison writes "A Description of England."

1580
Francis Drake circumnavigates the world.

1582
Gregorian calendar is adopted by some nations.

1585
Hideyoshi becomes Japanese ruler.

1587
Mary, queen of Scots executed; the Roanoke Colony is founded in North Carolina.

1588
The Spanish Armada is defeated by the English.

1590
Galileo experiments with the speeds of falling objects.

1594
Shakespeare writes *Romeo and Juliet.*

1595
The Dutch begin to colonize the East Indies.

1599
Shakespeare writes *Julius Caesar.*

FOR FURTHER READING

Peter Ackroyd, *The Life of Thomas More*. New York: Nan A. Talese, 1998.

Charles Avery, *Florentine Renaissance Sculpture*. New York: Harper and Row, 1970.

Otto Benesch, *The Art of the Renaissance in Northern Europe*. Rev. ed. Greenwich, CT: Phaidon, 1965.

Irwin R. Blacker, *Cortes and the Aztec Conquest*. New York: American Heritage, 1965.

Daniel Boorstin, *The Discoverers*. New York: Random House, 1983.

William J. Bouwsma, *John Calvin: A Sixteenth Century Portrait*. New York: Oxford University Press, 1988.

John Calvin, *Institutes of the Christian Religion*. Ed. John T. McNeill. Trans. Ford Lewis Battles. Philadelphia: Westminster, 1960.

E.R. Chamberlin, *Everyday Life in Renaissance Times*. New York: Capricorn Books, 1965.

Hamilton Cochran, *Pirates of the Spanish Main*. New York: American Heritage, 1961.

G.G. Coulton, *Life in the Middle Ages: Men and Manners*. 1910. Reprint, Cambridge, England: CambridgeUniversity Press, 1967.

Vincent Cronin, *The Flowering of the Renaissance*. New York: E.P. Dutton, 1969.

Basil Davidson, *The African Slave Trade*. Boston: Little, Brown, 1961.

Richard S. Dunn, *The Age of Religious Wars, 1559–1689*. New York: W.W. Norton, 1970.

Fray Diego Duran, *The Aztecs*. Trans. Doris Heyden and Fernando Horcasitas. New York: Orion, 1964.

Winston Graham, *The Spanish Armadas*. New York: Doubleday, 1972.

Ian Grey, *Ivan the Terrible*. Philadelphia: J.B. Lippincott, 1964.

Bernard Grun, *The Timetables of History*. New York: Touchstone, 1982.

J.R. Hale, *Age of Exploration*. New York: Time-Life Books, 1974.

E. Harris Harbison, *The Age of Reformation*. Ithaca, NY: Cornell University Press, 1955.

William Harrison, *The Description of England*. Ed. Georges Edelen. Ithaca, NY: Cornell University Press, 1968.

Thomas S. Kuhn, *The Copernican Revolution*. Cambridge, MA: Harvard University Press, 1966.

Albert Marrin, *Inca and Spaniard: Pizarro and the Conquest of Peru*. New York: Macmillan, 1989.

Robert F. Marx, *The Battle of Lepanto 1571*. Cleveland: World, 1966.

Garrett Mattingly, *The Armada*. Boston: Houghton Mifflin, 1959.

George L. Mosse, *The Reformation*. 3rd ed. New York: Holt, Rinehart, and Winston, 1963.

Linda Murray, *The Late Renaissance and Mannerism*. New York: Frederick A. Praeger, 1967.

Charles McKew Parr, *So Noble a Captain: The Life and Times of Ferdinand Magellan*. New York: Thomas Y. Crowell, 1958.

Robert Payne, *By Me, William Shakespeare*. New York: Everest House, 1980.

Alison Plowden, *Elizabeth Tudor and Mary Stewart*. Totowa, NJ: Barnes and Noble Books, 1981.

John R. Roberson, *Japan Meets the World: The Birth of a Superpower*. Brookfield, CT: Millbrook, 1998.

Rebecca Stefoff, *Ferdinand Magellan and the Discovery of the World Ocean*. New York: Chelsea House, 1990.

Time-Life Books, *The European Emergence: Time Frame A.D. 1500–1600*. Alexandria, VA: Time-Life Books, 1989.

John M. Todd, *Luther: A Life*. New York: Crossroad, 1982.

Hermann Voss, *Painting of the Late Renaissance in Rome and Florence*. Vol. 1. Trans. Susanne Pelzel. 1920. Reprint, San Francisco: Alan Wofsy Fine Arts, 1997.

INDEX